Chosen Instrument II

Chosen Instrument II

A History of the
Canadian Wheat Board:
New Horizons

William E. Morriss

Canadian Cataloguing in Publication Data

Morriss, William E.
    Chosen instrument II : a history of the Canadian Wheat Board : new horizons

    ISBN 0-660-18081-2
    Includes bibliographical references.
    1. Canadian Wheat Board – History
    2. Grain trade – Canada – History
    3. Grain trade – Prairie Provinces – History
    4. Grain trade – Government policy – Canada – History
    5. Grain trade – Government policy – Prairie Provinces – History.
    I. Canadian Wheat Board.

    HD 9049.M67 2000   338.1'7311.0971   C00-980086-7

Distributed by:
The Prolific Group
150 Wyatt Road
Winnipeg, Manitoba
Canada
R2X 2X6

Printed and Bound in Canada

Dedication

To Geraldine

CONTENTS

INTRODUCTION

Free trade in wheat, as an economic instrument, has been discredited by painful experience, and in any case, political considerations required that decisions on wheat production and prices be made by governments, rather than according to a romantic theory of interacting supply and demand. — Don F. Hadwiger

The above observation, written by an American professor of political science at Iowa State University, encapsulates a recurring theme throughout this second volume detailing the history of the Canadian Wheat Board to its Fiftieth Anniversary year in 1985. Hadwiger made that observation after being invited as a research scholar by the United States Department of Agriculture to study American wheat policy programs.

Indeed, it may have been an understandable sensitivity to "political considerations" by the then serving Commissioners of the Canadian Wheat Board, that has delayed publication of this history following the original volume, Chosen Instrument, A History of the Canadian Wheat Board: The McIvor Years. At that time we observed in the postscript that:

> This volume has traced the history of the Canadian Wheat Board to a point approximately midway in its first half century. We have covered an era dominated to a large extent by one remarkable man, George McIvor. In the first half of this endeavour to bring an understanding of the board's role and place in Canada's broader agricultural policy objectives, the author has had the benefit of a rich source of previously published material to guide him — particularly that of Charles Wilson and other observers of the early years. While research and writing on the second half of the first fifty years has been completed, those chapters largely break new ground. In

short, while many undertakings and initiatives that have impinged on the Wheat Board's operations have been reported, speculated, and commented upon in the popular press, there has not been a definitive recording of the background to those events. In being granted free and unimpeded access to the files of the Canadian Wheat Board, I found myself alone in unexplored territory.

In consequence of that privilege, granted by the commissioners of the Canadian Wheat Board, my research led me into heretofore unpublished personal correspondence, office memoranda, minutes of the board and the advisory committee of the board, minutes of grain agreement negotiations, and other personal classified material that might prove sensitive in the short term. Many of the principal personalities involved in that unfolding sequence of events remain on the national and international scene. It may be that, had some of them foreseen that their personal reactions were to be published, they would not have ventured them into the record, or upon consideration altered what was said or written. The dilemma that presents itself here is that the record would be incomplete without those personal reactions, which enliven and enrich any history.

Those words were written over 12 years ago, and while many of the fractious issues that marked western Canadian agriculture then have not yet been fully resolved, there comes a time, as Charles Wilson noted, when an adversary's confrontation is transformed into an enduring compliment. Hopefully that metamorphosis has taken place.

As noted in that postscript, the history of the Canadian Wheat Board would not be complete, nor would it be accepted with credulity, if it were written in isolation from such issues as the Crowsnest Pass grain-hauling rate debate, Feed Freight Assistance, the domestic feed grains policy, rail line abandonment, hopper car acquisitions, rationalization of the country elevator system, and the Operation LIFT controversy, issues upon which the Canadian Wheat Board was largely obliged to maintain an apolitical stance. All of these issues constitute a fundamental part of this current segment of the history of the Canadian Wheat Board.

Socrates sagely observed that, "Nobody is qualified to become a statesman who is entirely ignorant of the problem of wheat." As it was then, so it is today. The problem of wheat remains. It is intertwined in the most basic and fundamental policy decisions of almost all nations. And, among the surplus grain producing areas of our world, nowhere is that more true than in the United States and the European Economic Community. Neighbouring, as Canada does, upon the vast grain production capacity of the United States, the "politics of wheat" in that country impinge almost oppressively upon policy decisions in Canada. Thus, the history of the Canadian Wheat Board, as the chosen instrument of the federal government in the competitive, and more often than not subsidized, world grain market, cannot be written in isolation from decisions taken in Washington.

In consequence, what follows here is a history of two-and-a-half decades of bust and boom in Western Canada, predicated not only on the vagaries of a climactically sensitive semi-arid plain, but as often upon decisions taken by the United States in an abrasive confrontation with the European Community, over world market share in export subsidy wars.

Given the constant rhetoric from the United States, extolling the merits of the free enterprise open market system of price discovery for grains versus what is sometimes branded as "closed socialistic" wheat board systems employed in other countries, readers may find it ironic to find that the American government, which for the larger part of this century has propped up domestic prices by means of export subsidies, has on occasion turned to controls and embargoes to deflate the market. Such actions have been instituted both to influence domestic prices and as a weapon of diplomacy in world affairs. In short, the "romantic theory of interacting supply and demand," observed by Professor Hadwiger, is indeed a myth as far as world market prices are concerned.

It is not meant to imply here that the federal government in Ottawa was blameless in taking measures to both protect domestic consumers and to sometimes subsidize grain farmers through various means to counteract drastic drops in farm income. Such measures were, however, usually taken as reflex actions to counter external pressures rather than as an aggressive competitive stance. The Canadian treasury could ill afford to compete against those of the United States and the EEC.

In that regard it might be wise to briefly examine the origin and history of the Crowsnest Pass Grain Rate for the benefit of those readers not familiar with Prairie history. The Crow Rate, long regarded as a sacred right by Prairie grain farmers was, until recently, the subsidy advantage most vociferously cited by other competitors in the world grain market. It was also the most bitterly fought agricultural issue in Western Canada as will be seen in the following pages. The controversial Crow Rate had its origin in the desire of the Canadian Pacific Railway to build a rail line from Edmonton, Alberta, to Nelson, British Columbia, through the Crowsnest Pass in the Rocky Mountains. To do so they sought a subsidy or $3.4 million from the federal government. In consequence, an agreement was entered into in 1897 between the government and the CPR in which the subsidy was granted. In return, the CPR agreed to move grain from specific Prairie points to the Lakehead at Fort William, Port Arthur, Ontario, at a fixed rate in perpetuity. The agreement was confirmed by federal legislation on September 1, 1899.

For a short period at the beginning of the century, rates dropped below the Crow Rate as competition from other railways took effect. Then, during World

War I, the government allowed the rate to rise in recognition of wartime inflationary forces. However, in 1925, Ottawa reinstituted the Crowsnest Pass Rates
by statute. At the same time they were extended to include all grain shipped
from any point on the Prairies between the West Coast and the Lakehead. The
rate from Regina, Saskatchewan, to the Lakehead was 20 cents per hundred
pounds, or roughly one-half cent per ton mile.

At this writing the "Holy Crow" has been expunged from the statute books.

Also for the benefit of those readers unfamiliar with Western Canadian agriculture, and who may not have read the preceding volume of this history, a brief
review of the Canadian Wheat Board pooling system may be wise. As the basic
concept of the wheat board system, the pooling of returns from the sale of grains
grew from the upsurge of co-operative enterprise in Western Canada. Prior to
the beginning of each crop year — August 1, to July 31 — the commissioners
of the Canadian Wheat Board review market prospects for the coming year and
recommend to the federal government the level of "initial payment" to producers upon delivery of their grain to the board. That rate is normally set at a conservative figure which insures that there will not be a deficit in the pool at the
close of the crop year. Only upon rare occasions, as readers will see, has there
been a deficit to be paid from the federal treasury. Therefore, under normal circumstances, there remains a surplus in the pool accounts. After deduction of the
costs of the administration and operation of the Canadian Wheat Board, the
surplus funds are distributed as a final payment to producers on a pro-rata basis
according to the amount of grain they have delivered into the system.

Provision is made, should market conditions dictate, whereby the board may
recommend to the government increases in the initial payment during the crop
year. Should the "adjustment payments" be approved, they are paid out retroactively from the pool to farmers who have made deliveries under the original initial payment.

In its most simplistic form, that is the guiding principle behind the operations
of the Canadian Wheat Board. The early development of that system and a brief
history of agriculture in Western Canada leading up to the establishment of the
Canadian Wheat Board are covered in *The McIvor Years*. A review of the salient
points of that era need not be undertaken here, and it is suggested that a reading of that volume might well be a desirable prelude to a more complete appreciation of this current volume.

As in the preceding volume of this history, my thanks are extended to the
commissioners of the Canadian Wheat Board, all of whom are now retired, who
commissioned this work and allowed me free and unimpeded access to the files
and records of the board. My thanks are also extended to the large number of
other people for their assistance and tolerance of my persistent interruption of
their normal duties. Numerous past and current members of the staff of the

Wheat Board cheerfully answered my questions and guided me to long forgotten files. And, again as before, a special note of gratitude to the Board's librarian, Ruth Reedman, and her staff, who took time out to provide statistical material, pamphlets and other resources without which this history would have been incomplete. Also my thanks go to Bob Hainstock who succeeded me as editor and publisher of the Manitoba Co-operator for a short period and provided bound volumes of the paper dating back over the years of this history. I make no apology for making extensive use of references from that publication since, as the editor for an extended period, and particularly the period covered in this second volume, I have complete confidence in the accuracy and reliability of the primary sources.

Once more a special tribute to my wife Geraldine, who worked as my research assistant both during the original writing and the more recent re-editing of this second volume. With a passionate eye for accuracy, she checked, rechecked and revealed and corrected many of my errors, both of typography and omission.

Finally my thanks to Bob Roehle, Vice President, Corporate Communications for the Canadian Wheat Board, who renewed and spurred interest in this second volume, and to Brian Stacey, Manager of Planning & Evaluation for CWB Corporate Communications, who edited text, selected the photographs, prepared cutlines and organized arrangements for publication of the book.

CHAPTER I
THE NEW DOOR

When we wish to open a new door we must try many keys until we find one that fits.
— *L.C. Pu, China Resources Limited, February 17, 1961.*

From the mid-1950s world production of wheat, spurred by new technology, began a slow but steady climb. In 1950 it stood at 7.4 billion bushels and by 1958 had reached a new record of 8.71 billion bushels. At the same time world trade in wheat passed the one billion bushel mark, then rose above 1.3 billion bushels in three of the last five years of the decade. In this changing scene Canada's share of the world wheat trade fluctuated between a high 26.5 per cent in 1957 and a low of 20.5 per cent in 1960 when the new decade opened.

While Canada and the United States were still co-operating on holding the price line through informal meetings and through the International Wheat Agreement, which had been renegotiated in 1959 with 37 countries participating, American exports, financed largely through concessional sales under P.L.480 and other programs, were taking an increasing share of the expanding trade. By 1960, the United States held a 42 per cent share of the world market, exporting 662 million bushels of wheat in the 1960-61 crop year.

Over the last half of the fifties, Canadian wheat sales hovered slightly above and below 300 million bushels, slumping to just above 277 million bushels in the 1959-60 crop year. While Britain remained as Canada's principal market, with sales to the United Kingdom fluctuating above and below the 100 million bushel mark, there were ominous signs of change in the traditional European trade, which had so long dominated the importing side of the market. Subsidization of production by the European nations was leading to increasing self-sufficiency, with France achieving that goal and emerging increasingly as an exporter of wheat. Signing of the Treaty of Rome on March 25, 1957, had led to the formation of the European Economic Community, and while Britain had not yet joined, the six signatory nations were working toward what was to

7

become the Common Agricultural Policy of the EEC, promising further uncertainty in the once dominant European import market. The one bright spot for the Canadian Wheat Board was a steady increase in sales to the Japanese market. Wheat exports to Japan had risen progressively, from roughly 29.5 million bushels in the 1955-56 crop year to 46.8 million bushels in 1959-60. Even here, however, there were ominous signs as the Americans, increasingly frustrated over what was considered an inroad into a market that was theirs by right of development, were showing signs of stepping up competition in Japan. As well, 1960 was an election year in the United States. There was uncertainty as to what changes and initiatives might result from the election of a new administration.

Against this background, an extraordinary meeting took place in Ottawa on September 13, 1960. Present in the Department of Trade and Commerce offices, were representatives of the Department, the Canadian Wheat Board and the Board of Grain Commissioners for Canada.

All four commissioners of the Wheat Board were there: Chief Commissioner W.G. "Bill" McNamara, Assistant Chief Commissioner Bill Riddell, and Commissioners W. Earle Robertson and John T. Dallas. Also present were D.H. Treleaven, the Board's Secretary, and Dr. R.L. Kristjanson, Director of the Statistics and Economic Division of the Board. J.A. Roberts, who had replaced Mitchell Sharp as the Deputy Minister of Trade and Commerce, chaired the meeting. R.M. Esdale, Chief of the Grain Division, and Dr. Merle Menzies, Economic Adviser to the Minister, were also there. Representing the Board of Grain Commissioners was R.W. Milner, the Chief Commissioner. [1]

The agenda was a heavy one, covering marketing strategy and sales promotion for the coming year. McNamara was aggressively reorganizing the departments and administrative structure of the Canadian Wheat Board, and was seeking to bring the widely dispersed staff under one roof. Despite the fact that the mandate of the Board was still being extended for five-year periods, and the current extension would expire in 1962, the Board had obtained an option to purchase the old Customs Building adjacent to its head offices on Main Street in Winnipeg. Authorization was needed to tear it down and commence construction on a new building. Plans were also underway to install a computer to handle the Board's complex records and to facilitate payments to producers.

Pending the arrival of Trade Minister Gordon Churchill, discussion took place on implementation of a suggestion, made the previous June in Winnipeg, that a technical sales promotion program be undertaken. As the two Boards had discussed the matter previously, agreement was quickly reached. Dr. G.N. Irvine, Assistant Director of the Board of Grain Commissioners Research Laboratory, was made available to the Wheat Board to head the program for overseas technical missions. Cost of the project and recruitment of staff was to be jointly shared by the two Boards, with $250,000 authorized from the Wheat Board's special account to finance the operations. [2]

Authorization was then given for Milner to accompany McNamara on a trip to Japan. As Milner, his business done, left the meeting, McNamara suddenly turned the conversation to the prospect of opening a new market in the Far East. Could he combine his forthcoming journey to Japan with a visit to China? The Wheat Board had made a sale of approximately 3.8 million bushels of wheat to the People's Republic of China in 1958. But, aside from one cargo as part of the original contract, no trade had resulted in the following 1958-59 crop year.[3] Reports were now emanating from China that acute drought had persisted over several years and there was urgent need for food. McNamara suggested that the Canadian Trade Commissioner in Hong Kong be asked to apply for visas for himself and A.W. Cordon, the Board's Far East representative, to visit Peking.

Riddell, backed by Dallas, said he was fearful that there might be a change in American policy after the U.S. election — the presidency was being contested by John F. Kennedy for the Democrats and former Vice-President Richard Nixon for the Republicans — and trading arrangements with China might be negotiated by the U.S. "If Canada were not established in the area prior to such an eventuality we would, in all probability, lose out in the market."[4]

As discussion continued, Esdale was authorized by the Deputy Minister to immediately cable the Canadian Trade Commissioner in Hong Kong, indicating approval of the mission and requesting co-operation in obtaining visas. Trade Minister Gordon Churchill joined the meeting shortly afterwards, and after being briefed on the situation, agreed to the proposal for a fact finding and commercial sales mission to China.

The die was cast and the meeting turned to other matters. Approval was given for the opening of a Wheat Board office in Japan and for a preliminary study on a new Wheat Board building. McNamara then outlined the market outlook, which indicated commercial exports in the vicinity of 260 million to 265 million bushels. Unless substantial export assistance was forthcoming, a target of 300 million bushels would be difficult to reach. Shortly after the meeting adjourned, Esdale contacted C.M. "Max" Forsyth-Smith, the Canadian Trade Commissioner in Hong Kong. The search for entry through the "new door" was on.

During his subsequent trip to the Far East, McNamara visited Hong Kong and Canton and met with representatives of China Resources Limited, but little of substance resulted.

Then, two days prior to Christmas 1960, events broke with dramatic suddenness. On the morning of December 23, McNamara received a confidential trade memo, via London, England, that Australia had sold one quarter million tons of wheat to China, of which 40,000 tons would possibly go to Albania, and that a Chinese trade representative was seeking a visa to visit Canada. He cabled Forsyth-Smith in Hong Kong: "Understand Liu leaving for Canada can you confirm? Check rumour large Australian sale."[5]

Confirmation that Chris Perrett, of the Australian Wheat Board, had concluded a sale for 240,000 tons of wheat during a two-day visit to Hong Kong came back on December 24. Forsyth-Smith also reported that Liu Liang, a representative of China Resources Limited, Hong Kong agents of China, had planned to leave for Canada on that date, but that his visa had not yet arrived from Ottawa. Liu was now planning to leave December 31.

Several frantic days of trying to trace the movements and intentions of Liu followed. On December 28, it was reported he was arriving in Canada by CP Air via Vancouver and would be stopping off in Winnipeg for only half an hour en route to Montreal. This was cancelled and word was received that he was now coming via London and was due at Dorval Airport at 4 p.m. Thursday, December 29, accompanied by Yang Lu Liang, a British subject from Hong Kong who would be acting as secretary.

Immigration officials in Ottawa then reported that the Chinese officials would be arranging interviews, through the Royal Bank, with a steel company in Montreal, the Palmer Company of Canada, the Canadian Wheat Board, and one or two other industrial firms. Frank Rowan, Manager of the Wheat Board's Montreal office, was alerted to meet them on arrival. He did so and relayed a message to McNamara, who had gone to Vancouver over the holidays, that he would be receiving a phone call from the Chinese officials. The call to McNamara followed and arrangements were made for a meeting in Montreal on January 3, 1961.

Prior to that meeting, public disclosure of the Chinese mission had broken on New Year's Day. In London, England, a headline on the front page of the *Reynolds News and Sunday Citizen*, a leftist leaning newspaper that he did not normally read, caught the eye of J.B. Lawrie, the Wheat Board's European Manager: "FAMINE HORROR: Secret Peking Mission...CANADA-CHINA DEAL...Monster wheat sales despite U.S. protests."

Under that lurid headline was a story from the London paper's Toronto correspondent, Michael Cope. In light of subsequent events, particularly China's allegations of a breach of secrecy on the part of the Board, the story, though premature, was in some ways prescient. It read:

> Big international repercussions are expected from the arrival in Montreal of two top trade delegates from Communist China. Their mission is officially secret — but they hope to buy a large share of Canada's wheat surplus.
> And, in spite of inevitable protests from the United States, Canada is likely to sell the wheat. China needs it to

relieve areas threatened by famine after disastrous year of floods and drought.

The delegates, Yang Lu Liang and Liu Liang, are going on from Montreal to the Canadian Wheat Board headquarters at Winnipeg.

They say they will be here at least three months.

Two days ago, Peking Radio described the disasters which preceded the famine as "without parallel in the last century."

All but two provinces suffered drought, some for seven months. Then came 11 typhoons, giant floods and insect plagues. Experts estimated that half China's expected production may have been lost.[6]

The news report went on to predict anger on the part of the United States and "defiance" on the part of Prime Minister John Diefenbaker, who was "desperately seeking a big and immediate export market to counteract economic recession and widespread unemployment at home."

McNamara and Rowan met with the Chinese representatives in Montreal on January 3. During the two-hour meeting, Liu indicated China's interest saying they were anxious to do business and hoped to complete negotiations, but pointed out that he was having difficulty in persuading his principals to purchase Canadian wheat at a premium over Australian wheat. McNamara made a firm offer of 260,000 long tons of barley and 500,000 to 750,000 long tons of wheat with the price calculated in convertible sterling. The offer was for acceptance prior to the close of the market on January 5.[7]

The offer was not accepted: "China Resources considered our prices were so far out of line with Australian prices that they would not be accepting this offer."[8] Liu advised he was proceeding to Toronto later in the week. Arrangements were made to keep in contact with McNamara, who went to Ottawa for discussions with Department of Trade and Commerce officials. Negotiations resumed in Toronto's Royal York Hotel on January 8 and 9, with inconclusive results.

McNamara then returned to Ottawa, where he had a brief discussion with Agriculture Minister Alvin Hamilton, who had replaced Gordon Churchill as Minister Responsible to Parliament for the Canadian Wheat Board. (The transfer marked a precedent. While the Canadian Wheat Board Act specified that the Minister of Trade and Commerce was responsible for reporting to Parliament for the Canadian Wheat Board, the appointment of Hamilton was made by Order-in-Council. It was not until the 1962 session of Parliament that the Act was amended to specify that the duty could be assigned to any minister of cabinet.) McNamara then returned to Winnipeg. On January 12, McNamara received a phone call at his residence. Liu had authority from Hong Kong to negotiate on the volumes earlier specified.

Prior to that message, the Chief Commissioner had another phone call which lent urgency to closing the deal. Sylvestre Meyers of the Commodity Credit Corporation in Washington phoned to report a change in U.S. policy with respect to Spain and enquired as to how the negotiations were proceeding with the Chinese delegates. In a memorandum, McNamara reported:

> I indicated that no transaction had been completed but was hoping something could be worked out. He stated that he was also hoping we would be able to develop some business, and then went on to state that he was also hoping that the U.S.A. would be able to participate in this business. I did not comment on this remark but, to me, it was a clear indication that officials at Washington are also exploring the possibility of disposing of wheat to China. It might be that, if we do not button up this deal immediately, they will be moving themselves. [9]

The "inevitable protests" from the U.S., predicted by the press, were not in evidence, but buttoning up the deal was not to be easy. Finding a key to opening the new door was proving difficult. With the Chinese seeking concessions, the Board negotiators were having a difficult time explaining that, if price concessions were made, they would have to extend equally to all other Board customers.

Phone calls, telegrams and technical information continued to pass between the Board and Liu. Meanwhile, public speculation was growing and the Chinese were repeatedly insisting on complete secrecy. Finally, on January 18, Liu phoned McNamara to report that he had been authorized to negotiate on 300,000 tons of feed barley. Doug Treleaven, now Executive Assistant to the Board and who was to later become Assistant Chief Commissioner, left immediately for Toronto to continue the negotiations.

He found Liu not only ready to negotiate on barley, but also for 750,000 tons of wheat. The negotiations were long and painstaking. On January 20, Liu confirmed acceptance of the purchase of barley, but the wheat contract remained elusive. As bookings on the first cargoes of barley were now imminent, and news of such bookings would circulate through the trade, it was no longer possible to keep the negotiations totally secret.

On January 23, Agriculture Minister Hamilton made a brief statement in the Commons in Ottawa:

> I am pleased to report to the House that negotiations between the Canadian Wheat Board and representatives of

China Resources Company, Hong Kong, who are now in Canada, are continuing. The government is not yet in a position to make any announcement with regard to these negotiations except to advise that the Canadian Wheat Board anticipates that twelve cargoes of feed barley — approximately 120,000 tons — for nearby shipment out of our West Coast ports will be booked within the next few days.[10]

The statement had been carefully phrased by McNamara, who stressed to the minister that the Chinese were most anxious that no publicity should be given to the possible sale of wheat or further quantities of barley, because they wanted to make their freight arrangements first. They feared that announcement of a large sale would precipitate a rise in shipping rates.

As Treleaven continued the negotiations in Toronto, with Liu transmitting detailed reports to his superiors in Hong Kong and awaiting replies, and Treleaven likewise submitting lengthy reports on progress back to Winnipeg, tension was growing. In Winnipeg it became apparent that other forces were shaping in the background.

Forsyth-Smith reported from Hong Kong that he was under pressure from Liu's senior, L.C. Pu, to do some of the negotiating from there. He also reported that the Australian Wheat Board's Perrett had arrived back in Hong Kong. On January 24, Forsyth-Smith cabled Ottawa:

Impossible to stall Pu indefinitely and he insists on discussing negotiation with us. Our complete lack of information from you has placed us at a severe disadvantage as the only information is supplied by Pu...[11]

With Treleaven's negotiations at a critical phase in Toronto, McNamara suggested to Bob Esdale in Ottawa that a reply be cabled:

McNamara advises that at Liu's request discussions on a secret basis and in view of this understanding board has not kept minister or Ottawa officials informed. Only information which has been published was announced in Parliament yesterday after Liu's agreement to this release.[12]

Finally, on January 27, Liu and Yang having flown to Winnipeg, agreements covering the sale of 260,000 long tons of barley and 750,000 long tons of wheat were signed in the Canadian Wheat Board offices. The new door was ajar. It remained to find a key that would open it wide.

In the interim, the Board was faced with the problem of maintaining secrecy to the extent of the contracts. The railways, grain terminal companies and the Board's agents all had to be informed on the magnitude of the sales in order to plan and facilitate shipment, widening the chances of leaks. Additionally, departure of the Chinese mission via London for Hong Kong, had heightened speculation in the newspapers.

Officials in Ottawa had been given as little information as possible during the course of the negotiations in order to preserve the secrecy demanded by the Chinese, but pressure was growing on the government to reveal something in Parliament. On February 2 in Hong Kong, Forsyth-Smith outlined the pressures to Pu and pointed out that the speculation, now rampant, might have an even worse effect on freight rates than the facts. Pu said he would consult Peking by telephone and let the Canadian side know as soon as possible if an announcement could be made.

Before there was a reply from Peking, Alvin Hamilton rose in the Commons on February 3, to make a statement:

> Mr. Speaker, I am pleased to announce that the efforts of the government to sell grain to new markets have resulted in one of the largest grain sales ever consummated in the commercial field. Agreement with the China Resources Company of Hong Kong has been reached for the sale and shipment to China during the next few months of 40 million bushels of grain. [13]

Hamilton went on to outline the volumes and grades of wheat and barley and set the approximate total value of the sale at $60 million. While noting that the Canadian Wheat Board had negotiated the agreement "for the government," Hamilton put the emphasis on the government's role:

> I would like at this time to pay tribute to my predecessor who was in charge of the Wheat Board before he became Minister of Veterans Affairs (Mr. Churchill). He made the decision for representatives of the Canadian Wheat Board to go to China in 1958 and again in the fall of 1960. I have carried on with his plans for the expansion of wheat and flour sales to all parts of the world, but I feel that credit should go where credit is due. [14]

Alvin Hamilton's propensity for basking in the glow of the Wheat Board's initiatives and successes was to reach even greater heights in the very near future.

In Hong Kong, the announcement in the Commons had immediate repercussions. Forsyth-Smith cabled on February 6 to advise McNamara that Liu had called him and said the announcement in Ottawa had been "most upsetting," and had seriously embarrassed him with his principals in China who alleged that it was "a breach of a gentlemen's agreement." Despite that, Liu had urged that the board send an expert to Hong Kong to advise on loading and delivery problems, and gave the impression that further purchases were possible.

As evidence of interest by China for further purchases mounted, Doug Treleaven and Frank Rowan were despatched to Hong Kong via Tokyo. Arriving February 16, they were met by Liu and Forsyth-Smith and discussions were immediately opened. Prior to their arrival, a further sale of 60,000 long tons of wheat had been confirmed by an exchange of cables, and on February 20, Liu indicated to Treleaven that China was interested in a continuing long-term agreement.

Strict secrecy was observed on the additional sale, and elaborate precautions were taken to prevent any leaks on the new negotiations. Treleaven arranged to make direct reports by telephone to McNamara in Winnipeg, and Forsyth-Smith and the Trade and Commerce staff in Hong Kong agreed not to report back to Ottawa during the continuing discussions. Treleaven explained to McNamara:

> This is to some extent embarrassing since there have been no reports on the activities of the Hong Kong office. I was fearful, however, that some premature release on the new business might leak to the press and destroy all of the progress that we might have made in the last week in smoothing over with Cireco (China Resources Company) their annoyance at the earlier press release. [15]

It was suggested that McNamara inform Ottawa that the Trade and Commerce office in Hong Kong was co-operating in the "technical discussions," and that a report would be forthcoming when they were concluded. The "technical discussions" were now taking on a cloak and dagger atmosphere with the China Resources representatives crossing the border into China each night to telephone their reports to Peking and receive further instructions.

The key to opening the new door presented itself on February 23. Liu informed Treleaven, on a personal basis, that he thought it was possible to sell China from three million to five million tons of grain over the next three years. However, such a volume of business would require the Board to assist China in promoting trade to Canada on other goods, and the Board must "have more flexibility" in their payment terms. "It was clear that he had in mind some form of credit, possibly credit for one year with the buyer's option of prepayment." [16]

That evening at dinner Liu introduced a new negotiator in the person of Yu Tun Hwa, Assistant General Manager of the China Resources Company. Yu confirmed China's interest in a long-term, multimillion ton contract the next day. He hoped that McNamara, or some other Board member or official, could return to Hong Kong to conclude a new agreement. Treleaven carefully outlined the role of the Canadian Wheat Board as a marketing agency, with no authority whatsoever to enter into general trade discussions, or to arrange bilateral trade negotiations. He was sure, however, that the Board would co-operate to the extent possible in assisting the Chinese to establish trade contacts in Canada and facilitating discussions with appropriate government agencies. In respect to credit, Treleaven pointed out that there was no recognition, or diplomatic relations, between Canada and China, and the Board had neither the authority nor facilities to grant credit.

With Treleaven and Rowan scheduled to leave for Canada on the weekend, events moved swiftly. Prior to a scheduled tour of Hong Kong harbour on Saturday, February 25, Liu asked for a meeting. Treleaven reported:

> Mr. Yu opened the discussion by advising that after our initial discussions on future business prospects they had passed to their principals a summary of our talks and Cireco's ideas...They had some "news" for us to take home. Their principals had agreed in general with the estimates of purchases indicated by China Resources, but had indicated that in addition to five million tons of wheat they would require up to one million tons of barley over the next 2 ½ years — that is up to the end of 1963, with shipments to start immediately following the conclusion of the current agreement. [17]

Yu said it was now up to the Board to make firm proposals to conclude the sale. He requested that the Board reserve stocks of grain on the West Coast for China until negotiations on a new agreement could be concluded. With the ball in the Canadian court, Treleaven cabled Winnipeg, requesting reservation of the Pacific wheat and barley stocks pending re-opening of negotiations. The next day he left for home via Tokyo. In advance of Treleaven's arrival with a detailed report of the preliminary negotiations, McNamara alerted Ottawa and began preparations for a meeting with government officials to ascertain the availability of credit.

In the Hong Kong talks, Yu had introduced a note of urgency, saying that plans for the year's grain imports into China were always drawn up in the first three months of the year and negotiations should be completed by March 31. Further emphasis on despatch was lent by information from Forsyth-Smith in

Hong Kong, that Perrett had been negotiating with China Resources on behalf of the Australian Wheat Board. This probably accounted for Pu's absence from the Canadian negotiations after making a brief appearance. Perrett, however, unwisely revealed the negotiations to a reporter from the *South China Morning Post*, and said he might go to Peking to continue the negotiations.[18] For that indiscretion he was severely reprimanded by Pu and the Australian Trade Office believed that £28 million of business may have been jeopardized.[19]

Forsyth-Smith posted a delayed report on the negotiations to Ottawa while McNamara sent a proposal to cabinet. Under that proposal, the Wheat Board would obtain loans from the banks in order to extend credit to the Chinese. The bank loans to the Board would be backed by a government guarantee in the event of default. Thus, shortly after Treleaven returned to Winnipeg, McNamara, Treleaven and the Board's Comptroller-Secretary, C.E. Gordon Earl, proceeded to Ottawa to outline the new concept at a meeting of the Deputy Ministers of Trade and Commerce, Finance, Agriculture and External Affairs, and a representative of the Bank of Canada.

McNamara received word on March 9 that cabinet had authorized the Board to negotiate with China on the basis of credit not to exceed $50 million for a period of 180 days, but with the stipulation of at least 25 per cent cash. Armed with that authority McNamara, Treleaven and Earl left for Hong Kong on March 17, 1961, and booked into the Imperial Hotel. On March 22, they held a preliminary negotiating session in the China Resources offices in the Bank of China Building.

This time the Wheat Board representatives were greeted by Ting Ke-chien, General Manager and Managing Director of China Resources. Accompanying him were Yu, the Assistant General Manager, and Liu, Manager of the Industrial Products Department. Following the exchange of formalities, Ting indicated that he had delegated Yu and Liu to conduct negotiations on behalf of China Resources and asked who would negotiate on behalf of the Wheat Board. McNamara replied that, while Forsyth-Smith and C.J. "John" Small of External Affairs would sit in on the meeting, any deal would be between the two agencies.

In the initial stages, McNamara outlined the structure and operations of the Canadian Wheat Board. He pointed out that, up to that time, the Board had sold for cash only, although there had been occasions when buyers purchased grain through the private trade on credit using the medium of export credit insurance. In those cases the guarantee of credit was directly between the Canadian government and the government purchasing the grain, and such transactions did not involve the Wheat Board. However, the Chief Commissioner indicated flexibility: "I am not able to indicate how far the Board can go, but, as indicated, this is a new market and hence a new key is required to open this new door."

Ting replied that China was interested in a three-year agreement for substantial amounts of grain but:

> If my country cannot buy on credit, then the possibility of purchases on a cash basis is very small and even impossible. China has purchased both from Canada and Australia. Future business is not the same type of business since it must be on a basis other than cash. [20]

McNamara countered that he knew China was negotiating with Australia, and if China was paying all cash to Australia, anything other than a cash deal would not look good from a Canadian point of view. Ting simply replied, "The whole problem is the matter of competition. The country whose terms are more acceptable will obtain the business." The meeting ended on the promise from Ting that: "If the terms are suitable, the quantity involved will be large."

The ground rules had been set, but achieving an agreement was to prove a long, exhausting exercise. McNamara and Yu got down to business the next day with the Chief Commissioner making the first tentative offer of credit. Yu countered by agreeing that: "Canada has never before given such a proposition to a customer, but history is made by human beings so it is merely a question of creating our own history." He had in his mind no down payment and credit extending up to three years.

As the battle of wits continued — with three to four day intervals between meetings while Yu reported back to his principals in China and awaited new instructions — McNamara reported back to Bill Riddell in Winnipeg on March 30, that the weather was fine, "but one gets tired waiting around."

At the start of April, meetings began to take place on more regular intervals with seven negotiating sessions taking place up to April 10. At the meeting of April 7, Ting had reappeared and considerable progress had been made in narrowing the differences between the two parties. They were agreed on revolving credit up to a maximum of $50 million with a cash down payment of 25 per cent. However, McNamara was holding to a payment period of six months, while China Resources was pressing for extension of the period to nine months.

A draft agreement of "intent and undertaking" had been submitted to Peking covering the purchase of approximately five million long tons of wheat and one million long tons of barley, to be shipped between July 1, 1961, and December 31, 1963. At the close of the April 10 meeting, the Canadian delegation felt agreement was near and only the formality of signing remained. A vast number of details had been worked out with concessions on both sides. There was little to do but await the response from inside China.

Days of painful waiting followed. Then, unexpectedly, since McNamara had presumed the agreements would be signed in Hong Kong, an invitation came asking the Canadian Wheat Board mission to visit Peking. It was now presumed that the official signing would take place between the Wheat Board and China Resources' principals, the China National Cereals, Oils and Foodstuffs Import and Export Corporation (Ceroil). McNamara, Treleaven and Earl, accompanied by Yu and Liu, flew to Peking, but hopes of a speedy finalization of the contracts were soon dispelled. The deal was not yet locked up. McNamara and his companions met a new negotiating team consisting of Li Yu-sheng, Acting Director of Ceroil, Fu Hsing, Deputy Director, and two Deputy Department Managers, Tan Chao-van and Tang Chung-chiao on April 17.

In the courteous greetings which followed, Li invited the Canadian visitors to do some sightseeing in Peking. McNamara, after three weeks of negotiating in Hong Kong, was anxious to get home and explained that their time in Peking must be very short. He hoped that, within a few days, their business could be completed. The courtesies over, it soon became apparent that Li was a skilled bargainer. The question of the term of deferred payment was raised. Would the Board reconsider extending it to nine months rather than six? Over the next seven days there were ten negotiating sessions, at which not only the length of deferred payment was debated, but interest rates, quantities, grades, prices and a myriad of other details were again discussed.

On April 19, McNamara informed the Chinese that he had been to the British Embassy where he had received a cable from Ottawa authorizing him to extend the credit terms to nine months. Despite that breakthrough, there were further lengthy negotiating sessions, including three on April 21. McNamara, worn out through a month of negotiations, had to excuse himself from the final session which began at 10 p.m. and continued into the next morning. Finally, following a lengthy morning session on April 22, agreement was reached. After 20 negotiating sessions in Hong Kong and Peking, extending over 31 days and recorded in 91 pages of minutes, Li ended the marathon with the words: "We can proceed with the drafting." There had not been much time for sightseeing.

In Peking on Saturday afternoon, April 22, 1961, history was made with the signing of four documents. It was a long-term agreement negotiated solely by the Canadian Wheat Board on an agency to agency basis, backed by a guarantee from Ottawa on bank loans to extend credit to the purchaser. It was a pattern which would dominate large bilateral long-term agreements increasingly in the future. Signing on behalf of the Canadian Wheat Board were W.C. McNamara, C.E.G. Earl and D.H. Treleaven. Li Yu-sheng and Fu Hsing were the signatories for the China National Cereals, Oils and Foodstuffs Import and Export Corporation.

The documents, in both Chinese and English, included a long-term agreement from June 1, 1961 to December 31, 1963, under which China agreed to

C.E. Gordon Earl CWB Comptroller/Secretary and Executive Director during the sixties and early seventies.

purchase between three million to five million long tons of wheat and 600,000 to one million long tons of barley. Separate agreements were to be entered into at intervals, and at prices to be negotiated prior to each contract.

Two other agreements, representing the first contracts under the long-term agreement, covered the sale of 750,000 long tons of wheat and 360,000 long tons of barley to be shipped during 1961. Terms of the sales were 25 per cent cash with the balance payable within nine months at 5.5 per cent interest. The final document was a memorandum listing socialist countries, which were not Canadian commercial markets, to which China would be allowed to divert purchases. [21]

The signing ceremonies over, the Canadian team was hosted at a Peking duck dinner that evening and prepared to return to Hong Kong the following day. It was a harrowing journey. Not long after takeoff the aircraft, an aged Russian type, landed and they were informed that they could not go any further since it was becoming dark and the pilot chose not to fly over the mountains at night. The passengers were lodged overnight in an ancient walled feudal castle. The next morning Liu informed them that the plane was unserviceable and needed repairs. After three days of waiting, the party proceeded on the rest of the journey by train to Kowloon where they crossed the border into Hong Kong. [22]

In Hong Kong they were informed of a surprise development. Before leaving Peking, McNamara had transmitted news of the contract signing through the British Embassy to Ottawa. On April 26, Prime Minister John Diefenbaker rose in the Commons and announced that Agriculture Minister Alvin Hamilton was en route to Hong Kong "to discuss another grain sale." [23]

With all of the documents signed, sealed and delivered four days previous to that announcement, Hamilton was obviously moving in to take over the spotlight.

Treleaven and Earl left for Canada April 27 carrying the signed agreements. They declined comment on the negotiations at the airport. [24] On the last day of negotiations in Peking, McNamara had raised the subject of announcement of the agreements, pointing out to the Chinese that news of the sale would soon be known to the trade in Canada and that "ministers of the government like to talk about business." It was now apparent that the minister wished to make the announcement in Hong Kong in order to take credit for the already completed negotiations.

McNamara, who was booked out on a flight on the morning of April 28, prior to Hamilton's scheduled arrival in the afternoon, prepared a memorandum for the minister outlining details of the transaction. In it the Chief Commissioner warned:

> This long-term agreement should not be considered or announced as a firm sales purchase of commitment. It will be appreciated that the Chinese actual requirements or failure of both parties to negotiate satisfactory terms could substantially alter the quantities which will be sold during the period of this agreement. [25]

Hamilton declined comment to reporters, who met him at the airport on his arrival. The next day however, he announced at a press conference that an "agreement of intent" had been reached covering the sale of grain to China. Asked if the wheat sale under the agreement of intent would be the biggest one in Canadian history, Hamilton replied that he thought so. He told the press that he would not go to Peking to conduct discussions in respect of the agreement: "These discussions would be held in the Colony." [26] Asked if he was authorized to discuss credit with the Chinese representatives in Hong Kong, the Agriculture Minister replied, "We recognize in the field of credit that there is commercial credit, medium-term credit and long-term credit. In view of the situation in this part of the world, we would be willing to look at some form of commercial credit." Concluding the press conference, Hamilton said he hoped to fly home that evening and hoped to report to the Canadian House of Commons on his discussions the following Tuesday.[27]

After a day and a half in Hong Kong, Hamilton flew back to Canada and on Tuesday, May 2, announced details of the agreement in the Commons. After outlining the earlier cash sales, Hamilton added:

> Simultaneously with fulfilling the first order there have been discussions and finally negotiations between the Canadian Wheat Board and the China Resources Company concerning further amounts of grain involved and other factors. The Canadian government felt there should be an overall agreement to facilitate orderly marketing.
>
> I am now pleased to report that a long-term agreement has been signed. This long-term agreement covers the period of June 1, 1961, to December 1963. Under this agreement we have committed ourselves to provide up to six million tons of barley, wheat and flour. Of this amount approximately one million tons will be barley. To put this into approximate bushels and value, it would provisionally be 186.7 million bushels of wheat and 46.7 million bushels of barley, worth approximately $362 million.[28]

Noting that it would be beyond the resources of the Wheat Board to extend the required credit facilities for the quantities involved, Hamilton added:

> Accordingly the government, reflecting its intensive efforts to sell grain in volume to new markets, is prepared to guarantee to a maximum of $50 million the credit necessary for the Canadian Wheat Board to conclude these transactions on a short-term credit basis.[29]

The success of Hamilton's Hong Kong visit, in terms of personal political mileage, was reflected in the United Press International report of the announcement: "Mr. Hamilton made his report to Parliament after returning from Hong Kong where he personally closed the deal with a trading agency which acted on behalf of the Peking regime."[30]

On the day of the announcement in the Commons Treleaven, who had been engaged almost full-time in the negotiations since the first contacts in January, wrote to Jim Lawrie, the Board's European Manager in London, enclosing copies of the contracts and clippings from the *Winnipeg Free Press*. He could be forgiven for ending the letter on a caustic note:

> You will note that the announcement has been made in terms of an agreement reached between the minister and the Chinese authorities, and no mention is made in the official release of the wheat board participation in negotiations. One might well ask, as the trade has been doing all day, just what the board officials were doing in Hong Kong and China for a matter of six weeks!"[31]

McNamara had grave concerns about the actions of the Agriculture Minister:

> Unfortunately, the publicity that has been given to this transaction through the agency of the minister will, I am afraid, adversely affect future negotiations. We found the Chinese very keen, hard bargainers and now that these first two transactions have received so much public acclaim here in Canada, I am satisfied that they will take full advantage of the situation when we get together in about six months time to endeavour to negotiate further quantities.[32]

The Chief Commissioner's apprehensions were confirmed a short time later. Forsyth-Smith reported to him that he had sat next to L.C. Pu of China Resources at a dinner in Hong Kong:

> He remarked to me that Mr. Hamilton had done a great deal of talking about his part in the recent grain contract, that apparently Parliament had not been told it had been signed prior to Hamilton's arrival, and that obviously the government must consider it to be of tremendous importance. He mentioned that it seems, from a political point of view, the contract was most popular. I got the impression that the Chinese are softening us up for extremely tough negotiations on the next leg of the agreement.[33]

Little could be done about the cultivation of the myth of Alvin Hamilton as a super-salesman, and the Wheat Board quietly went about cementing its new relationship, including arrangements for the Chinese to send a delegation to Canada to view Canada's grain industry first hand. It must have been frustrating however, to read articles such as that in the *Montreal Star* in advance of a visit by a delegation from China the following September:

> Ottawa — When Agriculture Minister Alvin Hamilton was in China earlier this year setting up the more than $400 million grain deal which has just about moved all the surplus grain from the farms of Western Canada, he suggested to the men from Peiping that they might find it to their advantage to come to Canada and look at the entire grain operation. He also suggested that, since the Red China negotiators had helped solve a major grain problem in this country by buying up so much, some of their trade people might find it helpful to come here to see what they had to sell to Canada beside walnuts. [34]

In late September the Chinese trade mission arrived, and the first of a series of negotiating sessions on a second contract under the long-term agreement was held in Winnipeg on October 27, 1961. Four meetings took place in the Canadian Wheat Board building up to the end of the month. They resumed November 21, when the mission, headed by Li Yu-sheng, First Deputy Director of Ceroil, returned once again to Winnipeg. In the interim, the federal cabinet had authorized an increase in the credit guarantee by $50 million to a total of $100 million.

Nothing was finalized at the Winnipeg meetings but, shortly after the mission returned to China, McNamara received an invitation to go to Peking to conclude a second contract. The Chief Commissioner wired back that the pressure of business at home, and Board attendance at negotiating sessions on a new International Wheat Agreement, made a visit to Peking impossible. He suggested that, if some measure of agreement could be reached by telegraphic exchange, it might be possible for a Board member to meet briefly in Hong Kong in mid-January.

After a measure of agreement appeared to be reached on a suggested interim contract covering three to four months, McNamara and Treleaven left once again for Hong Kong on December 8, 1961. Prior to their departure, McNamara stressed that he must be back in Winnipeg by December 22. But once again negotiations proved complex. Seven negotiating sessions were required, between December 12 and 18, before a contract was signed. It covered shipment of 820,000 long tons of wheat and 190,000 long tons of feed barley from West Coast ports from January through May of 1962. McNamara cabled Hamilton that Ceroil was "not anxious for publicity at this time and especially request that prices are not disclosed if you decide some public announcement is necessary." On December 21, Hamilton announced the sale in a Department of Agriculture press release and placed the value of the contract at $71 million.

As predicted, the second round had been tough. It took a total of 14 negotiating sessions covered by 43 long pages of closely typed minutes to reach the agreement. However, the Board's bargaining position was strengthened since the Chinese negotiators were obviously concerned over availability of Canadian stocks of grain. Drought across the Prairies in 1961 reduced the wheat crop to 245.5 million bushels, compared to 481.7 million bushels in the previous year.[35] It was the lowest crop in 25 years, and combined with the new Chinese purchases, the Canadian carryover had been drastically reduced. Despite the hard bargaining, the Chinese, once having concluded a contract, lived up to the letter of the agreement and paid precisely on time.

It had been a momentous year for the Board. Preparation for the new building was well underway, along with provisions for acquisition of a computer to simplify accounting and records. A new office had been opened in Tokyo, and a new Department of Technical Services and Market Research had been set up to provide technical assistance to the milling and baking industry in overseas markets.

There were also changes on the board and in the senior staff during 1961. John T. Dallas, who had been appointed a Commissioner on July 10, 1958, resigned effective January 1, 1961, to return to Continental Grain. The vacancy was eventually filled by J.B. Lawrie, the Board's European Manager, on December 22, 1961. Doug Treleaven was appointed Manager of the London office and R.L. Kristjanson replaced him as Executive Assistant.

The pattern of Canada's trade on the world grain market was also undergoing dramatic change. The long-time traditional market in Britain was progressively diminishing. In 1961 the Chorleywood Process of breadmaking was introduced. Developed by the British Baking Industry Research Association in the small village of Chorleywood, half an hour out of London, the new process enabled British and European bakers to use higher percentages of their own domestic wheat, and less hard high-protein wheat from Canada, in producing an acceptable loaf.

In 1961-62, Canada's exports of wheat to Britain dropped to just under 86 million bushels. This decline was more than offset, however, by the new market in China, as the impact of the long-term agreement took effect. In the 1960-61 crop year wheat exports to China totalled 34.7 million bushels. The next crop year the China trade soared to 72 million bushels, replacing Japan as Canada's major market on the Pacific Rim.

On the political scene, the Progressive Conservative government of John Diefenbaker was nearing the end of its mandate. In the election of June 18, 1962, the overwhelming majority of 208 seats held by the Tories disappeared. Diefenbaker found himself leading a minority government. The Conservatives dropped to 116 seats in the 265 seat House of Commons, while the Liberals, under Lester Pearson, had regained ground and elected 99 members. The surprising upsurge of the Créditistes in Quebec, led by the fiery oratory of Réal Caoutte, resulted in that party taking 24 seats in that province. Thus, the Social Credit Party, with a total of 30 seats, virtually held the balance of power. There were also 19 New Democrats and one Liberal-Labour elected.

During the 1962 session of Parliament four amendments to the *Canadian Wheat Board Act* were passed. In addition to changing the responsibility for reporting for the Board from Trade and Commerce to Agriculture, as previously noted, rapeseed was added to the definition of grains under the act and provision was made whereby the Board might establish group life insurance and group medical-surgical plans. The mandate of the Board was also extended for another five years to August 1, 1967.[36]

With internal dissent now apparent in the Conservative ranks, the minority government did not last long in a turbulent House of Commons. John Diefenbaker was forced to go to the country again in 1963. On April 18, 1963, another minority government was elected. This time the Liberals held 129 seats to the Conservatives 99 and Lester Pearson became Prime Minister. Once again Social Credit represented the third largest bloc in the Commons with 24 seats, while the New Democratic Party won 17 seats. Mitchell Sharp was suddenly back on the scene as a Member of Parliament and minister in charge of the department where he had formerly served as the Deputy Minister. The Canadian Wheat Board was now reporting to Parliament through Sharp as Minister of Trade and Commerce.

Footnotes Chapter 1

1. *The Canadian Wheat Board Minute Book*, Vol. 26, p. 45.

2. *Ibid*, p. 47.

3. *Reports of the Canadian Wheat Board, Crop Years 1957-58, 1958-59*.

4. *Canadian Wheat Board Minute Book*, Vol. 26, p. 50.

5. Canadian Wheat Board File, China Resources Negotiations, January-April, 1961.

6. *Reynold News and Sunday Citizen*, January 1, 1961, p. 1.

7. Canadian Wheat Board Files, Office Memorandum, W.C. McNamara, January 4, 1961.

8. *Ibid*, January 13, 1961.

9. *Ibid*.

10. Debates of the House of Commons, January 23, 1961.

11. Canadian Wheat Board Files.

12. *Ibid*.

13. Debates of the House of Commons, February 3, 1961.

14. *Ibid*.

15. Canadian Wheat Board Files, D. Treleaven, letter to W.C. McNamara, February 26, 1961.

16. *Ibid*, W.C. McNamara Office Memorandum, February 24, 1961.

17. *Ibid*, Office Memorandum Treleaven to McNamara, February 28, 1961.

18. *South China Morning Post*, February 27, 1961.

19. Canadian Wheat Board Files, Forsyth-Smith, letter to W.C. McNamara, March 3, 1961.

20. *Ibid*, China Resource Negotiations, January-April, 1961.

21. *Ibid*.

22. Taped interview, C. Gordon Earl, June, 1984.

23. *The China Mail*, Hong Kong, April 27, 1961.

24. *South China Morning Post*, April 28, 1961.

25. Canadian Wheat Board Files, McNamara memorandum to Alvin Hamilton, April 28, 1961.

26. *South China Sunday Post-Herald*, April 30, 1961.

27. *Ibid*.

28. Debates of the House of Commons, May 2, 1961.

29. *Ibid*.

30. *South China Morning Post*, May 3, 1961.

31. Canadian Wheat Board Files, Treleaven letter to J.B. Lawrie, May 2, 1961.

32. *Ibid*, McNamara letter to J.B. Lawrie, May 5, 1961.

33. *Ibid*, Forsyth-Smith letter to McNamara, July 12, 1961.

34. *The Montreal Star*, September 16, 1961.

35. *Report of the Canadian Wheat Board, Crop Year 1961-62*, p. 16.

36. *Ibid*, p. 31.

CHAPTER 2
RED MENACE?

And you all know, security is mortals' chiefest enemy.
— *Shakespeare: Macbeth, III. v. [32]*

Prior to the return to power of the Liberal Party in Ottawa, the 1961 long-term agreement with China created a storm of protest from all sides.

With the inevitable outburst of protestations from Washington over Canada's "trading with the enemy," it was not long before the opposition parties in Ottawa and the Canadian media chimed in. Social Credit Leader Robert Thompson branded it as "the most irresponsible act of any government since confederation." Hazen Argue, the CCF House Leader, declared it to be the "flimsiest kind of transaction," and Liberal member Jack Pickersgill called for full information on the contract. [1]

As the formerly omnipotent majority of the Conservative government dwindled into minority in the 1962 election, fireworks over the China contract were anticipated when the House re-convened. Then China invaded northern India. Across Canada, editors thundered out against the continued sale of wheat to China. A sister nation of the Commonwealth was under attack. Even in the centre of the Canadian Prairies, the *Swift Current Sun* declaimed:

> It is all very well for Agriculture Minister Hamilton to say that "as a government, we intend to sell food to any nation regardless of the colour of their skin, their religious beliefs or their politics," but does this hold true when the purchaser nation is invading a member of the Commonwealth. [2]

Lubor J. Zink, in a syndicated news column from Ottawa, declared:

> Trade is, and always has been regarded by leaders of the Sino-Soviet Bloc as an important weapon in their openly

declared and openly waged war for world domination...By
trading with the enemy in this strange new form of mortal
combat, we are helping him to accomplish his aim. There is
nothing to beat such "policy" for suicidal stupidity.[3]

Against the backdrop of that volatile political atmosphere, the Canadian
Wheat Board was attempting to negotiate a further contract with China. On
November 19, 1962, Assistant Chief Commissioner Bill Riddell, accompanied
by Jim Lawrie and Gordon Earl, left for Hong Kong. The meetings with representatives of China Resources promised to be tough. For the Canadian team, the
dilemma was not whether it was politically palatable in Canada to sell more
wheat to China, but would the Board be able to meet growing competition and
sell any grain at all.

Jacques Lang, the peripatetic sales virtuoso of Dreyfus Grain, had just been to
Peking. He spent 20 days in China and Hong Kong and concluded a sale of
780,000 long tons of French wheat to the Chinese. The sale was at prices lower
than those earlier contracted by the Canadian Wheat Board and on terms over
18 months underwritten by the French government. While he would not reveal
the exact price, Lang was quoted as saying it was "extremely low." In total,
China had purchased 1.08 million tons of French wheat. In addition, they had
acquired 670,000 tons of wheat from Australia at prices rumoured to be 10 per
cent under the price Australia was offering it to the United Kingdom and other
European countries.[4]

Other democracies were having no hang-ups over trading with the
"Red Menace."

In Hong Kong, Riddell and his team were across the table from a determined
group of Chinese negotiators who knew they held the cards in a buyer's market.
In late November R.M. Esdale, of the Department of Trade and Commerce,
reported back to Ottawa that the Chinese were extremely disappointed with
Canada's performance regarding importation of Chinese goods, in contrast to
the Australian performance. Further, they were adamant that a longer credit
period was essential and drew attention to longer periods extended by Australia
(one year) and France (18 months). The Chinese also said that minimum quantities under the long-term agreement had already been purchased and unless
more favourable credit terms were made available, they might not purchase any
more wheat at that time.[5]

William Riddell, Assistant Chief Commissioner, during the period when the CWB broke into Chinese and Russian markets.

Even as these difficult negotiations were going forward, the Auditor General of Canada queried the power of the Wheat Board to borrow from the banks to extend credit to China: "On referring to the Canadian Wheat Board Act, R.S., c.44, it appears that the borrowing powers of the Board are restricted to making of loans for the financing of grain in store and that it lacks the authority to borrow for the purpose of financing credit sales."[6]

In a lengthy memorandum the Board's solicitor, Henry B. Monk, was able to satisfy the Auditor General that, under Section 11 of the *Canadian Wheat Board Act*, the Minister Responsible for the Board "may guarantee repayments of advances made to the Board on the security of grain or otherwise by any bank incorporated under the *Bank Act* for the purpose of carrying on its operations under the *Canadian Wheat Board Act*."[7]

Despite the public outcry against trade with China, and the questions of legality of the long-term contract, Riddell, Lawrie and Earl returned from Hong Kong early in December with a contract for a further 870,000 long tons of wheat to be delivered in the first six months of 1963. However, it had taken three weeks of bargaining — from November 19 to December 8 — to conclude the contract, and the credit terms had to be extended an additional three months from the previous nine months to one year. Authority for the extension had been given by Cabinet prior to their departure.

Concerned over the prospects of a continuing market in China at the expiry of the 1961 long-term contract, McNamara had despatched a lengthy letter to Alvin Hamilton outlining the insistence of the Chinese that they faced "discrimination" in the access of their goods into the Canadian market.

> As a marketing agency if the opportunity exists, and we think it does, to build up a steady continuing wheat trade with China it would be most welcome since such a development would broaden the base of our sales. Prior to the United States initiating its broad "give away" programmes under P.L. 480, [Public Law 480 and its broad implications on world wheat prices were fully outlined in *The McIvor Years*] we could expect to market a substantial volume of wheat in markets either traditionally importers of wheat or in need of wheat due to shortages brought about by natural calamities. Nowadays such marketing opportunities rarely exist. Many of our former markets now depend entirely on American aid. Coupled with this is the American propensity for moving into markets in need of grain due to crop failures under the P.L. 480 Sections — markets that would normally secure supplies commercially. All this limits the sale of Canadian wheat and makes it essential that we exploit every possible market, and especially those we are not frustrated in on account of American largesse.[8]

The Chief Commissioner again raised the subject with Hamilton in mid-January of 1963: "I told Mr. Hamilton that I was satisfied from reports received from Mr. Riddell and Mr. Lawrie, that there was little chance of our negotiating sales to China unless something was done to improve their trading relationship with Canada." McNamara suggested that, as a matter of goodwill, Canada should be prepared to send a trade delegation to Hong Kong to discuss the issue with China Resources.[9] He continued to press the matter with Ottawa through February and into March. However, on March 12, a phone call from Trade and Commerce informed Lawrie that the question of easing restrictions against Chinese imports had been considered by Cabinet and "it was shot down."[10]

By the end of April, as previously noted, a new government was in office in Ottawa and the Board was reporting to Mitchell Sharp. Sharp, who began a career in the grain business with James Richardson and Sons in Winnipeg prior to World War II, had negotiated grain sales and a most favoured nation protocol with the Soviet Union while he was Deputy Minister of Trade and Commerce in the previous Liberal regime. He proved to be more pragmatic than the Tories in his approach to China.

On April 29, the Board's London Manager, Doug Treleaven, was asked to trace the whereabouts of Lu Hsu-Chang, Vice-Minister of Foreign Trade for the People's Republic of China, who was reported to be in Europe discussing grain purchases. McNamara flew to London. On May 6, it was ascertained that Lu was at The Hague in the Netherlands. The next day McNamara and Treleaven flew to Holland and obtained an appointment with Lu.

They were cordially received and McNamara asked if two missions might institute dealings with Hong Kong, one dealing with textiles and the other a wheat agreement. Lu said that, if the Canadian side had any views on the problem of Chinese imports into Canada, that Bob Thomson, the Canadian Trade Commissioner in Hong Kong, should contact China Resources for a preliminary exchange of views.[11] Returning to London, McNamara immediately cabled Ottawa recommending that an exploratory mission, comprising representatives of various government departments, be sent to Hong Kong as soon as possible to discuss the whole problem of Chinese trade with Canada. On May 13, a reply came back. Sharp approved the mission.

In strict secrecy, V.L. Chapin, representing Trade and Commerce, M. Sakallaropoulo, Finance, and L. Howey, National Revenue, left Ottawa May 30 for Hong Kong via Vancouver. Doug Treleaven, who was to head the mission, flew direct to Hong Kong from his London base. J.W. Snell, the Board's representative in Tokyo, later expressed some frustration when he heard about the mission from the trade. McNamara had to mollify him in a long letter on June 12, pointing out the need for avoiding publicity as long as possible.

After four days of discussions with China Resources, Treleaven's delegation reported back June 8:

> Discussions with Cireco completed today. Chinese reiterated that in principle they were prepared to continue purchasing wheat in years ahead provided Canadian government were to reconsider its "discriminatory" treatment of Chinese

exports and provided also that satisfactory contract terms can be arranged. [12]

McNamara had just returned to work after several weeks of illness caused by a low-grade fever picked up in Europe, but the signal was all he needed. After discussions with Trade and Commerce in Ottawa on the extent of concessions that could be made on Chinese imports, particularly in the sensitive area of textiles, he flew to Hong Kong. There he was joined, on July 1, at the Repulse Bay Hotel, by Treleaven who had again flown in from London. As in 1961, negotiations on the second long-term contract were protracted. From July 2 to August 2, there were 24 separate negotiating sessions with China Resources. Treleaven detailed the painstaking details in 211 lengthy pages of minutes.

By July 27, agreement had finally been reached on access of Chinese goods to Canada amounting to $7 million annually. Basic terms of a three-year wheat contract were also agreed upon and Ottawa was advised. Deputy Minister of Trade and Commerce James A. Robertson cabled back to McNamara: "All here join warm congratulations and admiration for your efforts and look forward to earliest news successful conclusion. Minister proposes simultaneous announcement by government and Wheat Board..." [13]

The Chinese were now anxious to complete the first contract under the new long-term agreement. Finally, McNamara flashed the news to Roberts:

> Long-term agreement and sales contract signed 7 p.m. August 2. I have told the Chinese to expect Canadian publicity...The minister is therefore free to make announcement at any time along these lines. Please inform me soonest time of announcement and send text immediately after release. Leaving here Saturday afternoon. Arrive Winnipeg about noon Sunday. [14]

The long, complicated transaction was over. Simultaneous announcements were made from Ottawa and Winnipeg:

> The Canadian Wheat Board is pleased to announce the conclusion of a long-term agreement with China National Cereals, Oils and Foodstuffs Import and Export Corporation. This agreement is not a firm sales contract but rather a Declaration of Intent which sets out procedures to facilitate the sale and purchase of wheat through subsequent individual sales contracts. Under the agreement, the Chinese authorities have declared their intention to purchase from Canada three

to five million long tons (112.0 to 186.7 million bushels) of wheat over a three-year period August 1, 1963 to July 31, 1966. The Canadian Wheat Board has undertaken to make such supplies available to the Chinese Trading Corporation concerned with specific quantities, prices and shipping periods to be negotiated periodically.[15]

Agreement had not been reached without concessions. As noted, credit terms extended over 18 months as compared to one year in the previous contracts. In the first contract, covering shipment of 500,000 long tons of wheat from West Coast ports between August 1, 1963, and January 31, 1964, there had been price concessions. This, in line with the Board's policy of pricing to all purchasers on a similar basis, resulted in a lowering of the Board's posted prices.

Growing American frustration at the rapidly changing course of events was illustrated by a syndicated column from Washington that appeared in many U.S. papers. Quoting "authoritative U.S. sources," it stated:

> Washington — Canada's immense wheat sales to Red China are turning sour.
>
> While deliveries of the grain, which the Canadians peddled with zealous eagerness, are continuing on schedule, payment is not. Peking's instalments are steadily lagging.
>
> Authoritative U.S. sources estimate that the Communists are more than $100 million in arrears.
>
> Ottawa is giving no public hint of this disturbing situation. And naturally Peking is saying nothing either.
>
> But, Canada is sounding out U.S., British and World Bank officials on bailing out Red China by lending enough money to meet its overdue instalments on the $650 million wheat debt.
>
> In these hush-hush feelers, the Canadians apparently are thinking in terms of a loan of several hundreds of million dollars to the Communists.
>
> So far these backstage overtures have gotten no encouragement.
>
> What the next move will be remains to be seen. This matter has become known to congressional leaders, and they are watching it closely. Any attempt to provide Peking with funds to pay for wheat it bought from Canada over U.S. protests would precipitate a furious uproar.[16]

The "authoritative" story was a prime example of the type of wild rumour and speculation promulgated by opponents of the Canadian Wheat Board both abroad and at home.

Nothing could have been further from the truth. China had actually prepaid in December of 1962 and in the spring of 1963, in order to save on interest payments. On November 18, in a New York speech, Mitchell Sharp denied there was any truth in the statements. The Canadian Wheat Board refuted the article as being "issued with the intention of either hurting Canada or in a spirit of 'sour grapes.'" [17]

Coincidental with the appearance of that spurious article, a delegation, headed by Ting Ke-Chien, Managing Director of China Resources in Hong Kong, was being wined and dined in Canada as guests of the Canadian Wheat Board. They were hosted at a reception in Winnipeg's Fort Garry Hotel on November 4, attended by 95 representatives of the grain trade, the railways and the banks.

After touring Western Canada, Ting and his colleagues were again honoured at a dinner in Winnipeg's exclusive Manitoba Club on November 14. They dined upon, among other things, poached sole in champagne sauce, duck and wild rice. [18]

Seeding on the Prairies in the early sixties.

In Ottawa five days later, the delegation was again entertained, this time at the Royal Ottawa Golf Club, with Mitchell Sharp and other government officials present, along with another Chinese delegation headed by Hong Wai Chey, Manager of Teck Soong Hong Ltd. of Hong Kong, who had travelled to Canada to promote Chinese exports. Bob Esdale, Chief of the Grain Division of Trade and Commerce, was "surprised to note the heavy consumption of wine, and amused to note there were 19 cigars for 14 guests." A subtle jibe no doubt at McNamara's predilection for cigars. [19]

As these events were taking place, unknown to the rest of the world, a dramatic scenario was building up behind the Iron Curtain. A watershed in the post-war history of the world grain trade was at hand. After a period of early promise, during which Russia steadily exported grain, the new "virgin lands" in the Soviet Union were falling victim to the whims of a harsh and uncertain climatic environment. A major decision was being taken within the Kremlin walls. Following a massive crop failure, the Soviet Union was about to emerge as the "X" factor in the world grain trade. Nikita Kruschev, rather than calling on the population to tighten their belts, as Soviet leaders had done in the past, had chosen to make up the deficit with imports.

There would be no need for price concessions under forthcoming contracts under the long-term China agreement.

Footnotes Chapter 2

1. *Calgary Herald*, August 15, 1962, p.2.
2. *Swift Current Sun*, November 16, 1962.
3. *Brandon Sun*, November 13, 1962.
4. Canadian Wheat Board Files, D.H. Treleaven letter to W.C. McNamara, November 2, 1962.
5. *Ibid*, R.M. Esdale to Prime Minister John Diefenbaker, November 30, 1962.
6. *Ibid*, A. Maxwell Henderson letter to Alvin Hamilton, November 19, 1962.
7. *Ibid*, H.B. Monk memorandum to the board, December 5, 1962.
8. *Ibid*, W.C. McNamara letter to Alvin Hamilton, December 14, 1962.
9. *Ibid*, W.C. McNamara memorandum to the board, January 16, 1963.
10. *Ibid*, J.B. Lawrie, office memorandum, March 12, 1963.
11. *Ibid*, D.H. Treleaven, office memorandum, May 13, 1963.
12. *Ibid*, W.C. McNamara, office memorandum, June 10, 1963.
13. *Ibid*, J.A. Roberts, cable to W.C. McNamara, July 27, 1963.
14. *Ibid*, W.C. McNamara, cable to J.A. Roberts, August 2, 1963.
15. Canadian Wheat Board press release, August 2, 1963.
16. *St. Paul Pioneer Press*, November 14, 1963.
17. Canadian Wheat Board Files, W. Riddell letter to J.C. Brown, November 19, 1963.
18. *Ibid*, undated memorandum.
19. *Ibid*, R.M. Esdale, letter to W.C. McNamara, November 26, 1963.

CHAPTER 3

HOW MUCH HAVE YOU GOT?

I cannot recall a single case in history where people have been
starved into democracy.
— *Senator George Aitken of Vermont, 1963.*

Under ideal harvesting conditions across the wide expanse of the Canadian Prairies in late August 1963, the combines were gathering in a bumper crop of grain. As a result of the surge of grain exports through the new door, following signing of the record long-term agreement with China, farm stocks of wheat had dropped dramatically, standing at half what they were in 1961. Western farmers responded by sowing 27 million acres to wheat in the spring of 1963 and a record crop, estimated at over 700 million bushels was in prospect.

Despite the new sales, which had resulted in total exports of 331,367,218 bushels of wheat in the previous year, the bountiful yield posed a challenge for the Canadian Wheat Board with the promise of making it a year of surplus accumulation.

But, half-way round the world in the new virgin lands of Kazakhstan, which other exporting countries had been watching with apprehension as a possible competitor on world markets, the bright promise of the Canadian plains was not in evidence. Unknown to the rest of the world, Premier Krushchev's new granary of the Soviet Union had suffered a disaster.

In the Kremlin the decision had been made. Russia would open the curtain of their insecurity and admit a crop failure. Like the other rich nations of the world they would turn to the world market to make up the deficiency.

At the London office of the Canadian Wheat Board at No. 1 North Court, Great Peter Street, Doug Treleaven had "an interesting enquiry from the trade" on the morning of August 28, "with reference to completion of a new sales contract with Russia." [1]

Secrets are hard to keep in the complex and competitive labyrinth of the world grain trade where ship charterings and destinations, unusual gold or other currency transactions are tracked and watched in infinite detail by the merchants of grain represented by the multinational grain companies. It seemed that the Russians had come into the freight market on the Baltic Exchange for quotations on bulk wheat from St. Lawrence ports to Black Sea or North Baltic ports for September-October positions.

While the trade in London was curious to know whether the Canadian Wheat Board had negotiated a sale, their interest was piqued even more by the destinations reported. Given previous Canadian sales to the Russians, as far back as 1956, it was not unusual to see shipping booked via Canada's West Coast to Vladivostok. Those previous sales had been more a matter of logistics than actual need. The Russians found it more economical to distribute Canadian grain to its far eastern non-grain producing regions than to ship their own grain over long distances on the Trans-Siberian Railway. But from the St. Lawrence to European rather than to Asian ports? Was something big in the works? London agents of one of the "Big Five" multinationals, Bunge, relayed the query to their office in Winnipeg, where the manager was G.N. Vogel, later to become Chief Commissioner of the Canadian Wheat Board. They got back the reply that neither the Wheat Board nor the government was prepared to make any statement and did not wish to discuss the matter.[2]

McNamara relayed a confidential message back to Treleaven. Unusual things were indeed under way, the full implications of which were still unknown. An agreement had been reached on a sale of 300,000 long tons of wheat to the Soviets, half of which was to be shipped from the traditional West Coast ports and half from the St. Lawrence. The negotiations had been instituted on a government to government basis and Soviet Deputy Trade Minister S.A. Borisov was to arrive in Ottawa to begin negotiations with Trade Minister Mitchell Sharp on renewal of a Canada-USSR trade treaty. Under that treaty — detailed in The McIvor Years — Borisov, Mike Pearson, then Secretary of State for External Affairs, and Trade Minister C.D. Howe had signed a most favoured nation treaty in early 1956, and exchanged letters covering the purchase of 1.2 million to 1.5 million tons of wheat over the following three years. The grain sales had been negotiated by Sharp who was then Deputy Minister of Trade and Commerce.

Accompanying Borisov on the current trip was Leonid Matveev, President of Exportkhleb, the Soviet state trading organization. McNamara was flying to Ottawa on the following Monday or Tuesday to take part in the discussions. He was "hoping that, as a result of the discussions, that possibly an additional contract for this year, or some kind of long-term arrangement can be worked out with them."[3]

Events had moved with dramatic suddenness. They began when Jacques Lang, the London-based agent for Louis Dreyfus, flew to Moscow in mid-August hoping to close a deal for the sale of some Soviet corn on the international market. Lang was the "Russian connection" for the giant Dreyfus multi-national grain trading corporation. A gifted linguist, he had quickly learned the language from his Russian-born wife whom he met while interned by the Japanese during World War II in Shanghai.

In Moscow he met with Matveev. Matveev, who had given up an engineering career to become a grain trader, was well known in the closed circle of the international grain trade as a bargainer of legendary patience and stubbornness. With the advantage of inside knowledge on Soviet crop conditions, a closely kept secret from the rest of the world in those days before development of sophisticated satellite monitoring, Matveev had the reputation of always getting top dollar on intermittent exports of Soviet grain outside of the Soviet Bloc.

But this time Matveev was not selling. He told Lang that the Soviet crop had "drawn a blank." They were in the market for grain.

Following the agreement of February, 1956, a renewed Canada-Soviet trade agreement had been entered into in April, 1960, for a three-year period. Under it, the Soviets agreed to purchase twice as much from Canada as Canada imported from the USSR up to a maximum of $25 million, with half that amount being taken by the Soviets in grain. There still remained a commitment on behalf of the Russians to take up to 200,000 tons of grain.

McNamara, who first met Matveev during a visit to Russia several years previously and again in Rome during negotiations on the International Wheat Agreement, had raised the subject of the shortfall under the protocol when the Exportkhleb chief visited Canada in late August, 1962. Matveev had replied that he was not sure that Russia would require any Canadian supplies. But, during that visit, a firm friendship had developed between Matveev, who spoke fluent English, and McNamara as they discussed the world grain situation as exporters.

The rapport that developed was such that future correspondence and the exchange of New Year's greetings was on an informal first name basis. McNamara's letters to Matveev were always prefaced with "Dear Johnnie," while Matveev's salutation was a more effusive Russian greeting of "My dear friend Bill."[4] The month following Matveev's 1962 visit to Canada, R.V. Gordon, the Canadian Commercial Counsellor in Moscow, called on the Exportkhleb chief and reported back to McNamara:

> I spent about an hour with him and I must say that he is one of the most enthusiastic supporters of Canada and Canadians that it has been my privilege to talk to in the various countries in which I have been stationed. As well as being most interested in the technical aspects of the growing and distribution of wheat in Canada, he also spoke enthusiastically about his visit to Niagara Falls and Canadian football. He

seems to have become a convert to golf, and he and I are going to try to get something started on this line in Moscow, as we both think it is a game all businessmen should play.[5]

Throughout the fall of 1962 and the summer of 1963, the subject of the Soviet commitment was raised on several occasions with Matveev, during his visits to London. Jim Lawrie, the Canadian Wheat Board's European Manager, reported back to Winnipeg that Matveev had been non-committal on taking up the shortfall, although he had indicated there were some problems with the Soviet crop.

Now, with Lang in Moscow in mid-August 1963, the friendship that had developed between McNamara and Matveev was about to pay off in spades. Instead of purchasing corn, Lang was asked if Dreyfus would act as the agent of the Canadian Wheat Board in fulfilling the Soviet commitment under the Canada trade agreement. On August 20, McNamara received a cable from Matveev in Moscow: "Kindly be informed that we have got permission from the Ministry of Foreign Trade of the USSR to buy from you 250,000 — 300,000 tons of wheat on account of balance of commitments against the trade agreement..."[6]

In an exchange of cables over the next five days, agreement was reached for shipment of 150,000 tons of wheat out of West Coast ports and 150,000 long tons out of the St. Lawrence. Louis Dreyfus was to be the Wheat Board's agent for shipping of the grain over the next three months. Matveev would sign the formal contract on his arrival in Canada within the next few days.

Against this backdrop of a secure contract covering the next several months, and the prospect of further sales into the forthcoming year, McNamara, accompanied by his Executive Assistant, Larry Kristjanson, flew to Ottawa in early September. Bill Riddell, the Assistant Chief Commissioner, followed the next day.

In the international trade, speculation was rife. From London, Treleaven reported that one member of the trade had "very confidentially" indicated concern that, if there was an agreement between Exportkhleb and the Wheat Board, it might involve price concessions. There was also concern that the single agent, Dreyfus, would have inside knowledge which they could use to their own advantage in other areas by anticipating the Board's price adjustment at the time the contract was formally announced.[7]

With McNamara already in Ottawa, Jim Lawrie wrote back reporting on the developments: "In due course we will be hearing the details of the current negotiations but, in the meantime, there is nothing can be said other than it is an interesting development."[8]

As Sharp and Borisov began the ritual of negotiating a protocol on extension of the trade agreement in the Centre Block on Parliament Hill on September 3, McNamara and Kristjanson were meeting with Matveev a short distance away across the narrow stretch of the Rideau Canal. Beneath the green copper roof of the ageing, but still prestigious, Chateau Laurier Hotel, where so much of the history of the Canadian Wheat Board had been written in its formative years, they were meeting in Matveev's suite. A new chapter in Canada's grain trade was in the making.

Formalities on the previously negotiated sale over, Matveev indicated that the Russians were interested in further purchases. McNamara responded with his first tentative probe, "How much is Russia interested in?"

Matveev was not beating about the bush, "How much have you got?"

McNamara could hold a poker hand with the best of them, but the realization of what was at hand registered. His face dropped. Unprepared for such a massive proposal, he ventured that Canada might have 10 million tons in light of the bumper crop then being harvested. Matveev came right back, "We'll take it."

That evening Riddell arrived and was briefed on the startling turn of events. On that cool September evening, the Wheat Board negotiators walked over to Parliament Hill discussing the situation. Kristjanson had phoned Winnipeg following the afternoon meeting to obtain information on grades and quantities immediately available, and to ascertain port capacities and other relevant logistical information on transportation.

Frank Rowan, by now Sales Manager in Winnipeg, had tentatively calculated the amount that could be moved in relation to other commitments. It was obvious that slightly over five million long tons was the maximum that could be accommodated through the overall handling system. Back in Winnipeg the lights of the new Canadian Wheat Board building burned late as a multitude of details and equations were worked out.

In Matveev's suite the next day, McNamara presented the preliminary estimate of maximum deliveries. The Exportkhleb chief was disappointed and angered. He had counted on more and felt that he had been misled by the preliminary estimate of 10 million tons, which was obviously physically available in Canada.

Dan Morgan in his book on the Big Five multinational grain companies, *Merchants of Grain*, reported that, "McNamara of the Wheat Board and Matveev were incommunicado in an upstairs suite for days. Sometimes McNamara stumbled out of the room, rushed to the hotel bar and downed a whisky and muttered, 'It's big.'"[9]

While that colourful anecdote imparts a measure of drama to the narrative, the record shows that McNamara had no need to stumble from the room for spirituous sustenance. Both he and Matveev had legendary capacities for matching each other in hospitality while still retaining their wits. The room was not dry. Nor would McNamara, knowing representatives of the multinationals were in the hotel, publicly breach the confidentiality insisted upon by Matveev.

Incommunicado they were, but behind the scenes a multiplicity of details were being put together. The railways, lake shippers and port authorities had to be contacted and ship bookings arranged before the magnitude of the deal was revealed.

Having been mollified, to the extent that the quantity limitation was one of logistics, and not physical stocks of wheat in storage and on farms, Matveev was nonetheless still pressuring for larger amounts of grain. Having made the decision to enter the market, the Soviets wanted as much as they could get from Canada and other sources before turning to their ideological enemy, the United States, to fulfil an obviously urgent need.

The master contract on the previously negotiated sale of 300,000 tons was officially signed by the Board and Exportkhleb on September 6, but it was not until Tuesday, September 10, that the Canadian Wheat Board issued a brief press release covering the cash sale and estimating its value at approximately $22 million.[10] Meanwhile both agencies were reporting back to their government representatives on Parliament Hill where the trade agreement protocol was being negotiated. There was little to negotiate. The Russians wanted Canadian grain, and as much as they could get. There was no need for a two for one quid-pro-quo reciprocal trade agreement with a monetary limit, as embodied in the 1960 trade pact. The only questions to be settled were the upper limits on quantities available, price and credit terms.

As in the Chateau Laurier negotiations, the Russians were putting governmental pressure on Canada to increase the quantity commitment. The Wheat Board provided a memorandum to Mitchell Sharp to counter the pressure from Borisov. Sharp outlined three questions to be settled: the quantity of wheat involved in the transaction; the credit terms available; and the question of possible diversion of flour to Cuba. Reading from the Board's memorandum, Sharp informed the Soviet delegation:

> I first want to assure Mr. Borisov that we are most anxious to supply the greatest quantities of wheat in the shortest possible time to the USSR. You may be assured that every facility of the Canadian government will be made available to the Canadian Wheat Board and the Canadian grain trade in order to facilitate the movement of wheat. But as practical men involved in grain marketing problems we must be realistic. It would not be to the advantage of either this government or your own to enter into a commitment which was impossible to fulfil.
>
> I would also wish to suggest to Mr. Borisov that Canada, under the terms of the International Wheat Agreement, has commitments to supply wheat to signatories of that agree-

ment. This government must honour its commitments under the terms of this international commitment.

Finally on the question of supplies, as an exporter of long standing, Canada must view this situation from the standpoint of the long term as well as our short term commercial interests. We are aware of the fact that harvesting conditions in all of Europe are extremely unfavourable this fall and our steady customers will require increased quantities of wheat during the coming year. We cannot ignore the requirements of these markets when they are in difficulty.

In view of these considerations my government has instructed the Canadian Wheat Board to limit the volume of wheat and flour to be offered to a maximum of 5.3 million long tons of wheat and 500,000 tons of flour. [11]

As to credit, Sharp said the government was ready to back up to $200 million through export credit insurance on terms of 50 per cent down and 25 per cent at six and 12 months. The question of diversion of flour to Cuba would be delayed pending discussion with External Affairs. [12]

Finally, on the morning of September 16, McNamara and Matveev signed the master agreements in a public ceremony. It was followed by the signing of the trade agreement protocol and an exchange of letters covering the wheat transaction by Borisov and Sharp. The Canadian Trade Minister then held a press conference.

Around the world the Dow Jones commodity news service teletypes clattered out the news:

> Ottawa - DJ - Russia today signed the biggest wheat-purchase pact in Canadian history ordering nearly $500 million worth of wheat and wheat flour for delivery in the next 10 ½ months.
>
> The order is for 198 million bushels of wheat and flour equal to another 29.5 million bushels.
>
> Trade Minister Sharp and S.A. Borisov, Russia's First Deputy Minister for Foreign Trade, signed the deal as part of a new three-year trade agreement between Canada and the Soviet Union — the signing took place shortly after 11 a.m. EDT at a press conference in Parliament's Centre Block.

In exchange trading pits and grain trading offices around the globe, traders gathered round the teletype terminals which had momentarily ceased their clatter as the reporter relayed further details to the operator. The bell, signifying urgent news, clanged again and the despatch continued:

> Add - Wheat Deal - Ottawa - DJ - The Soviet has also agreed to buy a further 18.7 million bushels of wheat or flour equivalent in the third year of the trade agreement.
>
> The shipments during the current crop year extend into the second year of the trade pact which was made retroactive to April this year, the expiry date of the previous three-year agreement.
>
> Russia recently purchased 11 million bushels of Canadian wheat for shipment this year. The new undertaking brings total shipments in the current crop year to Russia to about 239 million bushels of wheat and flour.
>
> Flour shipments alone will exceed total Canadian flour exports to all countries during the 1962-63 crop year.
>
> The wheat is being sold on a one-price basis and it covers all grades at Canada's option.
>
> Basis of the payment is 25 per cent cash for each shipment with one third of the remainder after six, 12 and 18 months. The Export Credits Insurance Corporation is extending facilities up to a maximum of $200 million at any one time. Effect of this ceiling is that a substantial portion of the Soviet purchases will be made for cash, Trade Minister Sharp said. [13]

The teletypes paused again, but in the offices of the multinationals action was already underway. Without waiting for the details that followed, arrangements were being made for their top traders to converge on Ottawa. Jacques Lang, of Dreyfus, and Patrick Mayhew, representing a New York trading firm, were already in Ottawa. At one stage during the negotiations Lang, who had negotiated his firm's agency part in the 300,000 ton sale by the Canadian Wheat Board, met with Matveev. The Russians were in a buying mood. Lang sold him 1.3 million tons of Australian wheat as an agent of the Australian Wheat Board. [14]

Now, with Sharp's announcement of the magnitude of the Canadian sale, the top echelon of the world's great grain houses beat a trail to the Chateau Laurier, seeking Matveev's favour. There was Michel Fribourg of Continental; Frederic Hediger of Garnac; Leopold Stern from Dreyfus in New York; Walter Saunders and Robert Diercks of Cargill, as well as representatives from Bunge. [15] They were there, not to jockey as agents of the Canadian Wheat Board where the commissions were a slim fraction of a cent a bushel, but to attempt to sell part of the huge stockpile of grain that had built up in the United States. There was more room to manoeuvre for profits in such a transaction.

Despite the U.S. Export Control Act, which directed the President to prohibit exports that "would make a significant contribution to the military, or economic potential," of nations threatening U.S. security, President Kennedy took a political gamble on October 9, 1963. He authorized the sale of up to four million tons of wheat to the Soviet Union. With a huge national shipping fleet exerting political pressure through the Seafarer's Union, Kennedy specified that half of any such grain sales be carried in American flag vessels. Not only did this make shipments more expensive, since American shipping rates were well above other world carriers, but the Russians, while willing to concede the crop failure, did not wish to have vessels bearing the Stars and Stripes offloading grain at their ports — particularly in continental Europe. Russian crews were also not anxious to drop anchor at U.S. ports where they were sometimes accorded hostile treatment. No matter how urgently the Soviet required grain, there was an apparently insurmountable barrier to which Russian pride would not bow. The traders left empty-handed.

For all that, the announcement of the huge Canadian sale must have been particularly galling to the United States Administration. Secretary of Agriculture Orville Freeman may well have winced at one portion of Sharp's prepared announcement:

> In taking the necessary measures to see that maximum supplies of Canadian wheat are made available, the Canadian government and the Canadian Wheat Board will be inspired both by pride and sense of deep humility that once again the bounty of nature and the skills and efforts of our farmers and of all associated with the handling of grain will be happily combined to help meet the need for daily bread throughout the entire world. [16]

Freeman could look around at a $7 billion budget for the USDA, and over one billion bushels of government-held stocks, built up under the price support program. While the United States had exported 638 million bushels of wheat in the 1962-63 crop year, in comparison to Canada's 331 million bushels, 75.3 per cent of the American exports had been by concessional sales, barter or donations. Only 24.7 per cent had been cash sales. Against this, only 1.74 million bushels of Canadian exports had gone out under the Colombo Plan and other government programs. The remainder were commercial sales. [17]

Freeman's dilemma had been graphically described the previous April when Time Magazine did a cover story on him:

> Hope, springing eternal, argues that the farm mess will somehow, some day, just go away. Maybe the growth rate of

the U.S. population will catch up with farm output, perhaps export markets will open up and swallow the surplus. But projecting present trends, the Agriculture Department foresees farm capacity running ahead of population growth until 1980 and beyond. Any export markets for U.S. farm goods may well narrow in the years ahead: Europe's Common Market, customer for nearly half of U.S. farm exports, is building up a tariff wall against agricultural imports.[18]

Now, here was Canada, with no hang-ups about trading with the Communists, following up the second long-term China agreement with a massive sale to the Soviet Union. The strain on the now shaky price stabilization compact between Canada and the U.S., which had already evinced itself in the Japanese market, was growing.

Nonetheless it could be argued that, to a large extent, the United States benefited from the huge Canadian sale. With the sudden entry of the Russians into the world market, world trade in wheat soared to over two billion bushels for the first time in history, exceeding the old record of 1.75 billion bushels set in 1961-62.[19] With the Canadian grain handling system strained to the limit in exporting 594, 547,631 bushels of wheat in the 1963-64 crop year, and turning away potential new commercial markets, the United States was able to expand its exports to 849.5 million bushels.[20] At the same time, the percentage of U.S. exports under governmental programs dropped as dollar, or regular commercial sales, expanded by more than 200 million bushels.[21]

Finally, when the Russians accepted that Canada could not supply more grain in that year, due to logistical constraints, Continental sold one million tons of U.S. wheat to the Soviet Union in January 1964. With Matveev still holding off on paying the additional shipping costs for U.S. grain, a breakthrough was made when Continental proposed a plan whereby the multinational would be able to claim additional export subsidies to compensate for the cost of using American ships. Cargill followed suit with a sale of 750,000 tons of wheat the next month. However, U.S. taxpayers shelled out heavily to, in effect, subsidize American shipping interests. On the Continental Grain sale, which included 350,000 long tons of durum, the export subsidy was 72 and 73 cents a bushel on the durum and 65 and 66 cents a bushel on Hard Red wheat.[22]

For western Canada the sales were a bonanza. Fertilizer and farm implement sales climbed. In Saskatchewan farm implement sales rose by 33 per cent in 1963.[23] Sales of seed wheat also soared as Prairie farmers made plans to sow a record acreage to wheat and to cut back on coarse grains in 1964.

In the Soviet Union, the trauma of turning to world markets with a massive outlay of hard currency, after the glowing promises of self-sufficiency to come from pouring capital into the new lands, eventually sealed the fate of Nikita Khrushchev who became the first Soviet leader to be ousted into retirement. The clandestine occupation of biting political humour in Moscow resulted in a story wherein one man asks another if he had heard there was to be a new Nobel prize for agriculture, and guess who was going to get it? "Why Krushchev of course. He is the first man in history to plant wheat in Siberia and harvest it in Canada."

For the Canadian Wheat Board, signing of the contract triggered a hectic period of activity. Construction of the new building on Main Street, renovation of the old building and merging of the two structures was completed during 1963 at a final cost of $4,103,411 with the effective date of occupancy on December 1. [24] Consolidation of the staff, now numbering 609 people, under one roof and computerization of records and accounting functions proved invaluable in meeting the challenge posed by the unprecedented surge of activity.

The Russians were obviously anxious to move as much grain as possible in the shortest possible time, and wished to assist in the correlation of the mass of detail on contracts with the trade acting as agents of the Board on shipping arrangements. Matveev obtained permission for three of his officials to remain in Canada for the entire period of the wheat and flour shipments. Nikolai A. Belousov, Director of the Grain Department of Exportkhleb, worked out of the Wheat Board's Montreal office, while Leonid N. Kalitenko, Exportkhleb's London Representative, was given an office in the Board's Winnipeg building. Alexandre I. Naumov, Exportkhleb's Representative in Amsterdam was stationed in Vancouver to co-ordinate West Coast shipments.

Matveev also stayed on in Canada and visited Winnipeg in early October, where he advised McNamara that all of the 5.3 million tons of wheat had been booked and that all of the flour and all the wheat except 1.03 million tons had been purchased on a cash basis. He indicated that, if total interest charges under the credit arrangements were above five per cent, Exportkhleb would not exercise the credit option on the remaining wheat. Eventually all of the sales were carried out on a cash basis.

On his return to Eastern Canada, Matveev and Belousov, accompanied by a Board representative, began a tour of terminal elevator facilities at Quebec, Trois Rivières, Halifax and St. John. Obviously still anxious to obtain additional Canadian grain before turning to the United States, the Russians were querying port officials on handling capacities at the ports over the winter months.

It was the beginning of persistent pressure on the Canadian Wheat Board to contract a further one million long tons of wheat for delivery in the 1963-64 crop year. On October 17, McNamara received a telephone call from Campbell Malcolm, a member of the National Harbours Board. Under close questioning from the Russians, Malcolm had indicated that additional capacity could be handled out of the St. Lawrence. He stressed to McNamara that it would be new business. The Chief Commissioner was obliged to advise Malcolm, "that the National Harbours Board should not get into the business of selling grain."[25]

Three days later Belousov visited the Board's Winnipeg headquarters and met with Assistant Chief Commissioner Bill Riddell. Exportkhleb wanted to buy additional quantities and the Harbours Board had indicated it was possible to ship it out. Riddell explained that, because of labour difficulties, the Board could not take any new commitments. Further, the cost of moving wheat to Trois Rivières by rail was 36 ½ cents a bushel, as compared to water rates of 13 ½ cents. Additionally, wheat prices had advanced 8 ⅜ cents since that last contract. Therefore, the cost to the Russians of wheat from the St. Lawrence ports would be 31 ⅜ cents a bushel higher than the wheat already purchased.[26] Despite the increased costs, the Russians were still interested. Kalitenko approached Jim Lawrie on October 29 to broach the question further. He was given no encouragement.[27]

The pressure resumed November 22, when Matveev again visited Winnipeg. He had returned from Washington and reported that Russian negotiations in the U.S. had failed, mainly due to the American shipping position which would cause a doubling of the freight costs. He said the Soviet Union still required wheat and were prepared to purchase, especially in the period January to April, 1964. McNamara gave Matveev little hope for additional shipments from the St. Lawrence and discussions turned to a possible early opening of the Hudson Bay port at Churchill in the coming season. Matveev was interested and indicated that the Soviet Union would co-operate with respect to the use of icebreakers for entering the northern port.[28]

Shortly afterwards, Matveev returned to Moscow but the pressure didn't stop. Two days before Christmas 1963, McNamara picked up the phone to find an irate Donald Gordon on the other end of the line. Kalitenko and another Russian had visited the CNR President in Montreal. They were still pressing to secure another one million tons of wheat out of the St. Lawrence. Gordon was told he was being approached because the Wheat Board indicated the railway could not supply the cars.

> I pointed out that nobody was blaming anybody, but the minister had stated in the House of Commons and at public meetings there was a demand for all the wheat this year which Canada could sell, and it was a matter of transportation, which included cleaning, terminal facilities, etc., as well as the lake and rail movement of grain, which were the limiting factors. This seemed to satisfy Mr. Gordon and he indicated that, if the question were referred to him again, he would advise the Russians that additional supplies from Canada were problems solely in the hands of the Wheat Board.[29]

The Russians were not the only buyers exerting pressure on the Board for new contracts or additional supplies. In the aftermath of the huge Soviet sale, a delegation from Koospol, the Czechoslovakian state purchasing agency, arrived in Winnipeg on October 1. The Czech's were seeking 300,000 tons of wheat, preferably No. 4 CWRS. McNamara was obliged to advise K. Jiracek, Deputy Manager of Koospol, that the limit would be 120,000 tons and it would have to be No. 2 and No. 3 grades. Queried about capacity from the West Coast, McNamara explained that the Board had already had to refuse a request from Japan for barley due to the tight shipping situation. [30]

It was indeed a seller's market. Eight days later a delegation from the Japanese Food Agency met with the Board. Taketo Nikai, leader of the five-man delegation, was seeking a portion of the Board's commitment over the next eight months to be made up of feed wheat. McNamara was unable to make the commitment, despite protestations from the Japanese that, unless the commitment was made, the Japanese might not contract the previously agreed upon 100,000 tons a month from Canada. [31]

Two weeks after that, the Board met on October 24, to consider requests from a number of small purchasers. Unable to meet the demands, the Board decided that Frank Rowan should contact the trade to ascertain what "long" stocks they had available to fulfil some of the requests. A number of the approaches, such as those from Italy, Rhodesia (now Zimbabwe) and Brazil, had to be rejected outright. [32]

Early in 1964 a new customer appeared, accompanied by Charles Kroft, President of McCabe Grain. On January 9, a delegation from East Germany met with the Board in Winnipeg. Their chief spokesman, Willi Claussen, indicated that the German Democratic Republic would like to enter into an agreement for 500,000 tons of wheat over a three-year period, but that such an agreement would be based on obtaining grain in the current crop year up to July 31. McNamara welcomed the approach but was unable to fulfil the request for immediate deliveries. He suggested that stocks might be available in the 1964-65 crop year and that the East Germans should begin early negotiations with the federal government in Ottawa on credit. [33]

In February, 1964, the close personal friendship that had evolved between McNamara and Matveev was cemented even further. McNamara and his wife Margaret arrived in Moscow on February 13 as guests of Exportkhleb. During the 12-day visit to Moscow, Leningrad and the Black Sea resort of Sochi, the McNamaras were treated with lavish hospitality by their Russian hosts. Little was discussed on future business as the McNamaras were taken to visit points of historic interest and entertained at the ballet, opera and at variety shows. Climax of the trip was a dinner given by the Soviet Ministry of Foreign Trade. It was hosted by Borisov, the First Deputy Minister of Trade, who had just returned from New York. R.A. Ford, of the Canadian Embassy in Moscow, reported back to External Affairs in Ottawa:

There is no doubt there is a warm personal regard for the McNamaras by Exportkhleb officials, and this was signified by the fact that Mrs. Matveev and Mrs. Belousov were present at most of the functions. Russian wives of Ministry of Foreign Trade officials seldom appear publicly.[34]

Prior to that celebration cementing the new relationship between Canada and the Soviet Union through grain sales, a Chinese Resources delegation had arrived in Winnipeg early in December, 1963, to negotiate a second contract under their current long-term agreement. This time there were no price concessions. With prices rising in the wake of the Soviet sale, the Chinese were anxious to secure as much grain as possible. McNamara pointed out:

The Canadian wheat supply situation has changed considerably from what it was when earlier sales contracts between our two organizations were completed. We are faced with a situation where the demand for Canadian wheat, particularly out of our Pacific ports, is far in excess of our ability to transport grain to those ports and load grain at the ports.[35]

The Chinese delegation was disappointed that the Wheat Board could only enter into a firm contract for 500,000 long tons of wheat between February 1 and June 30, 1964, with discussion on a possible further one million tons for the July to December period to take place in the following April or May.

It had been an unparalleled year for the Canadian Wheat Board, now firmly settled under one roof in its new building. In its annual report for the 1963-64 crop year, the Board was able to report:

A strong advance in the general level of world wheat prices occurred during the 1963-64 crop year. Following the large sale to the Soviet Union, the continuing strong demand and tight shipping schedule for Canadian wheat, along with higher asking prices by competitors, led the board to increase its asking prices. Board quotations for No. 1 Northern Wheat in store the Lakehead averaged $1.92 ¾ per bushel during August and September. The upward movement in prices began in October with the season's monthly average high of $2.08 being achieved in February and March.[36]

The welcome price advance was not to last long. South of the border the United States was viewing these developments with a jaundiced eye. The

Administration, headed by President Lyndon Johnson following the tragic assassination of President John Kennedy on November 22, 1963, was about to abandon the route of co-operation and to wield its economic power even more aggressively in the world wheat market.

Footnotes Chapter 3

1. Canadian Wheat Board Files, D.H. Treleaven letter to W.C. McNamara, August 28, 1963.
2. *Ibid.*
3. *Ibid,* W.C. McNamara letter to D.H Treleaven, August 30, 1963.
4. Canadian Wheat Board Files.
5. *Ibid,* R.V. Gordon letter to W.C. McNamara, October 4, 1962.
6. *Ibid,* Matveev cable to McNamara, August 20, 1963.
7. *Ibid,* Treleaven letter to McNamara, September 3, 1963.
8. *Ibid,* Lawrie letter to Treleaven, September 6, 1963
9. Dan Morgan, *Merchants of Grain,* Penguin Books, 1980, p. 158.
10. Canadian Wheat Board press release, September 10, 1963.
11. Canadian Wheat Board Files, memorandum to Mitchell Sharp, September, 1963.
12. *Ibid.*
13. *Dow Jones News Service,* September 19, 1963
14. Dan Morgan, *Merchants of Grain,* p. 159.
15. *Ibid,* p. 163.
16. Canadian Wheat Board Files, Mitchell Sharp, September 16, 1963
17. *Report of the Canadian Wheat Board, Crop Year 1962-63,* pp. 7,8.
18. *Time Magazine,* April 5, 1963.
19. *Report of the Canadian Wheat Board, Crop Year 1963-64,* p. 5.
20. *Ibid,* p. 12.
21. *Ibid,* p. 8.
22. Canadian Wheat Board Files, Frank Rowan memorandum to board.
23. *Wall Street Journal,* February 13, 1964.
24. *Report of the Canadian Wheat Board, Crop Year 1963-64,* p. 30.
25. Canadian Wheat Board Files, McNamara memorandum to board, October 18, 1963.
26. *Ibid,* R.L. Kristjanson memorandum, October 21, 1963.
27. *Ibid,* J.B. Lawrie, memorandum, October 30, 1963.
28. *Canadian Wheat Board Minute Book, Vol. 29,* pp. 97, 98.
29. Canadian Wheat Board Files, McNamara memorandum, December 23, 1963.
30. *Canadian Wheat Board Minute Book, Vol. 29,* pp. 52-54.
31. *Ibid,* pp. 67-70.
32. *Ibid,* pp. 81,82.
33. *Ibid,* pp. 139-142.
34. Canadian Wheat Board Files, R.A.D. Ford letter to Department of External Affairs, January 23, 1964.
35. *Ibid,* W.C. McNamara letter to Ting Ke-chien, December 3, 1963.
36. *Report of the Canadian Wheat Board, Crop Year 1963-64,* p. 15.

CHAPTER 4
THE BIG STICK

In 1965 the United States abandoned the route of co-operation, instead threatening to use its economic power competitively in the wheat market. It ended its price partnership with Canada and emphasized its new independence by becoming reluctant to renew its membership in the International Wheat Agreement.
— Don F. Hadwiger, Federal Wheat Commodity Programs.

January 25, 1965, was a busy day in the offices of the Canadian Wheat Board. Bill McNamara had just returned from another intense session of negotiations in Hong Kong. A press release on the new contract had been prepared and was being distributed:

> The Canadian Wheat Board is pleased to announce under the provisions of the Second Long-Term Agreement with China a further sales contract has been signed to provide for the export of 700,000 long tons, five per cent more or less, of wheat, of which 620,000 tons will be shipped from Pacific ports February through June, and the balance of 80,000 tons shipped from St. Lawrence River or Atlantic ports during the same period. Assuming the full tolerance is taken, this amounts to slightly over 27 million bushels. [1]

Few realized what was to follow in the wake of what had become a routine announcement of continuing sales to China. It was to precipitate a traumatic series of events which were to send world grain prices tumbling.

Finalization of the contract with China Resources had been achieved in a somewhat shorter period than some of the previous negotiations. McNamara had gone to Hong Kong to begin the round on January 5. Accompanying him was Garson N. "Gerry" Vogel who had been appointed as the fifth

Commissioner of the Board on September 1, 1964. No stranger to the grain trade, Vogel had joined the Grain Division of the Department of Trade and Commerce in Ottawa, following his discharge from the Canadian Army at the end of World War II. He left his position as Chief of the Division some time later, to return to his home town as Vice-President and General Manager of one of the multinational grain traders, Bunge Corporation Limited, in Winnipeg, before accepting an appointment to the Board.

All through the negotiations in Hong Kong, McNamara and Vogel had been haunted by the necessity of maintaining a wary stance on price concessions. There were visible signs of unrest in the United States over holding the price line in the face of expanding sales by other exporting nations into commercial markets.

Quarterly meetings in Washington between representatives of the United States Department of Agriculture and the Canadian Wheat Board, where pricing information and relevant data were exchanged, had been abandoned. But an informal exchange of pricing changes and details of agreements between Canada and the U.S. was continuing.

Robert G. Lewis, Deputy Administrator of the Agricultural Stabilization and Agricultural Service of the USDA, was one of the officials contacted by the Wheat Board when pricing changes were instituted. Lewis clearly outlined the changing atmosphere in the United States in November 1964 in a speech at Kansas State University. Commenting on the International Wheat Agreement of 1962, he noted that it was a "gentlemen's agreement" which had never really been put to the test in supply circumstances which would warrant application of its minimum price provisions:

> The reason is that it simply isn't practical to expect 50 or so importing countries, many of which are not well developed financially or politically, to pay cash prices above the going market price under a treaty which provides no penalty that can be made to stick. The Wheat Agreement itself has no teeth in it by which its provisions can be forced on its member nations. It is the withholding power of the United States and Canada, exercised outside the agreement but within its full view and approbation, that actually "enforces" the minimum price policies written into the agreement. And it is supplies available from the U.S. and Canadian reserves that insure supplies for importing countries at prices within the range in case of short crops. [2]

Lewis then went on to point out that other exporters, particularly Australia, Argentina and France, failed to participate in the stocks-withholding and price-strengthening efforts of the U.S. and Canada. "Their policy is to undersell wheat from the United States and Canada, so as to clear out each year's production by the time a new crop comes along."[3]

While Lewis acknowledged the support of Canada in maintaining an "umbrella" on prices, administrators in the United States were perturbed that, when reserve stocks were sold outside of the IWA, the U.S. exports were on concessional terms while Canada's sales were primarily into commercial markets, particularly the Communist countries where the Americans were locked out by law. Lewis explained that abundant supplies and lagging export demand for wheat in 1964, in contrast to the exceptionally strong demand and huge export sales of 1963, had focussed sharp attention from the trade, producers and government administrators in the United States onto "this inadequacy" in the present world system:

> The immediate reflex action response of many is to urge an increase in the United States export subsidy, thus slashing the net export price of U.S. wheat in order to compete more aggressively...A world "price war," although in the short run it would be questionable in gaining an expanded share of the market for U.S. wheat, it might very well result in restraint upon wheat production in the longer run. To the extent that U.S. wheat producers could outlast producers of other countries at low wheat prices, or could retain the assistance of subsidies from the U.S. government, the proportionate share of the world commercial wheat market enjoyed by the United States could be enlarged.[4]

It was a blunt warning that patience was wearing thin on the part of U.S. legislators and that the "big stick" of the U.S. Treasury might be brought out and waved menacingly. Thus, knowing the political climate in the United States, McNamara had negotiated cautiously in Hong Kong as the Chinese sought concessions on price levels. He cabled back to Bob Esdale at Trade and Commerce in Ottawa on January 12:

> It is our view that sterling price levels at or near Aug. 1/63 sales contract completely unrealistic and it would be in our interest to break or suspend negotiations at this time rather than to reduce prices to this extent.
>
> Personally feel any major reduction in prices for higher grades would create a real problem with U.S.A. and would be better off to pass up sale to Chinese at this time rather than to so drastically lower prices.[5]

Despite these apprehensions, McNamara was anxious to complete a sale. In mid-1964 the massive exports to the Soviet Union under the 1963 sale had dwindled off. There was a record world wheat crop of 9.3 billion bushels in the 1964-65 crop year, due principally to a Soviet harvest of 2.1 billion bushels, as compared to 1.47 billion bushels in the previous disastrous year. Western European crops were also up some 200 million bushels with 130 million bushels of that increase coming from France alone. [6]

As a result of that bountiful output, Russian imports of Canadian wheat dropped to a scant 10,199,167 bushels as compared to 234,378,150 bushels in the previous year, and competition on world markets intensified. [7] On the Canadian Prairies farmers increased wheat acreage in 1964 to almost 27.2 million acres, but crop conditions were not as favourable as in 1963. However, an above average crop of 544.4 million bushels resulted. [8] With carryover stocks again building, the Board needed sales.

In Hong Kong the Canadian negotiators believed they had found a solution to the pricing dilemma that would not offend the sensitive situation in Washington. Harvesting conditions had been difficult and Canada was carrying large stocks of lower grade wheat. As a consequence, Washington had been informed, as early as the previous October, that Canada might have to widen price spreads on lower grades in order to dispose of them for feeding purposes. If the Chinese would take a large proportion of their needs in the form of No. 5 Northern, considered a non-milling grade, then a discount could be offered on that grade while, at the same time, prices on the milling grades could be maintained.

Consequently, agreement was reached that China would take 60,000 long tons of No. 3 Northern at the posted prices with no discount. On 350,000 tons of durum China would pay a premium of four cents a bushel over the Board's regular asking price for durums, basis the Lakehead. The bulk of the contract, 400,000 long tons of No. 5 Northern, were offered at a 12 cent discount below the Board's previous asking price.

On Monday morning January 25, the press release on the China contract having been prepared and sent out, McNamara lifted the phone at 11 a.m. and called Lewis in Washington, "to bring him up to date on our new Chinese contract." After detailing the contract, McNamara reminded Lewis that Canada had a large surplus of No. 5 wheat in Peace River and northern Saskatchewan and that the Board was very pleased to have disposed of that wheat into the Chinese market. "I also said that it would be beneficial to the North American durum position to have this quantity of durum moving into this new market at this time. Mr. Lewis agreed that this should be beneficial." [9]

Lewis was told that the Board might be forced to make some adjustments in spreads on its quoted prices, basis the West Coast, and Washington would be advised of the changes the next day. "Mr. Lewis thanked me for this information

CWB Commissioners, 1967-68. From left to right are Doug Treleaven, Gerry Vogel, Bill McNamara (Chief Commissioner), Jim Lawrie (Assistant Chief Commissioner), and Larry Kristjanson.

but made no suggestions or comments with regard to the proposed price adjustments tomorrow." [10]

There would be no waiting for tomorrow. Three hours later the blow fell. At 2 p.m. the phone rang in McNamara's office. It was Lewis. The United States was increasing its export subsidies, thereby reducing prices by 12 cents a bushel, on Hard Red Winter wheats and Soft wheats on all coasts. Further, they were increasing the subsidy on all flour by 27 cents a hundredweight. [11]

Shocked at the sudden and drastic reductions, McNamara remonstrated that he had not indicated major reductions in spreads and that the increased subsidy on flour could not be related to Canada's price decline on No. 5 wheat because, as Lewis was aware, Canada was not exporting flour milled from No. 5 wheat. It was obvious to McNamara that the U.S. had been looking for an excuse to lower their wheat prices, and "they have seized upon the Chinese No. 5 wheat price as the excuse for so doing." [12] The Chief Commissioner's arguments had little effect. It was to be a hectic week.

The next morning McNamara phoned Lewis to tell him that, in view of the 12 cent reduction on all wheat except Spring wheat, the Board was forced to make some adjustments. They ranged from 7 ½ cents reduction on No. 4

Northern to two cents on No. 1 Northern. On the lower grades, Nos. 5, 6 and Feed wheat out of Pacific ports, the Board was raising prices by two cents a bushel. He also informed Lewis that the Board had heard from London that Argentina was making enquiries as to how much more they could cut their prices without violating the minimum under the International Wheat Agreement. McNamara suggested that some of the problems could be ironed out at a forthcoming IWA meeting and that prices could be stabilized at current levels. [13]

Lewis responded that their chief problem was not with Canadian prices, but with prices from Argentina and Australia. In the afternoon, Lewis called again to say that, in view of the Canadian price increase on No. 5 Northern, the U.S. was raising its prices on Hard Red Winters. However, they were increasing the subsidy and reducing the price on Spring wheat by six cents a bushel at all coasts. [14]

At a Washington press conference on January 27, Lewis denied there was a "price-cutting war," but rather a "reflection of market developments on Soft wheat in the southern hemisphere, Argentina and Australia, which countries have tended to dominate the market for low grade wheat."

In what was to become a familiar and continuing pattern over the years, U.S. export subsidy increases were applauded by American producers, who placed blame for the price competition on the Canadian Wheat Board:

> The National Association of Wheat Growers today charged that the Canadian Wheat Board is so anxious to sell that it is willing to drag all producers of the world into a cut-throat price war as a result of Canada's cut-rate 26 million bushel wheat sale to Red China on January 25.
>
> The Association further contended that it is quite obvious that Canada lowered her prices in order to sell to China and commended the USDA for promptly raising the export subsidy 10 cents per bushel and the flour subsidy 22 cents per hundredweight. "Why don't the Canadians use their surpluses to feed hungry mouths throughout the world," the Association asked and stated that this recent move is "like gasoline on the embers of apprehension" in other exporting countries. [15]

Lewis again called Winnipeg on Thursday, January 28, with news of further cuts in U.S. prices by way of increased export subsidies of up to 10 cents a bushel. Referring to criticism of Canada by the National Association of Wheat Growers, he declared it was not inspired by the USDA. McNamara was less than convinced: "It appears obvious to me that the criticism had been previously prepared and was no doubt inspired by USDA officials at some level." [16]

In that frantic week, U.S. prices declined by as much as 25 cents a bushel on Hard Red Winters out of West Coast ports, with drastic reductions on other varieties from all ports. Canadian prices also declined, but not to the extent of those in the U.S. There were further gradual reductions in American export prices, but the Board attempted to hold the line, and did not match them, so that the spread for Canadian wheat and wheat from other sources was wider at the end of the crop year than it had been for many years. The net result was that Canadian Wheat Board asking prices for No. 1 Northern, in store Fort William, Port Arthur, declined from $2.05 ¼ per bushel in August 1964, to $1.93 ½ at the end of the crop year in July 1965.[17]

What must have been the ultimate frustration for McNamara occurred in mid-February. T.H. Yu, Assistant General Manager of China Resources in Hong Kong, wrote to McNamara to report that they had "commenced a smooth performance on the contract we signed on January 21." It was the contract seized upon by the Americans to trigger the price war. After his polite opening paragraph, Yu delivered a stinging rebuke:

> The price for the new business is really high. We recall during our negotiations we repeatedly suggested that the price should be lower than that of the August, 1963, contract to be reasonable and in keeping with the market trend, but you were insistent that there would not be a price drop. As old friends we had full confidence in your word and used our influence to convince our principals to accept what we then considered too high a price. The turn of events proves our idea of price at the time was objective and reasonable. When the contract was not ten days old you were unable to maintain your price which dropped substantially. Objectively speaking, the price should drop and should have dropped much earlier. So we committed an error in the course of our negotiations, specially as the principal negotiator, I should have insisted on a price lower than that of the August 1963 contract, but I did not do so. What is more, we did use our influence to convince our principals to accept your high price. By doing so, we have lost considerable prestige before our principals, and it will greatly weaken our competence in making future recommendations to them. I cannot but feel that you had already planned a price drop but delayed the action only until the signature of the contract with us. As a long-time and big buyer, our principals not only have failed to get their customary and usual favourable price, but have to suffer a heavy loss. In the circumstances, we express our regret over this matter.[18]

McNamara dictated a diplomatic reply to Yu's charges. After pointing out that he had made the point in negotiations that there was a danger that, if Canada lowered prices to complete the contract, such action might precipitate a decline not only in the price of wheat but other basic agricultural commodities. He concluded:

> The point that I am endeavouring to make is that it would appear that the level at which we sold our wheat to you precipitated the decline which has since developed. However the point that you raise in your letter, to the effect that we had already planned a decline in our price but had delayed the action until we had completed our contract with you, is not correct. We appreciate that many factors enter into the level at which wheat trades in the international market and it is our view that the recent decline is at least partly due to the level at which your organization has been successful in purchasing wheat, not only from Canada but also from other suppliers. As a major importer of wheat, your country secures a direct benefit by this lowering of prices and I am sure your principals will appreciate the part that your organization played in this regard. [19]

By now it was apparent that the International Wheat Agreement's pricing formula was disintegrating with some of the signatories selling below the fixed minimum. As a consequence, the fifth IWA, negotiated in 1962, expired in tatters on July 31, 1965. It was extended by protocol without amendment for a one year period. It was later extended for another year in 1966. The price and quantitative obligations under the pact ceased as of July 31, 1967, when only the administrative provisions were extended for another year.

Canada had played a leading role in the IWA and had been a strong supporter since its inception in 1949, with the Canadian Wheat Board taking a major role in the recurrent negotiations. In 1965 Canada would have preferred to renegotiate the 1962 convention. However other participants, particularly the United States, preferred to work out a new arrangement under the "Kennedy Round" of negotiation of the General Agreement on Tariffs and Trade. This resulted in the one-year extensions of the IWA as the new talks progressed.

In 1964, negotiations started under the Kennedy Round for a more comprehensive pact covering domestic as well as international trade policies for all grains. The result was that, in May, 1967, at Geneva, a memorandum of agreement was signed in regard to the key elements to be included in the new pact. Subsequently a full negotiating conference was convened in Rome in July, 1967, to produce a complete arrangement. The conference, attended by representatives of 52 governments, concluded negotiations in August on the International Grains Arrangement to come into effect July 1, 1968.

The IGA consisted of two legal instruments, a Wheat Trade Convention and a Food Aid Convention, under which 4.5 million metric tons (tonnes) of grain (approximately 165 million bushels) per year would be made available to needy countries. The United States and the European Economic Community were the principal contributors to the Food Aid Convention, supplying 42 and 23 per cent respectively, while Canada was committed to supply 11 per cent.

The Canadian Wheat Board, in its annual report of 1966-67, noted that the Wheat Trade Convention was quite similar in scope and approach to the IWA of 1962, and declared: "Of paramount importance was the general increase in minimum and maximum prices for Canadian wheat of approximately 21 cents per bushel, basis No. 1 Northern in store Fort William/Port Arthur." That bright hope, of increased prices and stability, was soon to be dashed.

In the spring of 1966 Canadian prices had strengthened following negotiation of a new three-year contract with the Soviet Union, averaging $2.09 ¾ a bushel for No. 1 Northern in the closing month of the 1965-66 crop year. Throughout the 1966-67 crop year the Board continued to maintain its price near the maximum under the extended IWA. But, late in the year, there was a decline as American prices dropped. As the 1967-68 crop year began, competition intensified and the Canadian Wheat Board tried desperately to hold the line. It was at some cost, as their report for that year outlined:

> Harvest of a bumper world wheat crop in the autumn reduced import demand and increased export competition. Concern grew about price instability as the United States, the world's largest wheat exporter, declared that in the absence of a formally accepted international agreement on prices, it would consider 1967-68 to be a "free year" in regard to export pricing.[20]

As prices steadily weakened on the world market, the Board refused to drastically lower prices to levels which would jeopardize the coming into force of the International Grains Arrangement. "This meant that wheat prices could not be competitive at all times, and may have caused some loss of sales in 1967-68."[21]

The policy was pursued because, in the Board's judgement, the implementation of the IGA and maintenance of price stability was in the long-term interest of Western Canadian producers. Despite that effort, which resulted in increasing spreads between Canadian prices and those of other exporters, the Board's asking prices declined from $2.04 at the beginning of the year to a low of $1.90 ¼ in November of 1967. As the price decline set in, Trade Minister

Robert Winters, who had succeeded Mitchell Sharp when he moved to the Finance portfolio, rose in the Commons on September 27, 1967, to announce that the federal government would guarantee Western farmers a price above the then current $1.70 initial payment, pending implementation of the IGA:

> I am determined that everything possible should be done to ensure wheat prices will strengthen further and that wheat will trade within the range agreed to at Geneva, but not yet ratified.
>
> When the agreement is ratified it will stand on its own feet. But pending ratification and only until that date, the government is prepared to make up the difference between the agreed schedule of Geneva minimum prices, related to approximately $1.95 ½ basis No. 1 Northern in store the Lakehead, and any wheat sold by the Canadian Wheat Board below this level during the period August 1, 1967, and July 1, 1968. [22]

As a result of that interim selling price guarantee, implemented under Order-in-Council 1968-640, the Federal Treasury made a payment of $9,741,611.46 which was allocated to the applicable wheat pool accounts. [23] The hope of a renewal of international co-operation and price stability, upon the coming into effect of the IGA, was quickly dashed. There were some upward adjustment of prices to the new IGA minimums on its inception, but the pact faced very difficult problems right from the start. The 1968-69 world crop set a new record of over 12 billion bushels. It followed upon a 10.8 billion bushel crop the previous year and an 11.2 billion bushel crop in 1966-67.

In addition, large forward purchases had been made by importing nations at pre-IGA price levels. The resale of these stocks, the large sale of new high-protein wheat offered by Australia at prices only slightly higher than the minimum negotiated for their soft wheat, and unresolved freight differentials, established competitive prices in major markets below the IGA minimums. Compounding those problems, was the fact that some traditional importing countries, as well as some non-IGA members, such as the Soviet Union, offered significant quantities of wheat on the market at whatever price was required to move it.

Canada attempted to restore order by appealing to the Prices Review Committee, set up under the IGA, by asking that body to establish prices for new grades and qualities coming into prominence which were not listed in the schedule of the Convention, plus establishment of related prices for wheats available from non-member countries. It proved impossible within the Committee to reach consensus on such price levels. The Canadian Wheat Board was obliged to report:

These efforts to make the IGA a viable instrument which
could function effectively were not successful as short-term
interests took precedence over long-term interests for most
importing as well as some exporting members. Thus, the
Arrangement did not have the stabilizing effect that had been
expected. Price competition intensified and export subsidization, particularly by the EEC and the U.S.A., grew as the
crop year progressed.[24]

Finally, in March 1969, the Board informed the Prices Review Committee that
it could no longer strictly observe the IGA minimum prices as established for
Canadian grades and was forced to meet the competition. The price slide was on.
Without co-operation from the United States, Canada could not hold the line
alone. From then on it was dog-eat-dog and the IGA was a dead instrument.

In the 1969-70 crop year downward pressure on prices continued to be severe
as international wheat supplies hit record levels. The forlorn hope of the United
States legislators, that a price war "might very well result in restraint upon wheat
production in other nations," was not bearing fruit.

Wheat was the basic foodstuff — a survival imperative — for many nations.
They would seek self-sufficiency as far as possible, no matter what the cost in
relation to abundant supplies available at lower prices on the world markets.
The hard lesson, that price cutting in international markets will not materially
expand demand, was yet to be learned. (Nor has it been even today.)

For Canada the cost of attempting to stem the decline, by holding within the
agreed price limits of the IGA, was reflected in the percentage of world trade
captured by the Canadian Wheat Board in the 1967-68 crop year. With total
wheat exports of 336 million bushels, Canada's share of the market fell to a new
low of 17.9 per cent as compared to 26.3 per cent in the previous crop year.[25]
As the decade of the 60s ended, prices slid even further. From a high of
$1.85 ⅝ in August 1969, the price dropped to $1.73 per bushel during the
closing month of the 1969-70 crop year in July 1970. On the farms of Western
Canada the bins were bulging with a record carryover of 540 million bushels
of undelivered wheat.[26]

Over the decade the world grain market had undergone marked changes in
structure and volume. It was now clearly divided into three distinct compo-
nents; the first being that commercial, concessional and Communist markets.
Canada dominated the new Communist sector of the market for two principal
reasons: the political climate in the United States militated against trade with
China; and the American shipping regulations, whereby half the exports were
obliged to be carried in U.S. flag carriers, inhibited sales to the Soviet Union.

Of no less importance was the preference for state purchasing agencies to negotiate with the Canadian Wheat Board. It was not only a case of the convenience, and philosophical acceptance, of negotiating on an agency to agency basis. Another major factor was that long-term agreements, for assured supplies at stable prices on credit terms backed by the Canadian government could be established. On the other hand, the U.S. subsidy system often prevented the private trade from making forward sales. The uncertainty of fluctuating U.S. subsidy rates left the multinational traders vulnerable to loss if the rate dropped during the period of the contract.

To counter this latter deficiency the United States had, in early 1964, announced a change in their wheat export subsidy policy whereby subsidies were quoted up to 12 months in advance in relation to wheat futures prices. This change imposed problems for the Wheat Board in keeping a close watch on U.S. prices and sales in order to remain competitive. [27]

Despite the frustrations of 1965, occasioned by the onset of the price war, it was in other respects a successful year for the Canadian Wheat Board. Even as the critical letter of February 17, from Yu of China Resources, was enroute to Canada following the January agreement with China, another letter was passing to Ting Ke-chien, Managing Director of China Resources in Hong Kong. In a letter of February 19, McNamara broached the possibility of Bill Riddel and his wife visiting China: "While Mr. Riddel's trip would not be for business, I am sure he would like to have the opportunity, as I did, of meeting the principals of China National Cereals, Oils & Foodstuffs, while in Peking..." [28]

In the absence of Ting, it was Yu who replied on behalf of China Resources. Any recriminations appeared to be forgotten. They would welcome the Riddels to China and suggested a late April or early May visit. When Air France Flight 195 arrived in Hong Kong on Sunday, April 18, 1965, the Assistant Chief Commissioner and his wife were aboard.

Prior to leaving Hong Kong for Mainland China on April 21, Riddel cabled back to McNamara that, while there was no indication of undertaking negotiations following his return to Hong Kong, he was very hopeful. He asked that Gerry Vogel and Dave Yates, the Board's Vancouver Manager, hold themselves in readiness in the event they were called upon. After 18 days, during which the Riddels were entertained at Canton, Hangchow, Shanghai, Peking and Wuhan, they returned to Hong Kong on May 9. They were met by Vogel and Yates who had flown in the previous day. The Chinese were ready to negotiate and, on May 2, a new contract was signed.

McNamara wired to Bill Snell at the Tokyo office: "Please extend to Riddel, Vogel, Yates, sincere congratulations Chinese contract. Although price adjustments will create some difficulties, satisfied we can work them out without upsetting our friends. This additional business with China will create great satisfaction to all concerned."[29]

As usual, negotiations had been intensive with the price issue deadlocked until the final day. The Board had, however, sold the Chinese another 1.5 million long tons of wheat to be delivered from July 1965, through April 1966, and the price concession was minimal.

Announcement of the sale was delayed while McNamara, acutely aware of the drastic American reaction to the previous China sale, contacted Washington. This time the response was more moderate. The Board lowered its West Coast offering price by two cents on lower grades and the Americans followed with a two cent drop on all West Coast Hard wheat shipments. When the Board raised prices by two cents the following day, May 27, the Americans followed suit. The status-quo remained.

However, when an addendum to the May 21 contract expanded the sale by 625,000 long tons, the response from Washington was icy. When J.H. Warren, Deputy Minister of Trade and Commerce, phoned John Schnittker at the USDA in Washington, the U.S. official "questioned the Canadian policy of advocating high prices and selling wheat at distress prices."[30] But there was no price reaction. That sale marked the end of the Board's second long-term agreement with China, with the Chinese taking the maximum under the agreement of five million long tons of wheat, or approximately 186.7 million bushels.

There was a short respite before the Board found itself negotiating another major contract in 1965. Severe drought had again struck the virgin lands of South Kazakhstan and Western Siberia. The Russians were back in the market. As before, the initial overture came with dramatic suddenness.

On the morning of July 19, a telegram was laid on McNamara's desk. Following a cheery "good morning" salutation from Moscow was a terse message from Matveev:

> To satisfy traditional requirements of our Far East for wheat and determine possible sources of supply for covering above requirements, I shall appreciate your opinion concerning possibilities ship from Pacific starting from September 1965, up to five hundred thousand tons of Manitoba four only or, if impossible, partly Manitoba three, but not higher grades. Looking forward to hearing from you soon. Best Regards.[31]

The next day McNamara telexed back setting out a proposed monthly shipping schedule and giving the previous day's prices in store Vancouver of $1.87 ½ per bushel for No. 3 Northern and $1.79 ½ for No. 4 Northern. Matveev came right back: "We agree purchase mentioned wheat quantity for shipment from the Pacific with fixation of firm prices basing on quotations stated in your telex."[32] In contrast to the extended China negotiations, the Russians moved quickly. Nicolai Belousov, Vice-President of Exportkhleb was applying for a visa and would fly to Winnipeg within a few days to complete the documents.

When Belousov arrived in Canada on July 30, it was as a member of a trade mission headed by the Soviet Deputy Minister of Foreign Affairs, N.G. Ossipov. In the interim, a formal contract had been completed between Exportkhleb and the Board, expanding the telexed agreement to 700,000 long tons of wheat to be shipped from the West Coast. Signed on July 30, announcement of the contract was held back until August 5.

It was now clear the Russians had more than "traditional Far East requirements" in mind. McNamara and Vogel, accompanied by Executive Assistant Larry Kristjanson, hastened to Ottawa to meet with the Russian trade mission. Ossipov suggested that they would like to negotiate with the Board in some locale other than Ottawa or Winnipeg, so that they could deal privately and away from interference of the trade by phone or personal visit. Mitchell Sharp arranged with the Canadian Pacific Railway to have accommodation made at the posh Seigniory Club at Montebello, Quebec.

In the luxurious privacy of the Laurentian hideaway, negotiations commenced on August 3. With Ossipov as the principal Russian negotiator, it soon became apparent that the Soviet delegation wanted as much grain as the Board could logistically move through the system. With the previously negotiated China sale, plus the new 700,000 ton Soviet contract, Pacific ports were completely booked. Attention turned to tonnages that could be moved from September through the next June at St. Lawrence and Atlantic ports.

Board officials broke for talks with the railways after the first day. At a meeting, also attended by Sharp, the railway presidents put pressure on the minister by registering dissatisfaction over new labour legislation calling for a 40-hour week, which they claimed would cut back their capacity by 20 per cent. The meeting was difficult with the railways seeking higher rates for winter movement to the Atlantic ports. After McNamara outlined the proposed program, the railways sought to have the winter movement cancelled.

It was symptomatic of a problem that was to plague the Canadian Wheat Board increasingly over the next two decades as the railways sought persistently to apply pressure for removal of the fixed statutory Crowsnest Rate for hauling grain. McNamara explained:

> We took the position that the USSR could not be expected to take a flood of grain in the fall and spring and tie up their fleet for the winter months. My own feeling is that the railways always were using this to press their case with the

government. When we told them cutting back on the winter program would cut back on fall and spring, they backed away from original positions of wanting to cut back on Atlantic movement.[33]

The same day that McNamara was outlining these difficulties to Ossipov and the Soviet negotiators, his Assistant Chief Commissioner was back in Winnipeg loading another barrel in the Board's sales arsenal. On August 3, Bill Riddel wrote to Ting Ke-chien, Managing Director of China Resources in Hong Kong, recalling the invitation to visit Canada to "review matters of mutual interest," he had made earlier. He had a new long-term agreement in mind. Riddel's renewed invitation was to lead to another meeting at Montebello, this time with the Chinese.

Meanwhile, at the current meeting, McNamara and Ossipov agreed to the issuing of a press release in Winnipeg the following day on the preliminary 700,000 ton sale "to keep the grain trade off balance." They then returned to negotiations. With obvious pressure on the transportation system, McNamara pressed for shipments out of Manitoba's northern port of Churchill. Belousov declined:

> We appreciate your efforts to maximize the movement of wheat through Churchill. However, after very careful consideration of the matter with our Marine department and with Sovfracht, we regret to inform you that we could not obtain their agreement to a movement ex Churchill…[34]

Agreement on the Russian contract was reached after one week. On August 10, the contract was signed and the next morning the negotiators, accompanied by Sharp, flew to Winnipeg for a press conference in the Canadian Wheat Board building. The announcement was a momentous one. In addition to the previously announced 700,000 ton sale, the Russians were taking 4.6 million long tons of wheat plus 400,000 tons of wheat in the form of flour. Total purchases in the two agreements amounted to approximately 222 million bushels. Just over one week into the 1965-66 crop year, the Board was off to a flying start. When the final tally was made, wheat exports hit 584,905,946 bushels in 1965-66.[35]

It was evident that the transportation system was going to be under strain throughout the crop year, and on August 13, the Board met with the railways to set out car requirements. This was followed by a meeting, convened by Sharp, which resulted in the setting up of a Rail Transportation Committee. Composed of senior railway, grain trade and Wheat Board officials, the committee was able to co-ordinate, review and improve the overall flow of grain to the Lakehead. Later, in January 1966, a similar committee was set up at Vancouver under the chairmanship of Bill Riddel, who had retired as Assistant Chief Commissioner of the Board on September 30, 1965. Jim Lawrie replaced him as Assistant Chief Commissioner on October 1, and Doug Treleaven and Larry Kristjanson were appointed Commissioners.

Treleaven's place as London Manager was taken by Bill Snell, who moved from the Tokyo office, and Gordon Earl was appointed to the position of Executive Director. The Tokyo position was filled temporarily by T.C. Barnes and W.E. Wellman took over as Tokyo Manager before the end of the crop year.

Prior to Riddel's retirement, he received a letter on August 25, from China National Cereals, Oils and Feedstuffs in Peking. The Wheat Board's invitation had been accepted and a seven-man mission was making preparations to visit Canada as the Board's guests. The mission arrived in Canada in the midst of a general election campaign. After visits to Vancouver and Calgary, their arrival in Winnipeg coincided with a two-day campaign visit by Prime Minister Lester Pearson. For the minority Liberal government, negotiation of a new long-term agreement was obviously ardently desired to improve their previously desolate political fortunes on the Prairies. (There is no record, however, of a meeting between Pearson and the Chinese delegation.)

In any event, McNamara used the pre-election political climate to advantage when negotiations eventually got under way. Following a week in Winnipeg and visits to Fort William, Toronto and Montreal, the Chinese and the Wheat Board officials opened formal talks at Montebello on October 21. McNamara found that the Board really had two negotiations underway at the Seigniory Club. Reporting to Treleaven, who was still in London awaiting arrival of Snell as his replacement as London Manager, McNamara wrote:

> The first and possibly the most difficult — as you will appreciate — was with members of the Canadian Establishment. They were very reluctant to make any concessions on Chinese imports but I had the whip hand politically and, though I did not have to use it too strenuously, they all realized that they would have to up the maximum limitations. As the Chinese only posed a maximum of $10 million, I persuaded the Establishment that we would not try to bicker or negotiate this figure but accept it outright. [36]

The Chief Commissioner had another problem in keeping the negotiations secret. Dow Jones News Service began telexing Winnipeg as early as October 16, asking for details of a rumoured agreement: "In view of conflicting reports on size and value of wheat deal with Red China and the fact that these reports have been widely printed may we request a clarifying statement be issued promptly to eliminate widespread confusion." That, and following telex queries were simply marked "not acknowledged" by Kristjanson. But, if the Commissioners were remaining tight-lipped, government ministers, faced with an upcoming vote on November 8, apparently were not. McNamara reported:

> The fact that our minister decided to "leak" the information on Monday, prior to the signing on Tuesday, caused us some embarrassment and some concern because I was just afraid that at the last moment Ting might have advised us that his principals had changed their minds. However, all's well that ends well.[37]

It had ended well indeed. The new long-term agreement was signed October 27, and details were announced the next day at a press conference in Winnipeg attended by Sharp, who had been present at the signing in Ottawa. The Chinese had declared their intention to purchase from three to five million long tons of wheat over a three-year period beginning August 1, 1966, with specific quantities, prices and shipping periods to be negotiated periodically.

The Chinese Corporation and the Board further agreed that, prior to May 1, 1966, consideration would be given to increasing the quantities involved to a minimum of 4.5 million tons and a maximum of 7.5 million tons, or alternatively extending the three-year agreement to five years, involving a minimum quantity of 7.5 million tons and a maximum of 12.5 million tons.[38] Even with his eye on the forthcoming polls, Sharp, in contrast to his predecessor Alvin Hamilton, gave full credit to the Wheat Board when he told the press:

> I am delighted about this massive wheat agreement and I would like to extend my heartiest congratulations to the Canadian Wheat Board. The board deserves the highest praise for the successful effort they have made to develop the Chinese market. The total value of wheat shipments under this agreement will range from $200 million over three years to a possible limit of $900 million over a period of five years. Based on past experience I am confident that the quantities purchased will be closer to the maximum figure. On this basis, this would be the largest single wheat agreement ever concluded by the Canadian Wheat Board. Not only Prairie wheat producers but all Canadians will benefit from the income from these sales.[39]

He added that, by a separate agreement, the limitation on imports of "sensitive" Chinese goods into the Canadian market had been increased from $7 million in each year to $10 million.

The expectations of the agreement were realized. In the three years of the agreement to July 31, 1969, China contracted 232 million bushels of wheat, some 64.8 million bushels above the minimum quantity specified. In the latter difficult years of the decade, when the massive Soviet purchases subsided, China was Canada's largest market.

For Prime Minister Pearson and his Liberal Party, the anticipation of political rewards in the election, held just over one week later, were not borne out. The ardently sought majority government again eluded them. It was another minority House with 131 Liberals, 97 Progressive Conservatives, 21 New Democrats, nine Creditistes and two independents being elected on November 8. On the Prairies there was one lonely Liberal seat in Manitoba.

In the fractious personality conflict between Pearson and John Diefenbaker, the government did not live out its franchise. With both major parties having elected new leaders, the electors went to the polls again on June 25, 1968. This time the Liberals, headed by Pierre Elliott Trudeau, achieved their long-sought majority, taking 155 seats to 72 for the Conservatives under Robert Stanfield. "Trudeaumania" which marked the 1968 election, contributed to breaking the Liberal political drought on the Prairies. Five Liberals were elected in Manitoba, two in Saskatchewan and four in Alberta.

In the interim between the elections, the Canadian Wheat Board was finally recognized as a permanent institution after 32 years of existence. On August 1, 1967, Sections 23 and 34 of the Canadian Wheat Board Act were repealed and no new sections to replace them were enacted. Those sections had required the legislated powers of the Board to be reviewed and re-enacted by Parliament at intervals, and the Board's mandates had been extended for five-year periods. The amendment to the Act made this no longer necessary. At the same time, a further amendment was made allowing cabinet to designate the minister to whom the Board was to report. This meant that responsibility for reporting to Parliament on behalf of the Board could be designated to any one of the ministers instead of being assigned to a specific portfolio. [40]

That latter amendment was to be given a thorough workout over the next decade. One of the freshmen Liberal members, elected in the Saskatoon-Humboldt riding of Saskatchewan, was a serious 36-year-old former Dean of Law at the University of Saskatchewan and Rhodes Scholar, Otto Lang. Soon to become Minister Responsible to Parliament for the Board, while at the same time holding a succession of diverse portfolios, Lang was to play a major part in a turbulent era of change in Western Canada.

The studious, hard working newcomer quickly caught the attention of Prime Minister Trudeau and in July, one month after being elected, he was appointed to the cabinet as Minister without Portfolio. Working with Trade Minister Jean-Luc Pepin, then Minister Responsible to Parliament for the Board, Lang soon turned his attention to perceived problems facing the Prairies. After a short period, during which the fledgling minister increasingly became involved in initiatives dealing with the Western grain economy, Lang was appointed as Minister Responsible for Reporting to Parliament for the Canadian Wheat Board by Order-in-Council P.C. 1969-2002, on October 15, 1969.

The first report of the Canadian Wheat Board, for the crop year 1968-69, delivered to the new minister, set out a grim and deteriorating picture. There were deficits in all of the pool accounts, including wheat, oats and barley. Only once before, since the Board assumed monopoly control of the three grains, had there been a deficit in a pool resulting from an initial payment to farmers being higher than the realized sales prices, less administrative costs. It occurred in the 1956-57 crop year when the oats pool showed a deficit of $2,188,200.80 on sales of 32.4 million bushels of oats for $22,821,229. That deficit was caused, in large part, by a heavy crop in a year of sluggish sales for oats which resulted in carrying charges of $3,826,327 on unsold holdings.[41]

Now, for the first time there were deficits of $39,787,979 in the wheat pool and $9,834,516 in the barley pool, as well as a deficit of $1,143,161 in the oats pool.[43] In addition to that there was a special payment of $6,555,614 to farmers who had delivered durum wheat to the Board during the crop year. While there was no separate pool for durum and, under the terms of the Canadian Wheat Board Act, all grades and classes of wheat were considered one grain, the government by supplementary estimates authorized the payment to the Board for distribution to producers of durum, since the sales of that grain had shown a profit. Without the special vote, the profit on durum sales would have been used by Treasury to offset the losses in the general wheat account.

While the $39,787,979 deficit in the wheat pool account was seized on by critics of the Board, including spokesmen for some American farm associations, as an inordinate subsidization of Western farmers, it represented a loss of only six per cent in total wheat sales totalling over $668,625,682 during the crop year. And, given that the Board had made wheat sales totalling over $18.04 billion over the previous 25 years, any "subsidization" inherent in the Treasury payment represented a scant two-tenths of one per cent in relation to those total sales. In comparison to the heavy subsidization by almost all of the other exporting countries, any government assistance to Western Canadian farmers through the operations of the Canadian Wheat Board was minimal indeed.

Beside that bleak news for the federal Treasury there was an all-time high payment of $79,760,320 allocated to the pool account for wheat under the Temporary Wheat Reserves Act. The record federal payment resulted from carrying charges on 479,573,159 bushels of wheat as of August 1, 1969.[43] Under the terms of the Act, the government reimbursed the Board for all commercial holdings of wheat above a basic stock of 178 million bushels. Farm stored wheat was not taken into the equation. Canada's carryover of wheat at July 31, 1969, had reached a record 851 million bushels.[44] Sagging exports, increased competition and declining prices in the face of four consecutive world grain crops in excess of 10 billion bushels, showed little prospect of improvement for Canadian sales.

In large part, the pool deficits and lagging export sales at the end of the decade of the 60s, were a legacy of Canada's determined effort to adhere to the pricing provisions of the International Grains Arrangement, which had been breached by almost every other exporting nation. Seized of this near critical situation, Lang almost immediately implemented a series of far reaching initiatives. Coming from an academic background in law, and with little practical experience in the grain industry, the new minister's active and analytical mind probed into all aspects of the trade with dramatic, and often highly controversial, results.

Over the coming decade no sector of the grain economy was to be left untouched. While the outcome of many of the policy initiatives are still in dispute in many quarters, one thing must be conceded — Otto Lang showed great political courage. The 70s were to become a decade of drastic change.

Footnotes: Chapter Four

1. Canadian Wheat Board press release, January 25, 1965.
2. Robert G. Lewis, speech to the Third National Wheat Utilization Research Conference, Kansas State University, November 5, 1964.
3. *Ibid.*
4. *Ibid.*
5. Canadian Wheat Board Files, McNamara cable to Esdale, January 12, 1965.
6. *Report of the Canadian Wheat Board, crop year 1964-65,* p. 5.
7. *Ibid,* p. 10.
8. *Ibid,* p. 16.
9. Canadian Wheat Board Files, McNamara memorandum to the board, January 25, 1965.
10. *Ibid.*
11. *Ibid.*
12. *Ibid.*
13. *Ibid,* January 26, 1965.
14. *Ibid.*
15. Journal of Commerce, Washington, January 28, 1965.
16. Canadian Wheat Board Files, McNamara memorandum to the board, January 28, 1965.
17. *Ibid.*
18. Canadian Wheat Board Files, T.H. Yu letter to McNamara, February 17, 1965.
19. *Ibid,* McNamara to T.H. Yu, February 24, 1965.
20. *Report of the Canadian Wheat Board, crop year 1967-68,* p. 12.

21. *Ibid.*
22. Debates of the House of Commons, , September 27, 1967.
23. *Supplementary Report of the Canadian Wheat Board, crop year 1967-68,* p. 6.
24. Report of the Canadian Wheat Board, crop year 1968-69, p. 11.
25. Report of the Canadian Wheat Board, crop year 1968-69, p. 15.
26. *Ibid,* crop year 1969-70, p. 26.
27. Canadian Wheat Board Files, G.A. Torgerson memorandum to R.L. Kristjanson, January 30, 1964.
28. *Ibid.* McNamara letter to Ting Ke-chien, February 19, 1965.
29. Canadian Wheat Board Files, May 21, 1965.
30. *Ibid,* McNamara office memorandum, July 15, 1965.
31. Canadian Wheat Board Files, July 19, 1965.
32. *Ibid,* July 21, 1965.
33. *Ibid,* R.L. Kristjanson, Notes on Meeting Held in Ottawa, August 3 to August 10.
34. *Ibid,* N.A. Belousov letter to McNamara, August 10, 1965.
35. *Report of the Canadian Wheat Board crop year 1965-66,* p. 16.
36. Canadian Wheat Board Files, McNamara letter to Treleaven, October 28, 1965.
37. *Ibid.*
38. Canadian Wheat Board press release, October 28, 1965.
39. Canadian Wheat Board Files. prepared statement Mitchell Sharp, October 28, 1965.
40. *Report of the Canadian Wheat Board, crop year 1966-67,* p. 31.
41. *Ibid,* crop year, 1956-57, pp. 17, 18.
42. *Supplementary Report of the Canadian Wheat Board, crop year 1968-69,* pp. 5, 10, 13.
43. *Ibid,* p. 6.
44. *Ibid,* p. 1.

CHAPTER 5
THE NEW BROOM

*The Canadian government's decision to pay farmers not to grow
wheat in 1970 bewilders and frightens us. Bewilders us because it
reveals a fundamental sickness in our supposedly modern economic
system. Frightens because it tempts the Providence of God who has
blessed our country with such enormous agricultural potential.*
— Saskatchewan Catholic Weekly, March 8, 1970.

Canada's grain industry moved toward the volatile and controversial decade of
the 1970s in an atmosphere of bleak frustration. Trade Minister Jean-Luc Pepin
summed up the unprecedented situation facing the Canadian Wheat Board at
the first inaugural meeting of the newly instituted Canada Grains Council in
Winnipeg on September 26, 1969. The minister, in what was to be his last
speech as Minister Responsible to Parliament for the Canadian Wheat Board,
reviewed his one-year tenure in that capacity and his association with the grain
industry:

> Some industry! Important, complex, frustrating, challeng-
> ing, altogether fascinating. Some year! Strikes, unfavourable
> harvest conditions, cold, record world crops, declining trade,
> price conflict, numberless questions in the House, the cre-
> ation of the Grains Council, yesterday's sale to China. The
> roughest year in Canadian wheat history, I'm told; which
> makes me happy for my predecessors. [1]

The grain industry problems besetting the Quebec Cabinet Minister, and
occupying over half of his working day, were indeed complex and overwhelming
as he attempted to cope with a mounting crisis. Although it had not yet been
revealed, an unprecedented deficit in all of the Wheat Board's grain pools was
building as figures were compiled for the recently ended 1968-69 crop year. On

western farms the bins were bursting with over half a billion bushels of undelivered wheat. Entering the new crop year on August 1, the commercial storage facilities across the West and in export positions were clogged with a further 466 million bushels of wheat. In the rain-sodden fields of western Canada men and machines were desperately trying to garner a rapidly deteriorating 684 million bushel wheat crop. At country elevators, and on the farms, urgently required grain dryers were being acquired on an emergency basis wherever possible.

Bill McNamara, Chief Commissioner (centre) talks to the Sales Review Committee, a group of internationally-known, grain marketing specialists appointed to review Canadian grain sales policies. From left to right are: V. Lester from Vancouver; Dr. J. Schnittker, former U.S. Undersecretary of Agriculture; Dr. M.W. Menzies (Chair), a prominent Canadian grain policy advisor; A.T. Baker, Alberta Wheat Pool; A.P. Van Stolk, a grain market advisor to the European Economic Committee; and Dr. J.L. Leibfried, Executive Assistant to the CWB.

Compounding the situation, some country elevator companies, unable to cope with the high-moisture grain being delivered, forwarded unprecedented quantities of high-moisture grain to terminal positions without consideration of the impact on the entire system. This overloaded the drying capacity at the terminals, particularly Vancouver, and caused severe congestion in the entire system. This, more than anything, convinced planners that better control of car-loadings was essential, and was to result in a new "Block Shipping System."

On the world scene, the International Grains Agreement had broken down as the world wheat crop swelled to a record of over 12 billion bushels. Pepin and officials of the Canadian Wheat Board had attended two hastily called wheat exporters' ministerial meetings in a last desperate attempt to salvage the pricing arrangements under the ailing international agreement. At the first, held in Washington on July 10 and 11, 1969, the United States agreed to defer price cuts temporarily pending assurances from the European Economic Community, which had emerged as an increasingly aggressive exporter by means of export subsidies, that the EEC would use restraint in what were perceived as U.S. markets.

But, at the second meeting held in London on August 1, 1969, the uneasy truce reached in Washington broke down. The EEC delegates were intransigent on increasing prices to match proposed rollbacks to higher prices by the U.S., Canada and Australia. From London the message flashed back to Canada: "Meeting ended with no agreement on any accommodation to deal with current critical situation...There was no communique issued after the meeting, nor were there any agreed conclusions."[2]

The cost of Canada's unilateral attempt to stabilize and inject some backbone into the IGA by holding the price line had been heavy. While world wheat trade in the 1968-69 crop year was over 1.65 billion bushels, Canada's share of that trade was a slim 306 million bushels, or 18.3 per cent of the market. That slump was occasioned in part by the fact that the Soviet Union had sought and obtained a deferral on the three-year contract entered into in June 1966 for the purchase of 336 million bushels of wheat between August 1, 1966 and July 31, 1969. In the first two years of the contract, the Russians took delivery of only 173 million bushels of wheat. Despite strong representations from Canada, the Soviets took only 15.6 million bushels in the final year, leaving an outstanding commitment of 132.8 million bushels at the end of the 1968-69 crop year.[3]

Within the various segments of the grain industry there was dissension and internal strife as the crisis in grain marketing grew. In an inflation-heated economy there was labour strife resulting in strikes and stoppages of grain movement. The railways, openly showing increasing disenchantment with the low statutory Crowsnest Rate for hauling grain, were retiring aging boxcars from their fleets at an alarming rate without replacements. At the same time the railways, pleading financial inability to repair and maintain grain hauling branch lines, were allowing the Prairie rail network to fall into disrepair. In the grain trade itself arguments abounded over allocations of rail cars between the Wheat Board and the private trade handling non-board grains and oilseeds, particularly in respect to rapeseed, an expanding crop on the Prairies and the dominant article of trade on the Winnipeg Commodity Exchange.

Given that background of gloom and divisiveness, Pepin could be forgiven any feeling of relief he may have experienced as he was about to relinquish the reins of responsibility for reporting on the Canadian Wheat Board to Otto Lang within the next three weeks, as he delivered his address at the press conference announcing formation of the Canada Grains Council.

The Canada Grains Council concept had been born out of the hope that the divisiveness within the trade might be defused by having all of the diverse interests associated within a single organization to discuss interrelated problems and reach a consensus. The concept was advanced as a Liberal Party plank by Pierre Trudeau during the June 25, 1968, election campaign. At the first organizational meeting, held in late January, 1969, in Winnipeg's Fort Garry Hotel, Pepin heralded the new advisory council as "the hope of the wheat economy from now on."[4]

That bright hope was not to be fulfilled. Major farm organization representatives to the Grains Council, sensing that the new organization was intruding into farm policy through controversial resolutions, withdrew from the Council. Roy Atkinson, President of the National Farmers Union, announced that his organization was withdrawing from the organization in the first year. In 1973 the powerful Prairie Pools, led first by Saskatchewan Wheat Pool, renounced their memberships, leaving United Grain Growers as the principal producer representative on the Council.

From then on the Canada Grains Council, under Dr. Donald Dever, a federal appointee as Secretary-General, was seen primarily as an ally of the private trade in its opposition to the Canadian Wheat Board.

In later years, when he had retired from public life, Otto Lang, who was instrumental in the formation of the Grains Council and who had appeared at the inaugural meeting along with Pepin and Agriculture Minister H.S. "Bud" Olson, defended the principal of having the diverse group, ranging from producers through the co-operative and private grain handlers and the railways and shipping interests assemble together. However, Lang admitted that it had provided a public platform for those interests opposed to the Wheat Board.[5]

That "Board bashing," in part, spurred the withdrawal of the NFU and Pools, both strong supporters of the Canadian Wheat Board, from the Council. The Wheat Board, accorded only advisory status at its own request to the Council, and without direct membership, could not defend itself against attacks from the private trade and minority farm groups within the Council. Thus, rather than achieving consensus amongst the disparate groups, the divisions were sometimes exacerbated by the public exposure.

Symptomatic of the clash of interests was a letter Bill McNamara received from Pepin as Minister of Industry and Commerce within four days of the September 1969 Grains Council meeting. Pepin commented that several of the representatives at the meeting had "publicly and in private conversations" indicated concerns about the transportation and handling of grains:

> "I would appreciate your views about the concerns the trade expressed. Is there a need for special measures by Ministers of the Government or is it sufficient to leave this problem for the Board to work out with co-operation of the Grain Transportation Committee?"[6]

McNamara's reply was somewhat ascerbic:

> There is no doubt, as a result of very severe congestion that
> developed at the end of the crop year, that everyone engaged
> in the grain business — our Board as well as the private trade
> — is encountering marketing difficulties...Most of the
> traders are not in favour of the quota system, nor are they in
> favour of any restrictions on the transportation of commodi-
> ties in which they are primarily interested. I think this is a
> natural reaction insofar as they are concerned. On the other
> hand, I cannot agree with their contention that, because they
> are responsible for the merchandising of grain other than
> wheat, oats and barley, producers of these non-board grains
> should get a priority on deliveries to country elevators or on
> the limited transportation...In conclusion, I do not think
> there is any action the Ministers of the Government can take
> at this time, and I think that you would be well advised to
> leave it to us, along with the railways and the trade, to work
> out this problem.[7]

With Lang's accession to responsibility for reporting to Parliament on behalf
of the Canadian Wheat Board, he almost immediately set in motion the setting
up of another policy formulating body, the Ottawa Grains Group. Chaired by
Lang, the Grains Group consisted of personnel seconded from the various
departments of government involved in grain policy. It included the
Departments of Agriculture, Industry, Trade and Commerce, Transport and
Foreign Affairs. Among the civil servants assigned to the Grains Group were
R.M. Bryden, as Co-ordinator, and W.E. Jarvis, R.M. Esdale and R.J. Shepp.

In his first major address as Minister Responsible for the Board, Lang indicated that the winds of change were about to sweep through the whole grains
industry. Speaking to the annual meeting of United Grain Growers in early
November, 1969, the new minister observed that:

> Making the Canadian Wheat Board the whipping boy for
> everything that goes wrong in the Canadian grains industry
> has become a popular pastime...Those who have been anti-
> Canadian Wheat Board for years are taking advantage of the
> present marketing situation to rally their forces against the
> Board. Their attacks on the Board are unjustified...I am con-
> fident that, even in the declining market situation we have
> experienced over the last two crop years, Canada has sold

more grain at better prices than would have been the case if the Board's detractors had succeeded in wishing the Board out of existence. [8]

At the same time, Lang expressed concern that the Wheat Board had been asked to take on responsibilities and functions which detracted from its selling functions. Quoting from the preliminary report of a federal task force on agriculture that "at times the more general price and income problems of Prairie grain producers appear to have become the major preoccupation of the Wheat Board," the Minister indicated changes were in order:

> I intend to see if this is the case. The Board's efforts must be concentrated on selling. The Board should not be expected to administer or be heavily involved in any agricultural program which does not materially assist them in their selling function. [9]

In a further indication of what was to come, Lang dealt with a wide range of subjects, including transportation problems, storage costs, and the need for rationalization of the grain gathering system from country elevator to export position.

At the Canadian Wheat Board, initiatives had already been undertaken and implemented to deal with the transportation problems arising out of a complexity of shipping orders. During 1963 and 1965 the shipping system had been put to a severe test to meet the increased demands arising from the huge sales to the Soviet Union. In response to that handling and transportation emergency, the government appointed a Grain Transportation Committee. Chaired by the Chief Commissioner of the Canadian Wheat Board, the Committee included the Chief Commissioner of the Board of Grain Commissioners, the vice-presidents of Canadian National and Canadian Pacific Railways, and the presidents of three representative grain companies.

By 1967 the Grain Transportation Committee, which had been dealing with immediate problems as they arose, realized that the time had come for longer term reforms in the shipping order system. As a result, the Committee appointed a Grain Transportation Technical Group drawn from transportation experts within their own organizations. Over the next two years the Technical Group produced three reports: *Shipping Orders, A Proposal For a Co-ordinated Shipping Order System,* and *The Movement of Grain Through West Coast Ports.* The first report analyzed the weaknesses and redundancy in the shipping order system and the overlapping authority of the participants, including the Wheat Board, the elevator companies and the railways. A sub-committee was then appointed to draw up recommendations.

The result was a proposal for a "Block Shipping System." The Technical Group's report set out a list of priorities and objectives which included: meeting all short-term and long-term demands by the Wheat Board and the private trade, making the most efficient use of country and terminal elevator storage and handling facilities, and making the most efficient use of car equipment and train service.

To meet these objectives, it was recommended that the Wheat Board, as the major claimant upon transportation, take the initiative in the continuous planning of grain movement and in keeping an up-to-date inventory of the kinds and grades of grain in all positions. The Board would also maintain regular consultations with the railways and elevator companies on planning the Board's shipping programs in order to assist them in planning their own operations.

Although the Board would continue to place shipping orders with the elevator companies in proportion to the relative volume of their business, it would discontinue issuance of orders specifying individual shipping points and would now issue them in terms of "blocks" of shipping points. Blocks were defined as a series of shipping points connected by the same railway line on an operational basis embracing as many as five train runs. Thus, the shipping orders were to be related directly to the actual operating units of the railway.

So far as the elevator companies were concerned, they would now become their own masters in respect to elevator operations within each shipping block. The Board would allocate their shipping orders relative to the business they had done within each shipping block and leave it entirely to the elevator companies to assign their share of the orders to elevators within the block. The orders would specify the kinds and grades of grain to be shipped and there would be no overlapping or duplication of orders. There would be one matching order for each car. Accordingly, when the companies transmitted these orders to the railways, the railways would know exactly at what elevator they must spot the cars to fill the orders, and elevator managers would have advance notice of the specific grain they must load into each car. The railways could spot cars with precision without having to make allocation decisions in the process.

A further advantage was that the elevator companies, having control over their own loading operations, would be able to maintain their rate of unloading at export terminals in compatibility with their rates of load in the country, thereby improving railway efficiency by avoiding congestion of cars under load in terminal yards.

Following the report of the Technical Group, test blocks were established at Medicine Hat, Alberta, in February 1969, and at Dauphin, Manitoba, in March 1969. In the June-July period a further nine blocks were placed in operation. The experiments proved so successful that the whole Canadian Wheat Board designated area, consisting of 48 shipping blocks covering 1,431 shipping points, was integrated into the Block Shipping System by February 1970. The first tangible results were a substantial reduction in the in-transit time for cars between loading and unloading, resulting in a faster turnaround, enhancement of marketing opportunities and more efficient operation of country elevators.

While recognizing the efficiencies stemming from the Block Shipping System, Lang gave notice that he intended to go even further to streamline the transportation system on a long-term basis. Upon its formation, the Ottawa Grains Group was immediately assigned a number of priority projects, including a feasibility study on modernization of the elevator and transportation system to effect grain handling economies. Other study projects included: the most effective marketing system for oilseeds, including rapeseed and flaxseed and the most effective system for marketing oats and barley.

As these studies and related matters got underway, it soon became evident that research activities and promotional programs being undertaken by the Canada Grains Council were conflicting with the work of the Grains Group and infringing upon the responsibilities of the Canadian Wheat Board.

On April 10, 1970, George Heffelfinger, Vice-Chairman of the Canada Grains Council, and its Secretary-General, Don Dever, were called to Ottawa for a meeting with the Grains Group. Lang lost no time in pointing out that:

> Because the terms of reference of the Grains Group and the Canada Grains Council are so similar, effective liaison must be maintained to serve the common purpose which can only suffer if the two bodies work in practice, however unintentionally, at cross purposes. [10]

After pointing out that there had been "commendable liaison" on the part of the Council with respect to its study and report on the revision of the Canada Grain Act, and a proposal for a new quota system and protein grading, the minister raised several points where improvement was needed. The most conspicuous instance, which generated misunderstanding and reaction, was the Grains Council's proposal for a market intelligence and development service. Further, said Lang, there had been no consultation with government on the Council's proposed study of the export pricing of Canadian grains, "which directly overlaps the responsibility of the Canadian Wheat Board and policy review within the Grains Group." [11]

The Board of Directors were also taken to task for unanimously endorsing membership applications from the Carman Farm Business Association and the Saskatchewan Association of Rural Municipalities and submitting them for approval to the annual meeting. Lang questioned whether the organizations were eligible for membership under the Council's bylaws and declared that they should have been submitted for approval to the government. He bluntly warned:

> If the Council members feel that they can only survive on an independent basis, in the sense of self-determination of their activities and projects, and that continuous liaison and regard for government interest in such problems would compromise their independence, then the Council and government should be aware that they are on a collision course. [12]

Despite that blunt warning there were indications that the Canada Grains Council was still bent upon an independent course. On May 7, 1970, Bryden wrote to J.W. Warren, Deputy Minister of Industry, Trade and Commerce, that "through the intervention of the Grains Group," the Grains Council had altered its Secretary-General's proposal for establishment of a market intelligence and development service abroad to one of sending two or three technical missions to the Caribbean and Latin American countries to explore possibilities for introducing barley into local feed use in replacement of widely-used American corn. Representatives of the Wheat Board, the Trade Commission Service and the Grains Group participated with the Council in formulation of the proposal.

Provided the proposal was submitted in acceptable terms, the Grains Group was prepared to recommend that 50 per cent of the cost of the mission be met by the federal government. Lang observed:

> Although the Grains Group has represented on several occasions that the proposal and draft budget would have to be submitted through it to obtain federal government acceptance, I am not altogether certain that Dr. Dever has taken aboard this suggestion. To assure that the matter is dealt with properly, I should be grateful if you would have the Trade Commission Service notify me of any direct communication they may receive from Dr. Dever. [13]

As the diverse studies and initiatives got under way, Lang met for the first time with the Advisory Committee to the Wheat Board on January 21, 1970, to outline the formation and objectives of the Grains Group. Foremost among the immediate problems was an "urgent" review of production patterns. At the same time he announced appointment of a committee to review the Wheat Board's delivery quota system. Members of the committee included: E.A. Boden, Vice-President of Saskatchewan Wheat Pool; W.G. Winslow, General Manager of United Grain Growers; and Dr. J.L. Leibfried, Executive

Assistant to the Wheat Board. Appointment of a Transportation Co-ordinator at Vancouver was also announced along with studies on long-term transportation needs.

The Advisory Committee was also introduced to David Suderman who had been appointed earlier that month to head up a new Department of Information Services established by the Board. In addition to developing and maintaining liaison with the news media, the department was set up to undertake specific programs designed to provide producers and the grain trade with more complete information on developments in the domestic and international markets for grain, Board policies and operations and developments of importance to Prairie grain producers. With an air of urgency everywhere, impelled by the critical domestic and international situation, the Wheat Board was modifying its previous low-profile image of working quietly in the background.

Shortly after that meeting, the full import of Lang's overall strategy to shape a new course for the Prairie grain industry became apparent. On the afternoon of February 9, 1970, the teletype in the Canadian Wheat Board offices began to clatter and over the next 13 minutes outlined the first indications of what was to become one of the most controversial programs ever instituted in western Canada. Addressed to McNamara from Bob Esdale at the Grains Group, the 11-page proposal was titled: "Program to Keep Land From Producing Wheat in 1970." It was shortly to turn into "Operation LIFT" (Lower Inventory for Tomorrow).

Pointing to farm-held stocks, which were climbing toward the 522 million bushel mark, the message was as follows:

> Not only is the farmer having to store this wheat at his own cost, including the erection of many new bins or storage outside with likely deterioration through the summer and fall, but this huge stockpile has a serious price depressing effect on world market prices and domestic feed prices. In addition, the urgent task of rationalizing the grain handling and transportation system, which at present cannot call forth and move what the market demands, is unduly hampered by the continual clogging of the system that these stocks inevitably involve. [14]

The objective set forth was to reduce stocks by at least 500 million bushels of wheat within the next two years by reducing the size of the 1970 and 1971 production (or just 1970 if practical). The program was "to be designed in such a way that only 20 million to 21 million acres remained in production thereafter, about four million acres of oats and nine million to 10 million acres of barley, and that other crops do not increase out of line with demand." To achieve these desired future grain acreages, the program was to contain elements which would encourage diversion of some land out of wheat into forage and pasture for future livestock production. [15]

Elements of the package would include "an inducement of coercion to co-operate based on the size, the quota or the number of specified acres per farm," and "an incentive to co-operate based on the number of acres diverted from wheat." [16]

After setting out a number of alternative formulas to achieve the proposed acreage reductions, the message ended with the declaration that; "It is important that further plans be developed to prevent accumulation of surpluses of wheat again in 1971 or later, or of other crops in subsequent years." The main elements of such a program were to be: a new quota system related to demands and needs; early announcement of annual quota levels for all crops each year; a five-year grassland program; a much stronger and more intensive outlook program covering annual and five-year prospects; a comprehensive agricultural adjustment program; and restrictions on new land entering agriculture.

At the Canadian Wheat Board there were grave reservations about the implied use of the delivery quota system as an "inducement of coercion" to cut back on wheat acreage. Of equal concern was the further implication of confidence in the ability of the Ottawa planners to forecast changes in market demand, not only for one year but up to five years, and to thereby institute supply-management in crop production through acreage recommendations.

The Board's long experience with variable yields, due to the whims of yearly weather patterns and sudden volatile changes in the world marketplace, clearly indicated caution on such an approach. Further, the Commissioners were confident that the farmers, looking at their bulging bins and reduced delivery opportunities, would make their own individual decisions to diversify and cut back on wheat production, particularly if the recommendations of the Quota Review Committee resulted in a delivery system more attuned to bringing forth the particular grains suited to market opportunities and demands.

But in Ottawa the push was on. Events were now moving inexorably toward a unilateral decision by Canada to take drastic action in the hope that other exporting nations would follow the lead in wheat crop reductions.

On February 18, Lang met in Washington with Secretary of Agriculture Clifford Hardin and senior officials responsible for U.S. grain policy. The Americans were told that Canada was in the final stages of developing a program designed to achieve a major reduction in wheat acreage. A decision concerning the program would be taken immediately and announced later that month. Noting that the program would represent a substantial cost to the Canadian Treasury and further burden on the Canadian industry, Lang stressed that the success of Canada's action, in achieving its full and effective implementation and maximum benefit to the world wheat economy, would depend importantly on the willingness of others to take complementary measures. It was agreed that it would be opportune to convene a meeting at the ministerial level with other grain exporting countries for a full explanation of the Canadian program as a basis for reviewing co-operative and complementary action that might be taken by other exporters to reinforce the Canadian program and its beneficial effects.

On Lang's return to Ottawa, messages were despatched to Brussels, Canberra and Buenos Aires, outlining the Washington meeting and suggesting a meeting of the major exporters in the latter part of March. Two days later, on February 27, Lang rose in the House of Commons and outlined Operation LIFT. Pointing to the growing carryover of wheat, equivalent to nearly two year's disappearance, the Minister declared that, unless strong action was taken immediately, the prospect was for heavy movement out of wheat into coarse grains and oilseeds:

> The wheat producer is in a position in which he must attempt to increase his cash return. In large measure this would lead to increased acreage in other crops. Our stock positions, particularly in oats and barley, are already high. A further increase in these crops this year would result in burdensome surplus and lower prices for these products. This would create extreme difficulties for producers whose income normally depend on sales of these crops…The government proposes to implement a program to reduce wheat acreage and to encourage farmers in the Wheat Board designated regions to hold this land out of production of any crop this year. [17]

The program outlined to achieve the acreage reductions was comprised of a carrot and a stick. The carrot was an estimated $100 million program, to be administered by the Department of Agriculture, whereby western wheat farmers, who reduced wheat acreages below 1969 levels and increased summerfallow by the same amount, would receive compensation payments of six dollars an acre for additions to summerfallow, or ten dollars an acre for additions to perennial forage acreage. Compensation payments would be available to a maximum of 22 million acres of additional summerfallow and two million acres of additional perennial forage. A maximum of 1,000 acres for any individual producer would be eligible for compensation payments.

The stick made use of the Canadian Wheat Board's delivery quota system. In effect, farmers who did not comply with the acreage reduction program were to be severely limited in their privilege to deliver wheat under quota in the coming year. Land seeded to wheat was specifically excluded from the producer's quota base. Wheat delivery quotas would be based on a total of: 25 per cent of summerfallow acreage as stated in the producer's 1969 permit book; total acreage of summerfallow in 1970; and the amount by which acreage in perennial forage in 1970 exceeded the acreage in perennial forage in the previous year. The "inducement of coercion" had appeared.

Quotas for oats, barley, Soft Spring wheat, and other crops to which delivery quotas applied, were to be based on acres seeded to each crop in 1970. In addition, the producer could choose to allocate any or all of his acres qualified for wheat to any other crop instead of wheat. [18]

While Lang assured the Commons that he had discussed the program fully with the leaders of farm organizations in Western Canada, and that in many respects it had been improved by the adoption of their recommendations, reaction from the farmers was less than enthusiastic. An indication of their hostility toward the program was given in answers to a questionnaire circulated by a Conservative Member of Parliament, Jack McIntosh, in his constituency of Swift Current-Maple Creek. Asked if the LIFT Program offered a solution to their problems, 336 of the 400 respondents said no, 19 said yes and 45 had no opinion. Asked if they were able to participate in the LIFT Program, 272 replied in the negative, while 68 said yes and 60 offered no opinion. [19]

Lang's proposed meeting of ministers from the major exporting countries for late March was delayed. Finally held May 4 and 5 in Ottawa, it was chaired by Agriculture Minister H.A. Olson. After an outline of the LIFT Program by Lang, the other exporters detailed measures taken by their respective countries.

The United States had already announced a program for 1970-71 at 43.5 million acres for wheat. Australia, where drought conditions had cut back on the crop, had reduced producer deliveries to 318 million bushels, down 40 per cent from 1968-69. Argentina, which had suffered a series of short crops and had actually imported wheat in the previous year, had virtually no carryover. The EEC representatives gave little by way of commitment except to outline a proposed long-term rationalization program.

Doug Treleaven, who attended the meeting along with other Commissioners of the Canadian Wheat Board, said it was difficult to objectively assess the results of the meeting because no specific policy commitments were involved. [20]

The impact of the LIFT Program was equally hard to assess. Overall plantings of the six major crops on the Prairies in the spring of 1970 dropped to 35.1 million acres from a total of 44.22 million acres in 1969. Wheat acreage showed a dramatic drop, falling to 24.4 million acres in 1969 to 12 million acres in 1970. However, there were increased acreages in all other crops except oats, which showed a slight decline from 5.63 million acres to 5.26 million. Plantings of barley rose from nine million acres to 9.5 million, while rye rose from 859,000 acres to 944,000 acres. The most dramatic increases were shown in the oilseeds sector. Flaxseed jumped over one million acres, from 2.32 million acres to 3.35 million, while rapeseed acreage doubled, rising from 2.01 million acres in 1969 to 4.05 million acres. [21]

While $140 million had been allocated to the program, the final tally showed that the federal Treasury paid out $63,192,415 to 101,038 farmers who participated in Operation LIFT. Administrative costs of $2,211,745.38 brought the total cost to the government to $65,404,160.38. [22]

As the 1970-71 crop year began, the Grains Group in Ottawa were putting forward a new longer-range program to supersede Operation LIFT. Basic to the planning was the premise that the full 86.5 million acres of improved land in Western Canada could not be used between 1971 and 1975 with normal

Garson N. (Gerry) Vogel was Chief Commissioner of the CWB from 1971 to 1977. It was a period marked by a sharp growth in world wheat trade, stronger prices and grain transportation problems.

summerfallow of 26 million acres, unless markets were expanded substantially above the present levels. The primary objective, as the Ottawa planners saw it, was to allocate the Prairie land base in rational relation to market prospects.

Continued emphasis was to be placed on diverting land from wheat to other crops, particularly barley, in order to compete in a rapidly growing world trade in feed grains. Unlike the relatively static milling wheat market, the world feed grain market, dominated by U.S. corn, had expanded dramatically over the previous decade. World export trade in feed grains jumped from 29 million tonnes in 1960-61 to 42.8 million tonnes in 1969-70.23 Canada had been only a residual supplier into this expanding market and barley was seen as the only real prospect for sales expansion. Commissioners of the Board had pressed this point in discussions with the Grains Group.

To achieve those objectives, Lang proposed a number of wide-ranging reforms. *The Temporary Wheat Reserves Act*, passed in 1956, under which the federal government paid storage charges on all commercial stocks of wheat in excess of 178 million bushels, was seen as an incentive towards wheat production. The federal payment was added to the Board's wheat pool for distribution to farmers, thereby creating a disparity between final returns on wheat and other crops. With a heavy commercial carryover and lagging sales, it was estimated that the *Temporary Wheat Reserves Act,* under which payments had soared to $71,329,837 in the 1969-70 crop year, was adding as much as 15 cents a bushel in returns to farmers for wheat.[24] Therefore the Act would be terminated and wheat would become less of a preferred crop as future initial prices would be reduced accordingly.

In order that barley should improve in relative profitability, assuring sustained production to aggressively compete against U.S. corn on the expanding world feed grains market, the initial payments would be supported as required should world prices fall below the level which would generate adequate supplies, and the Board could vigorously pursue a policy of expansion of annual barley exports towards 200 million bushels. (This, implied a deliberate federal export subsidy commitment by the federal government for the first time since monopoly control of wheat and feed grains was assumed by the Canadian Wheat Board. At all other times initial payments were set at a level below anticipated final returns from the market.)

To compensate farmers for the loss of the *Temporary Wheat Reserves Act* an income stabilization fund was proposed. To be jointly financed by the producers and government, it would make payments in any year when the farmers' income from the sale of the six major crops fell below the previous five-year's average returns. It was also proposed that the income stabilization fund be available to offset losses which might occur in the pools for the three Board grains.

At the Wheat Board there was considerable concern over the wide-ranging proposals. Larry Kristjanson noted that the recommendations called for a redistribution of the timing of income from grain sales, rather than an income transfer from the Treasury to the western producer. While agreeing with the forecast that the demand for feed grains would expand, Kristjanson observed: "It is, however, quite a different matter to forecast a specific level and guarantee that this level will be achieved regardless of the supply position of importing countries." [25]

McNamara outlined his reservations in a lengthy letter to the Grains Group:

> As we understand it, the main impact of the proposed program is to even out cash flow on an annual basis to the producers of western Canada. In other words, the program is designed to avoid the violent fluctuations in cash income that producers have experienced over the years.
>
> Under the Wheat Board Act, the Board distributes the returns, if any, as soon as a pool account can reasonably be closed. As far as the Board is concerned, its duty is to distribute the money as soon as it is practical. Any changes in this procedure would require an amendment to the Wheat Board Act. The sales experience varies tremendously from year to year and the amount of money distributed fluctuates widely, but as far as the Board is concerned it should be a decision of producers whether they want to change the system to even out their annual income. This sort of question should be decided by farm leaders in talks with the Government and the Canadian Wheat Board should not be involved in the judgement as to whether this should or should not be done.
>
> The exact mechanics of levelling the cash flow are not completely spelled out in the paper. We would want to become involved in the initial discussions of mechanics of the program to assure that the administration of the program would be such as to minimize any negative impact on our marketing operations. The Board is strongly of the view that marketing is our prime responsibility and we should not be involved in income distribution schemes that have a significant effect on the sales effort.
>
> There is one aspect of this paper that disturbs us greatly and that is the implied confidence in the ability to forecast changes in market demand. Past experience indicates that there is very little reason to have confidence in these market

forecasts. During surplus times, like the last two or three years, it is relatively easy to make judgements as to what should be planted in that, if an error was made there were ample stocks to take care of the problem. However, if we are entering an era where supply and demand are in better balance, very costly mistakes can be made in making these projections. One need only take a look at the forecast of the Agricultural Task Force with respect to required barley acreage this year to appreciate the magnitude of the errors that can be made.

The forecast in the paper that the demand for feed grains will expand is probably correct. However, it is evident that this year's experience is being used as a basis for forecasting the future. This is exactly the mistake that the Agricultural Task Force made last year when they projected needed barley acreage on the basis of the feed grain situation at the time the forecast was made. It is a common error in all these projections that have been made throughout the years to say that the current market situation is the marketing situation that will prevail in the future. [26]

McNamara's comments on the current barley situation and the previous forecast was in reference to an outbreak of corn blight in the United States which struck the hybrid varieties widely in use there, decimating yields and causing considerable turmoil in the market. Primarily as a result of the blight, the U.S. corn crop dropped from 116.4 million tonnes in 1969 to 104.4 million tonnes in 1970 — a drop of 12 million tonnes, or 472.4 million bushels. [27] At the same time demand for feed grains on the world market rose to a new record, climbing from 42.8 million tonnes in 1969-70 to 46.1 million tonnes in 1970-71. However, the price impact of the U.S. corn shortfall was somewhat blunted by substantial quantities of lower grade wheats that moved into the feed grains market.

Recognizing that, with the heavy farm carryover of wheat and the impact of the LIFT program, that a large barley crop was in prospect, the Board had intensified its barley marketing efforts in the spring and summer of 1970. As a result, Canada was able to capture approximately 10 per cent of the world feed grains market with record barley exports of 179.6 million bushels, more than double the previous year's exports. [28] That upsurge in barley exports, combined with an increase of 90 million bushels in export wheat sales to 435.4 million bushels in 1970-71, resulted in a high level of country elevator shipments throughout the crop year. A total of 812.33 million bushels of grain were shipped from country elevators to terminals and to interior mills. [29]

The Canadian Wheat Board reported that shipments of this magnitude could not have been accomplished without the planning and co-ordination provided under the new Block Shipping System. When producer deliveries of barley fell to critical levels during the winter, an increase of 10 cents was authorized in the initial payment on March 1, bringing it to $1.01 a bushel. Deliveries thereafter returned to a more satisfactory level, but the result was a deficit of $10,945,327 in the barley pool.

Thus, despite the fact that the 1970-71 world wheat crop, estimated at 11.4 billion bushels, was the second highest on record and it was the fifth consecutive year that world wheat harvests had exceeded 10 billion bushels, there were signs of a turnaround. World wheat trade climbed 11 per cent to reach nearly two billion bushels. The Soviet Union had its second highest wheat crop on record at 3.66 billion bushels and exported a record 260 million bushels of wheat. Soviet imports from Canada slumped to 12.1 million bushels during the year, and as a result of the large Russian crop and consequent exports to other countries in the Soviet bloc, sales to other Eastern European nations dropped. Total Canadian sales to Eastern Europe were a slim 15,568,529 bushels. [30]

The decline in sales to the Soviet bloc was more than offset by increased sales to the United Kingdom and the EEC, and shipments to Asian nations rose by 56.9 million bushels, including a first ever sale to North Korea. Exports to South American countries also increased substantially with Brazil making its first purchases of wheat — 15.5 million bushels — from the Canadian Wheat Board. [31]

As Commissioners and employees of the Board fanned out to 63 countries on sales missions during the year in the drive to widen Canada's market base, a number of programs and initiatives were instituted within the Board. On March 16, 1970, a new Market Analysis and Development Department was formed with Dr. H.F. Bjarnason as General Director. Divided into two major groups, the department was responsible to the Board for: maintaining up-to-date files and personal knowledge on marketing conditions and outlook for all wheat importing areas and for particular grain and grain products; assessing crop year sales potential and recommending long-term market development programs for major wheat importing areas; keeping abreast of research and developments in technical areas (milling, baking, freight formula feeds, etc.) that have an impact on the market for western Canadian grain; maintaining and developing personal contacts and goodwill with, as well as providing market information to, buyers and others who may have influence in grain purchasing decisions; recommending and arranging for missions from overseas markets to Canada and for market promotion and development missions from Canada to overseas markets. [32]

In line with the restructuring of the organization during the 1970-71 crop year, the Board doubled its computer capacity as an interim step toward the ultimate installation of a new generation computer of significantly greater capacity than the combined unit then operating. As pioneers in the computer processing field, the Board's computers were working round the clock for up to seven days a week during the autumn peak load period, due to the heavy load imposed by administration of Operation LIFT and other programs.

Also, in October 1970, responsibility for administering all new sales of Prairie grains under medium-term credit of up to three years was transferred by the federal government to the Board. Prior to that time such medium-term credit sales were either insured under the Export Development Corporation Act, or under special guarantees extended by the federal government. Gerry Vogel, the Assistant Chief Commissioner, met with the banks to set up a $200 million blanket loan for credit use with the government underwriting the risk on a list of countries approved by Cabinet as eligible for the loans. [33]

One month earlier, the Board had appointed a Canadian Grain Marketing Review Committee. Charged with evaluating Canada's system of selling grain under changing conditions, this internationally composed commission was requested to report its findings and recommendations as soon as possible. The Committee, under the chairmanship of Dr. M.W. Menzies, a Canadian economic and grain policy consultant, included: Dr. John Schnittker, Professor of Economics at Kansas State University, and formerly Under-Secretary of Agriculture in the United States government; A.P. Van Stolk, President of a Rotterdam grain company and grain market adviser to the EEC; Vernon Lester, President of a Vancouver-based grain exporting firm; Albert Baker, former General Manager of the Alberta Wheat Pool; and Dr. J.L. Leibfried, Executive-Assistant of the Canadian Wheat Board.

The report of the Committee, submitted to the Board on January 12, 1971, fully supported retention of the Canadian Wheat Board:

> The principal theme of this report is the achievement of an integrated grain industry through the rejuvenation, modernization and co-ordination of centralized marketing, and all other elements of the system, building on the accepted structure and functioning of the Canadian Wheat Board. [34]

In a series of broad-ranging recommendations, the Review Committee said an income stabilization policy, with funds provided by the government and producers, was urgently needed to "relieve the marketing system of the pressures which build up in times of reduced deliveries or world prices." [35] However, the report made it clear that the administration of such a program should be outside the mandate of the Board:

> The entire system must be market oriented, providing cus-
> tomers with the kinds, qualities and quantities of grain they
> want at the right time and place, and at competitive prices.
> Income stabilization should not be the responsibility of the
> marketing system in an uncertain world. [36]

Revised quality standards for wheat, including protein grading, and a continued presence in the barley market, along with policies governing production
and inventories and changes in the Canadian Wheat Board organization were
recommended:

> Career opportunities should be given new attention
> throughout the grain industry. The proposals put forward in
> this connection for the wheat board can provide an example
> for the entire Canadian grain industry if they are imple-
> mented imaginatively. [37]

While finding that the marketing of rye, flaxseed and rapeseed outside of the
Board "seems to have worked reasonably well in the past," the Review
Committee noted that this had been due in part to the fact that the volume of
these commodities had been small enough, in relation to wheat and barley, that
the Board had been able to give them preferential treatment. It warned, however, that: "As rapeseed production increases, there is some doubt as to whether it
will be possible to leave rapeseed marketing outside of the increasingly integrated Board controlled system." [38]

Advocating changes in the delivery quota system, the Committee generally
endorsed the report of the Boden Committee, which had been delivered to Lang
on February 20, 1970, and said that "only to the degree consistent with efficiency of marketing should quotas be used for the equitable allocation of the
available market among producers." [39]

Upon its completion, the report of the Canadian Grain Marketing Review
Committee went forward addressed to Assistant Chief Commissioner
G.N. Vogel. In the interim, since appointment of the Review Committee, Bill
McNamara had retired on October 5, 1970, after 25 years of service with the
Board — nine of them as Chief Commissioner. Now 66 years of age,
McNamara was appointed to the Canadian Senate two days later on October 7.

An era had ended. McNamara was succeeded by Gerry Vogel, whose appointment as Chief Commissioner was delayed until early March, 1971. At the same
time, Doug Treleaven was named Assistant Chief Commissioner. Appointed to
the vacancy on the five-man Board was R.M. Esdale, who had previously served
with the Grains Division of Industry, Trade and Commerce from 1946 to 1970

and immediately prior to joining the Board was Marketing Co-ordinator of the Ottawa Grains Group. He joined Larry Kristjanson and Charles W. Gibbings, former President of the Saskatchewan Wheat Pool, who had been appointed a Commissioner on July 1, 1969.

Thus, as the 1971-72 crop year approached after a year-and-a-half of almost unprecedented change, there were new faces, new policies and a new outlook for a more aggressive and market-oriented Canadian Wheat Board.

On the political scene, Lang had begun an aggressive series of legislative changes aimed at fully implementing the changes recommended by the Boden Committee in the delivery quota system; changes to the grading system under the *Canada Grains Act*, including protein grading; implementation of a Prairie grain income stabilization program and termination of the *Temporary Wheat Reserves Act*.

Also on the Commons order paper was legislation to conduct a plebiscite among western farmers to see if they wished to continue to market rapeseed through the open market or have the responsibility transferred to the Canadian Wheat Board. In the background, the Grains Group was hard at work on a series of studies aimed at radical changes in the grain handling and transportation systems.

Lang, now appointed as Minister of Manpower and Immigration while still retaining responsibility to Parliament for the Wheat Board, kicked off his legislative campaign in late October, 1970, by tabling a 21-page "mini white paper" on Prairie grains policy in the Commons. [40] His proposal for an income stabilization program and termination of the *Temporary Wheat Reserves Act*, immediately came under fire from western farm organizations. The proposal that any deficits that might occur in Wheat Board pool accounts be recovered in the future from the stabilization fund was declared to be an abdication of responsibility by the government.

When a revised grains income stabilization plan was tabled in the Commons in mid-March, 1971, the clause specifying that Board pool deficits be reimbursed from the fund was deleted. At the same time, Lang announced that an interim payment of $100 million would be paid to Prairie farmers "to make up for relatively poor earnings this year plus ending of the *Temporary Wheat Reserves Act*." [41] The stabilization program was slated to come into effect at the start of the new crop year on August 1, 1971. But, when Parliament adjourned for a two month recess on June 30, the legislation remained on the order paper. Lang also ran into difficulties with Bill C-238, an Act to amend the *Canadian Wheat Board Act*, proposing changes to the grading system and changes in the grain delivery quota system. A controversial clause 15, providing for a plebiscite on the placing of rye, rapeseed and flaxseed marketing under the authority of the Canadian Wheat Board, was deleted in committee and a new Bill C-255 was drawn up to provide for the vote. However, at recess, that too had not been dealt with and remained on the order paper.[42]

Faced with the impasse on the key issue of the stabilization program in his wide-ranging plans, Lang mounted a Prairie tour to outline and defend his policies and proposed legislation. At the opening press conference, held in Winnipeg, Lang stirred up a hornet's nest of protest. Under questioning the minister confirmed that the $100 million interim payment, promised under the stalled stabilization plan, would not be forthcoming since the legislation had not been passed. At the same time, he said that federal payments under the *Temporary Wheat Reserves Act* would not be paid to the Canadian Wheat Board for distribution to farmers. While the wheat reserves legislation remained on the statutes, its repeal was included in the stabilization bill which remained on the order paper.

At the semi-annual meeting of the Canadian Federation of Agriculture, held the next week in Penticton, B.C., a demand was made that the *Temporary Wheat Reserves Act* payments, estimated at $61.6 million, be made forthwith, since the legislation had not been repealed.[43] Lang remained adamant and when Parliament readjourned, on September 7, he came under fire from the Opposition over non-payment of the funds. After two weeks of heavy pounding during the question period, the government brought forward Bill C-244, the grains income stabilization plan, for debate.

With the Opposition fighting to have an inflationary factor built into payouts under the stabilization plan, acrimonious debate raged until mid-October. Meanwhile, four Saskatchewan farmers filed suit against the Minister of Finance in a Regina court seeking payment of the funds under the *Temporary Wheat Reserves Act*. In the Commons, a compromise was reached with Opposition Leader Robert Stanfield, whereby sections of the controversial legislation would be passed and proclaimed, including the interim payment of $100 million to Prairie farmers and the rescinding of the *Temporary Wheat Reserves Act* retroactive to August 1, 1971.

Proclamation of other sections of the legislation would be delayed until the federal government met with Prairie agriculture ministers and farm organizations in an attempt to hammer out a more acceptable formula of payments which recognized the increasing inflationary costs faced by farmers.

But, the constitutional authority to retroactively rescind the *Temporary Wheat Reserves Act*, remained in doubt. Lang came under fire in the Senate from a fellow Liberal over that particular section of the legislation. Senator Eugene Forsey, a recognized constitutional expert, declared: "If I had been an opponent of the government when this feature of the legislation appeared, I would have said, 'The Lord hath delivered them into my hands.'"[44]

The Parliamentary compromise was blocked when the four Saskatchewan farmers refused to agree to an adjournment of the court case, scheduled for hearing in Regina on October 13. On October 12, Lang rose in the Commons to announce that the stabilization legislation was being withdrawn and the delayed payments under the *Temporary Wheat Reserves Act* were going forward to the Canadian Wheat Board for distribution to Western farmers. It was to be three years before another Western grain income stabilization bill would be introduced in the Commons by Lang in December 1974.

As Lang's master plan suffered that major setback, other legislation, aimed at streamlining the efficiency of the Wheat Board, went forward. The proposed changes in grading and delivery quotas were instituted by Order-in-Council and went into effect on August 1, 1971. Changes under the Canada Grains Act reduced the number of the top grades of wheat from five to three. As a first step, No. 1 and No. 2 Northern were replaced by a single new top grade, No. 1 Canada Western Red Spring wheat. On April 1, 1972, the Board began to offer this new top grade with guaranteed minimum protein levels of 14.5 per cent, 14 per cent and 13 per cent for shipment from the Lakehead and eastern positions at the beginning of the new crop year. This was followed by combining No. 3 and No. 4 Northern into a new No. 2 Western Red Spring wheat to be segregated on protein levels. The lower portions of the former No. 4 and No. 5 Northern were combined into a new No. 3 Western Red Spring wheat but were not marketed on a protein basis.

The Board was now in a position to compete with protein guaranteed grades offered by the United States and Australia and the Soviet varieties being sold into the United Kingdom and EEC markets. A call for Canada to meet that competition had been put forward as early as March 8, 1968, when the Advisory Committee to the Canadian Wheat Board noted that other wheat exporting countries had been improving wheat quality and their systems of grading to meet "radical changes in the milling and baking process, increasing the need for much more uniform quality than our present grading system allows."[45] The Committee asked the Departments of Trade and Commerce and Agriculture to set up a task force as a matter of urgency and make recommendations.

Also, as a result of changes to the delivery quota system implemented on August 1, 1971, the Board was able to more efficiently call forward the types, grades and quantities of grain in market demand. A number of the revisions recommended by the Boden Committee had been instituted at the start of the 1970-71 crop year, but the LIFT program had mitigated against full implementation of other major proposals. C.F. Wilson commented that the scope of the Boden Committee review and recommendations on quotas, which was completed in one month, was in inverse proportion to the brevity of the report and the time it took to produce it.[46] Its effect, upon implementation during the 1970-71 and 1971-72 crop years, was to virtually revolutionize the quota delivery system.

Objectives of the delivery quota system, as redefined by the Review Committee were:

> The primary objective of the delivery quota system for western Canadian grains is to enable the Canadian Wheat Board to bring into country elevators at the right time the kinds, qualities and quantities of all grain required to compete effectively for market demand. In the long-term interest of the agricultural industry it must reflect market demand back to producers.
>
> Secondary objectives which are desirable, if consistent with the primary objective stated above, include:
>
> 1. the allocation of delivery opportunities for grain in demand among producers as equitably as possible.
> 2. the provision to producers of freedom to deliver to elevators of their choice.
> 3. the promotion of orderly marketing and of efficiency in the operation of country elevators, the main function of these being to handle grain rather than provide storage.
> 4. the development of a system as simple as possible to administer and enforce. [47]

To achieve these objectives the unit quota, under which the producer could deliver 100 units of any grain he chose at the start of the crop year, and the specified acreage quota disappeared. The quota maximization and equalization policy, which congested elevators at the close of each crop year with grains that might, or might not be, in demand was eliminated. An "assignable acreage" was calculated and entered in each producer's permit book. The formula used to calculate such acreage consisted of four parts: land seeded to the six quota grains, summerfallow acreage, land in miscellaneous crop (any crop other than the six quota grains and perennial forage), and land in perennial forage up to one-third of the acreage in the three previous categories. [48]

While the farmer still listed his acreage seeded to the actual grains, producers were able to allocate their assignable acres to any grains they wished. A farmer, who might have a heavy carryover of one of the quota grains, could choose not to seed any acreage to that grain but still assign all, or part, of his quota acreage for delivery of his carryover crop in the coming crop year. The assigned acreage was listed in a separate column in the permit book, and it was upon this that the Wheat Board calculated its quotas to draw forth any particular grain. After harvesting was completed, producers could submit applications for one general acreage change on or before October 1 of each year.

Thus, the producer enjoyed a high degree of flexibility in the establishment of his quota base in relation to existing farm stocks of grain and his current land use. At the same time, the Board introduced non-cumulative quotas for wheat, oats and barley. Termination dates for each individual quota were announced when the quotas were authorized so that the producer knew the exact amount of time he had for delivery. And, for the first time, the Board was authorized to issue quotas on a grade basis.

In place of "over-quota privileges," a quota system was established for specialty markets. For example malting barley, on a selected and accepted basis, would qualify for carlot assignment at any time, provided the producer assigned 50 acres as a quota base or each carlot he intended to ship. Selected oats, rye for distilleries, rapeseed and flaxseed for crushing plants could also be shipped on an assigned area basis, but without requiring a prescribed number of assigned acres to do so. Special delivery permits were authorized to accommodate producers retiring from farming, for limited quantities of gristing (milling) for family use, and for deliveries made to purchase registered or certified seed.

The new quota system not only allowed the Board to more efficiently bring forward specific grains and grades tailored to market demands, it also gave clearer market signals to producers in planning their crop patterns. Additionally Lang, after consultation with the Wheat Board, instituted a policy of announcing initial payments and guaranteed delivery quotas by March 1, in advance of each crop year.

Following a short, but intense, period of innovation and change, precipitated in part by the frustrating closing years of the decade of the 60s, the machinery was coming into place for an unprecedented challenge in a suddenly changing and volatile world marketplace. A signal of the events, that were to shake and turn the world grain markets upside down, was given late in the 1970-71 crop year. In late 1969, the government and the Wheat Board had to choke back a bitter pill by not insisting that the Soviet Union fulfil its obligations under the 1966 three-year contract. In return for extension of the terms, the Soviet Union assured Canada that, in the event of need, they would turn to Canada first in the future.

At the Canadian Wheat Board, the progress of the 1971 Soviet crop was watched closely and with apprehension, as prospects for near record crop became apparent. Then suddenly, and unexpectedly, Nikolai Belousov, who had succeeded Leonid Matveev as chairman of Exportkhleb, applied for a visa to visit Canada on May 14, 1971. On June 4 in Ottawa, Wheat Board Commissioners Treleaven and Esdale completed a contract with Belousov. Not only had Exportkhleb taken the outstanding obligation of 1.03 million long tons of wheat under the 1966 contract, but a contract covering a further 2.22 million tonnes of wheat, to be delivered during 1971-72, had been entered into.[49]

With a large crop of its own assured, the Soviet Union had chosen to make significant purchases. It was a portent of things to come. The world market was about to turn upside down.

Footnotes Chapter Five

1. Canadian Wheat Board File 341, 1969-70.
2. Canadian Wheat Board Archives, Box 18.
3. *Report of the Canadian Wheat Board, Crop Year 1968-69,* p. 12.
4. *The Manitoba Co-operator,* February 6, 1969, p. 1.
5. Otto Lang, taped interview, July 1986.
6. Canadian Wheat Board File 341, Jean Luc Pepin, letter to W.C. McNamara, September 30, 1969.
7. *Ibid,* McNamara letter to Pepin.
8. Canadian Wheat Board File 343, 1969-70.
9. *Ibid.*
10. *Ibid.*
11. *Ibid.*
12. *Ibid.*
13. Canadian Wheat Board File 343, 1969-70.
14. *Ibid.*
15. *Ibid.*
16. *Ibid.*
17. Canadian Wheat Board File 341, 1969-70.
18. *Ibid.*
19. Canadian Wheat Board File 301, 1969-70.
20. Minutes of the Advisory Committee to the Canadian Wheat Board, May 13, 1970, pp. 6, 7.
21. *Report of the Canadian Wheat Board, Crop Year 1972-73,* appendix 1.
22. *The Manitoba Co-operator,* June 15, 1972, p. 1.
23. Report of the Canadian Wheat Board, Crop Year 1970-71, p. 11.
24. *Supplementary Report of the Canadian Wheat Board, 1969-70,* p. 6.
25. Canadian Wheat Board File 343, 1970-71.
26. *Ibid.*
27. *Report of the Canadian Wheat Board, Crop Year, 1970-71,* p. 10.
28. *Ibid.* p. 27.
29. *Ibid.* p. 39.
30. *Ibid.* p. 18.
31. *Ibid.* pp. 17, 22.
32. *Ibid,* Crop Year 1969-70, p. 46.
33. Minutes of the Advisory Committee of the Canadian Wheat Board, March 30, 1971.
34. *Report of the Grain Marketing Review Committee, January 12, 1971,* p. 5.
35. *Ibid,* p. 2.
36. *Ibid.* p. 5.
37. *Ibid.* p. 3.
38. *Ibid.* p. 41.
39. *Ibid.* p. 26.
40. *The Manitoba Cooperator,* November 5, 1970, p. 1.
41. *Ibid,* March 8, 1971, p. 1.
42. *Ibid,* July 22, 1971, p. 4.

43. *Ibid*, August 5, 1971, p. 1.

44. *Ibid*. October 14, 1971, p. 4.

45. Minutes of the Advisory Commitee to the Canadian Wheat Board, March 8, 1968.

46. Charles F. Wilson, *Grain Marketing in Canada, International Grains Institute*, p. 238.

47. *Ibid*.

48. *Report of the Canadian Wheat Board, Crop Year 1971-72*, p. 41.

49. Canadian Wheat Board Press Release, June 4, 1971.

CHAPTER 6

FULL CIRCLE

I emphasize that nobody knew then — neither the Department of Agriculture nor the trade — just how much the Russians would buy. The export traders were not telling each other how much the Russians were booking with them. The exporters did not tell the Department of Agriculture. Nor were the Russians talking. — U.S. Secretary of Agriculture Earl Butz, testimony before Committee on Agriculture of the House of Representatives, September 14, 1972.

Less than three months into the 1971-72 crop year there were clear signs that the Canadian Wheat Board, after setting a series of export records in the previous year, was embarked upon another successful sales program. The only limitation on the Board's ability to undertake sales appeared to be the capacity of the handling and transportation system to accommodate further commitments. Preliminary figures indicated that Canada had exported 696.8 million bushels of grain in the 1970-71 crop year. Wheat exports had risen to 434.5 million bushels compared to 344.7 million in 1969-70, while barley exports had reached a record 172.2 million bushels and rapeseed exports by the private trade soared to 46.8 million bushels, far exceeding the previous record of 22 million bushels.[1]

As a result of the improved export picture, and the Operation LIFT reduced 1970 wheat crop of 332 million bushels, Canada's carry over of wheat into 1971-72 had declined to 750 million bushels from the previous year's one billion bushels.[2] Acceptance by Lang and the Grains Group of the Board's contention that the world feed grains market offered new opportunities for sales was also paying off. Despite a record barley crop of 391 million bushels in 1970, the previous year's carry over of 200 million bushels had been reduced to 143 million bushels by the Wheat Board's aggressive sales thrust.[3]

The gloom that pervaded the outlook entering the 1970s was gone. In late February 1971, Lang announced in the Commons that the LIFT program "had succeeded fairly well, but there is no intention of repeating it." [4] By late October the sales picture had brightened even further. Exports of all grains were running well ahead of the previous year, with the exception of oats. The Board had negotiated very large forward sales of wheat and barley and reported that total exports of grain were likely to exceed 700 million bushels, including a possible 450 million bushels of wheat and 200 million bushels of barley. [5]

Aside from the logistical limitations in Canada's handling and transportation systems, only one thing marred the optimistic sales outlook. The United States was not sharing in what was increasingly becoming a seller's market. Faced with record wheat and corn crops, and the prospect of an increased carry over approaching one billion bushels of wheat and 1.4 billion bushels of corn, and a reduction of over 100 million bushels in wheat exports, the United States was increasing its export subsidies, thereby depressing prices on the world market.

In early October 1971, a meeting of the grain exporting nations was scheduled in Melbourne, Australia. The Soviet Union, Argentina and the EEC were invited to send delegates. However, the Soviets and Argentina indicated their inability to be present and the EEC cancelled out just prior to the meeting. The Russians for their part were now net importers and Argentina, after a series of short crops, was to all intents and purposes withdrawn from the market. Price relationships between exporters had been fairly good until September when the U.S. lowered its prices by three to five dollars a tonne.

7 St. Helen's Place, London, EC3, in the heart of "The City", where the Canadian Wheat Board maintained an office for many years. The United Kingdom was a large, high quality market during the sixties and seventies.

At the Melbourne meeting Canada and Australia, the latter having just suffered a severe drought which cut back the wheat crop by 24 per cent, sought to have the Americans strengthen their prices. The U.S. representative, Clifford G. Pulvermacher, General Manager of Export Marketing Services for the United States Department of Agriculture, agreed to narrow the price spread. But, while the meeting was in progress, his office in Washington increased the existing subsidy on wheat from nine cents to 16 cents a bushel.[6]

At a subsequent meeting with the Americans, held in Minneapolis later that same month, Canadian Wheat Board Commissioners Doug Treleaven and Charlie Gibbings outlined Canada's tight commitments and pointed out that the U.S. had "a virtual run at the market and there is no justification for continuing to depress prices."[7] The argument had very little apparent impact. The only undertaking made by the Americans was one to gradually move prices upward, "subject to market improvement."[8]

Reporting on the meetings to the Advisory Committee of the Wheat Board, Treleaven said one of the most disturbing results of the situation was that the Board might well be placed in a position of having to reduce its prices in a seller's market in order to keep faith with its customers who had purchased grain on a deferred price basis as far as six, eight or 10 months ahead. Gibbings echoed Treleaven's concern and found the U.S. position "incredible in the light of prevailing circumstances." He added, "The rationale for the U.S. position was impossible to fathom when, on the one hand, they agreed that the subsidy was too high but, on the other hand, appeared completely indifferent to the available market for the next six months."[9]

With Canada heavily committed to the limit of transportation and handling capabilities, and Australia and Argentina virtually withdrawn from the market, due to forward commitments and poor crops, evidence of the available market had been steadily mounting. After negotiating the 3.25 million ton contract with Canada on June 4, the Russians had bought 500,000 long tons of wheat from Australia, the first purchases from that country since 1965. Then, on September 23, France announced the sale of 750,000 long tons of wheat to the Soviets.

In late October A.N. Kosygin, Chairman of the Council of Ministers of the USSR, visited Canada and the United States. While in Ottawa, Kosygin enquired about the availability of Canadian barley and gave clear indications of continuing need for feed grains in the Soviet Union. It was becoming increasingly evident that the Russians were firmly committed to a five-year plan to dramatically increase livestock production and improve the diet of Soviet citizens. The continuing purchases through 1971 had been made despite a near record Soviet wheat crop of over 3.66 billion bushels. What would happen if the climatically vulnerable Soviet crop suffered a serious setback, as it had in the mid-sixties?

With a presidential election looming in 1972, President Richard Nixon had moved earlier in 1971 to quell farm belt discontent at the American exclusion from the burgeoning grain markets in Communist countries. In early June, Nixon lifted the 21-year old embargo on trade in non-strategic materials with Mainland China imposed by former President Harry Truman during the Korean war. At the same time, he suspended the 50-50 shipping rule, instituted by the Kennedy Administration, which required 50 per cent of grain shipments to be carried by American flag vessels. He also scrapped a rule requiring validating export licenses from the Department of Commerce for anything sold to the Soviet Union.[10]

The 50-50 shipping rule had proven particularly offensive to the Russians and they had made no purchases of U.S. grain since 1964. There was no immediate reaction to relaxation of the U.S. trade rules, but on November 5, 1971, Washington announced that Cargill and Continental Grain would sell two million tons of corn, 600,000 tons of barley and 300,000 tons of oats to Exportkhleb.[11] Prior to the U.S. sale, Wheat Board Commissioners Kristjanson and Esdale met with Belousov in New York to outline Canada's feed grain position and tight shipping schedule. As a result, on the same date, November 5, the Canadian Wheat Board announced that Exportkhleb was exercising its option under the June 4, 1971, contract to take an additional 250,000 tons of Canadian wheat, principally durums.[12]

There was only a short lull in the Soviet purchasing. As a result of an invitation from Belousov, a Canadian Wheat Board negotiating team, headed by Kristjanson, arrived in Moscow on February 15, 1972. By that time there were obvious indications that all was not well with the Soviet winter wheat crop. On February 4, a Soviet newspaper, *Selskaya Zhizn*, carried an article reporting that some regions of the Soviet Union had experienced strong continuous frosts and thin layers of snow so that soil, in some areas, was frozen to a depth of 150 centimetres. Farm leaders in these areas were urged to prepare for replanting in the spring, indicating that substantial winterkill of fall sown crops had taken place.[13]

On February 9, the *Financial Times* in London reported that the North Caucasus had been hit by unusually severe frost and lack of snow and that, in a large part of Ukraine, the Rostov and the Volgograd regions, as well as the "black soil" areas, were frozen to a depth of five feet or more. The Financial Times noted that this had happened only once since the mid-1940s, and that this area normally produced over half of the USSR winter wheat and contained the most efficient Soviet farmers.[14]

As Kristjanson and Belousov were engaged in week-long negotiations in Moscow, there were further clear indications that a serious situation was developing with respect to the Soviet crop. On February 18, *Pravda* published an unprecedented statement that the Central Committee of the Communist Party had met the previous day, together with all the First Secretaries of Central

Committees of Communist Parties and Chairmen of the Council of Ministers, plus 12 members of the Politburo and many ministers of the federal government, in order to examine "questions connected with the preparation and implementation of spring agricultural work, and also further development of the livestock industry."[15]

Despite all of these signs of a coming crop disaster, and warnings from Canada and other exporting nations as to their inability to meet the demand, the policy makers in Washington apparently slept on. It would lead to what became known in history as "The Great Grain Robbery."

On February 25, Kristjanson cabled Winnipeg that he was flying home with a signed contract covering a firm commitment for 3.5 million tons of wheat and an option for purchase of a further 1.5 million tons of wheat and flour. Due to large forward commitments, including heavy shipments under the previous 3.5 million ton Soviet contract through to June 1972, deliveries had to be scheduled from July forward and throughout the 1972-73 crop year. The option, if exercised, would have to be shipped in 1973.[16]

The agreement officially establishing the Canadian International Grains Institute in 1971 was signed by G.N. Vogel, Chief Commissioner, CWB and H.D. Pound, Chief Commissioner of the Canadian Grain Commission (CGC). Looking on (left to right) are R.M. Esdale, Commissioner, CWB; C.W. Gibbings, Commissioner, CWB; C.L. Shuttleworth, Assistant Chief Commissioner, CGC; D.H. Treleaven, Assistant Chief Commissioner, CWB; and F.M. Hetland, Commissioner, CGC.

The Canadian Wheat Board was now in the position of having to turn down further sales because of limitations in the transportation system. Meanwhile, the Commissioners were becoming increasingly concerned about U.S. export subsidies which were continuing to depress world prices. Gibbings and Treleaven attended a meeting with American and Australian officials in Hawaii and reported back that: "The outlook for stronger wheat prices at this point is very bleak." Argentina had again declined to attend since they did not have any wheat for export and might have to purchase wheat to meet their commitments. [17] Canada had raised prices slightly after the last Soviet sale and Australians were in favour of a price hike:

> However, the U.S. representatives were adamant that they could not endorse any increase in the price of their wheat. The reasons given were the fact that their exports this year have been rather dismal due to labour problems and high ergot content in spring wheat. This is also an election year and there is the complicating factor of export subsidies... [18]

On April 10, Kristjanson reported to the Advisory Committee of the Board that there were daily reports coming from Russia indicating continued bad weather. He noted that U.S. Secretary of Agriculture Earl Butz was in Moscow to discuss a sale of U.S. grain: "and this could result in perhaps the biggest grain sale ever and could possibly involve a long-term agreement." [19] That prediction was to be borne out in time, but for the present Butz returned from Moscow on April 12, without an agreement. He left behind a six-man team headed by Clarence Palmby, the Assistant Secretary of Agriculture. However, despite their now obvious urgent need for grains, the Soviet government officials were taking a tough bargaining stance and seeking concessional credit terms of two per cent interest over an extended period. The negotiations failed to produce any tangible results.

Reporting on his mission, Butz indicated optimism on an agreement for sale of American corn and soybeans to the Soviet Union:

> Russia has had a hard, cold winter with little snow cover. Even Moscow has had little snow. There has been considerable winterkill of wheat, and there is a definite lack of moisture. Both General Secretary Brezhnev and (Agriculture) Minister Matskevitch readily admitted this situation in our discussions. Russia can buy some wheat from Canada, Australia and France — but there is little corn available anywhere in the world except in the United States; and we are,

of course, about the only country with any soybeans available in any quantity. They want what we've got — and we've got what they want! So we talked about trade. [20]

Assistant Secretary Palmby met the Russians again in Washington on May 9, to renew high level talks about the proposed grain sale. At that short meeting — lasting an hour and fifteen minutes — the discussions focussed on credit terms. The Russians wanted two per cent interest over ten years. The Americans offered 6 ⅛ per cent for three years. [21] The Soviets showed no interest.

Possibility of a grain sale was again discussed at the Nixon-Brezhnev summit meeting, held in Moscow from May 22 to 29. On May 26, the Department of State told the Department of Agriculture that the Russians were willing to buy $130 million worth of grain from the United States in 1972, but were unwilling to commit themselves beyond that. [22] In Winnipeg, the Canadian Wheat Board was following this manoeuvring closely, in the hope that a substantial sale by the United States would result in termination of the American export subsidies and a consequent strengthening of world prices.

As reseeding of the winter damaged crops, and seeding of spring crops, got underway across the vast Russian steppes, there was another setback for Soviet crop prospects. The harsh winter was followed by searing drought, and as the temperature rose the Soviet need for imports rose with it. In Moscow, the experienced grain traders at Exportkhleb were aware of the consequences of a sudden and massive incursion into the export subsidized American market. With the American "target price" for export wheat set at $60 a tonne ($1.63 a bushel), basis No. 2 Ordinary Hard Winter, FOB Gulf Ports, it was very much in their interest to devise a strategy to keep it there. The Soviet Union had a massive need that could only be met on the American market. They would have to play their cards carefully.

The first indication that something was afoot was received in the Canadian Wheat Board offices on Friday, June 30. Gerry Vogel was away and Larry Kristjanson was preparing to leave on holidays. In the morning there were rumours that Belousov and other Russians were in Washington. Chicago wheat and corn prices had shown a slight rise and Cargill Grain made an enquiry to the Board asking how much barley Canada could make available for the Soviet Union in the next crop year. The resale barley market had strengthened by up to $1.50 a ton. Kristjanson left a memorandum, outlining the mornings events, for perusal by Vogel on his return to the office the following Monday: "With that optimistic note, I am off on my vacation." [23]

Kristjanson was to leave another, more lengthy, memorandum for the Chief Commissioner before he departed. The rumour of Belousov's presence in Washington was confirmed. At 3:45 that afternoon, Belousov called from

Washington wanting to know where Vogel was. He wanted to see someone from the Board in Washington in the middle of the next week. Would Vogel call him Tuesday morning in Room 1207 at the Madison Hotel? Kristjanson noted that Belousov "was going out of his way to indicate that he did not want to talk business to such an extent that there is no doubt in my mind that he has something specific in mind." [24]

Subsequent events were to reveal that Belousov, along with Alexander Kalitenko, and Paul Sakun of the Soviet Ministry of Foreign Trade, had booked into the Madison Hotel the previous day, June 29. At the United States Department of Agriculture offices in Washington, negotiations were underway at the ministerial level on a three-year line of credit to the Soviet Union for the purchase of grain.

Belousov, and his Exportkhleb buying mission, were not waiting for conclusion of the USDA talks on a U.S. Commodity Credit Corporation line of credit. They had something very specific in mind. Almost immediately after booking into the Madison, the Russians made a series of phone calls that triggered off the most intense and massive series of grain purchases in history. The "Great Grain Robbery" was underway. That Thursday the Exportkhleb team contacted almost all of the major international grain traders. Phone calls went out to Continental Grain Co., Cargill Grain, Bunge Corp., and Cook Industries. Later calls were made to Louis Dreyfus Corp. and Garnac Grain Co., Inc.

Continental was the first to be contacted — and the first to conclude a sale to the Russians. Michel Fribourg, President of Continental and Senior Vice-President, Bernard Steinwig, were in Paris when they were informed of the request for a meeting. Steinwig hurriedly packed and flew to Washington where he met with the Russians in the Madison Hotel on the evening of June 30. Belousov asked for firm price offers on four million tons of wheat and three million tons of corn. [25] That same day representatives of Bunge and Cook visited Room 1207 in the Madison, but went away empty-handed. The next morning, Saturday July 1, Continental was asked to submit an additional price offer on 500,000 tons of durum wheat. [26]

After arranging for negotiations to begin on Monday, July 3, in New York, Steinwig flew to New York to commence work on the offers and called Fribourg to return to the United States immediately. Over the weekend, Belousov and Kalitenko were entertained and shown the sights of Washington by Clarence Palmby, who had resigned as Assistant Secretary of Agriculture on May 12, 1972, to accept a position with Continental. [27]

Working over the weekend in New York, Steinwig had to assure himself of one thing before beginning final negotiations with the Russians. Would the U.S. government continue payment of export subsidies on wheat? He made arrangements to meet in Washington with Dr. Carroll G. Brunthaver, who had succeeded Palmby as Assistant Secretary of Agriculture.

There was a later conflict in testimony given by Steinwig and Brunthaver at a Congressional hearing. Steinwig, backed by affidavits given by two other Continental representatives, said he flew back to Washington on Monday, July 3, where he informed Brunthaver of the volume of wheat and corn the Russians were interested in, and asked if the wheat export subsidy would be maintained.28 He then flew back to New York where Brunthaver phoned him at 3:38 p.m. and assured him the subsidy would be maintained at the existing target price. Brunthaver said he could not recall the date of the meeting, nor any figures on volumes of grain involved. He was not expecting any agreements to be made before the U.S.-Soviet loan agreement was signed. [29]

When Vogel phoned Washington to contact Belousov on July 4, he found the Russian Exportkhleb team was in New York. Travel bookings, made by Kristjanson the previous Friday, were switched. Vogel, accompanied by Frank Rowan, flew to New York where they met the Russians in their New York Hilton suite of rooms on July 5 and 6. Belousov informed the Chief Commissioner that Exportkhleb would exercise its option, under the February 25 agreement, to take a further 1.5 million long tons of wheat for delivery in 1973. Exportkhleb also wanted one million tons of barley and wanted very much to buy it from Canada. Vogel promised to "squeeze to the bottom of the barrel" and make an offer accordingly. [30]

As this business was being transacted, negotiations were going on in another room of the suite with Continental Grain. That same day, July 5, the Russians signed a contract with Continental for 3.65 million tonnes of U.S. Hard Winter wheat, 350,000 tonnes of U.S. Soft White wheat, and 4.5 million tonnes of corn. [31] Indicating that he was dealing only with Continental, Belousov asked absolute secrecy.

Back in Washington, the ministerial level talks were still proceeding with the Soviet negotiators putting strong emphasis on their need for feed grains, particularly corn. It was reported, but never confirmed, that the Russians suggested in the latter stages of the negotiations that they might need some wheat. Possibly it could be included, along with the feed grains listed as eligible under the credit agreement?

When, on Saturday, July 8, President Nixon announced from the Western White House in San Clemente, California, that the U.S.-Soviet agreement had been signed in Washington, wheat was included in the list of eligible grains along with corn, sorghum, barley, rye and oats. The agreement called for purchase by the Soviet Union of $750 million worth of U.S. grain over three years, from August 1, 1972, through July 31, 1975. The United States would make available credit through the Commodity Credit Corporation for repayment in three years from the date of deliveries, with the credit outstanding not to exceed $500 million. The Soviet Union was obliged to purchase at least $200 million worth of grain in the first year of the contract.

In New York, Exportkhleb had already purchased over $450 million worth of wheat and corn from Continental, and negotiations were proceeding apace on contracts with other private traders. Between July 5 and July 20, the Soviet team bought 12.55 million tonnes of American grain. On July 10, they bought one million tonnes of wheat from Cargill and 750,000 tonnes from Dreyfus. The next day they contracted with Continental for 500,000 tonnes of durum and with Cook Industries for 600,000 tonnes of Hard Winter wheat. On July 20 there were three contracts; 850,000 tonnes of Hard Winter and 150,000 tonnes of Soft Winter from Continental and 200,000 tonnes of Hard Winter wheat from Garnac.[32]

In the middle of this frenetic round of negotiations and purchasing Belousov and Sakun, accompanied M.R. Kuzmin, the Soviet Deputy Trade Minister who had negotiated the U.S.-Soviet credit agreement in Washington, flew to Ottawa. Vogel met them there on July 17 and formal acceptance of the 1.5 million tonne option discussed in New York was signed. A further option was given to the Russians for 300,000 tonnes of wheat for shipment to Cuba in the last half of 1973. A new contract was signed for 200,000 tonnes of barley, to be shipped from Pacific ports between August 1972 and July 1973, as well as an option for 100,000 tonnes of barley for shipment from Churchill.[33]

Kuzmin then flew on to Moscow, while Belousov returned to New York to rejoin Kalitenko. The Exportkhleb team, having completed the first round of purchases, flew back to Moscow on July 21, to await the Soviet's July 25 crop forecast and further instructions. That report showed further deterioration, and on July 27, Belousov sent an urgent request to Washington for visas to return to the United States.

Belousov was back in New York on July 29. Another frantic round of buying began. Four contracts were finalized on August 1. Exportkhleb contracted with Continental for 1.75 million tonnes of corn, 100,000 tonnes of barley and 100,000 tonnes of sorghum, and with Dreyfus for 1.5 million tonnes of Hard wheat. The next day the Russians bought 600,000 tonnes of Hard wheat from Bunge and 350,000 tonnes from Garnac. Two days later, on August 4, they purchased 300,000 tonnes of Hard wheat and one million tonnes of soybeans from Cook. The final contract entered into by the Exportkhleb team was on August 9, for one million tonnes of Hard wheat from Cargill.

In just over one month, the Soviet Union had contracted for: 10.8 million tonnes of Hard wheat, 500,000 tonnes of Soft wheat, 500,000 tonnes of durum wheat, 6.25 million tonnes of corn, 100,000 tonnes of barley, 100,000 tonnes of sorghum, and one million tonnes of soybeans. It added up to a whopping 724,905,709 bushels of grain and oilseeds.[34]

Testimony before a U.S. Senate Committee later showed that, up to July 10, each of the international traders in turn had contacted the USDA indicating that the Russians were interested in contracts for substantial volumes of wheat and seeking assurance that the export subsidies would remain in force.[35]

By early August rumours of the enormity of the Soviet wheat purchases, amounting to one-third of the American exportable surpluses, began to circulate. As the international traders sought to cover their contracts through purchases inland, U.S. domestic prices began to rise. The export subsidy on U.S. Hard Red Winter, FOB the Gulf, which stood at two cents a bushel on June 30, began to climb steadily. It was nine cents on July 10. It reached 16 cents by July 30. Then, on August 3, the market on the Chicago Board of Trade went wild. On August 4, the subsidy jumped dramatically to 31 cents. By August 25 it had soared to 38 cents a bushel.

Under USDA policy, the grain exporting companies had the option when they received a contract to hold back on registration for subsidy payment for an indefinite period of time until they felt the subsidy rate was favourable. Once registered, the company was required to ship the quantity of wheat under the contract before the marketing year for that particular class of wheat expired. Failure to do so could result in penalties.

The cost of the Soviet sale to American taxpayers was now coming home to the American government. The Office of Management and Budget became alarmed at the potentially high subsidies to be paid as they watched wheat futures on the Kansas City Exchange soar upward. They feared that the prospective large subsidy payments would upset the budget plans, for both the Commodity Credit Corporation and the USDA. In addition, they felt continuance of the subsidy was contributing to domestic inflation by causing an increase in food prices. A meeting was held on August 25 between officials of the USDA and the OMB and agreement was reached to terminate the export subsidy.

Later that day, the international traders were called into a conference where Brunthaver informed them that the volume of export trade had caused fears of shortage of certain types of wheat in the U.S. He asked them to voluntarily disclose their sales commitments. Company representatives agreed to comply only if the information was furnished in a closed meeting. The media representatives at the meeting refused to leave and the conference broke up without any action. Later the same day, Brunthaver told the exporters they would have a one-week period of grace to register their past sales. The export subsidy would be increased from 38 cents to 47 cents a bushel for past export sales during the period of grace. After that the exporters would have to take their chances; the government could no longer protect the $1.63 export price.[36]

U.S. export subsidies on wheat were terminated on September 22, 1972. However, for the fiscal year 1972, over $333 million in subsidies were paid out, almost one-half directly resulting from the Russian grain sales. Designed to keep

U.S. wheat prices more competitive on the world market, the export subsidy policy had, on this occasion, held international wheat prices in check in the face of very strong demand for American wheat.

The impact on American consumers and taxpayers did not stop there. A Senate subcommittee, enquiring into the sales two years later found:

> The grain sales created a shortage in domestic supplies. This shortage drove up the price of bread and flour-based products. More importantly, the shortage resulted in increases in the price of feed grains. These increases meant it became more expensive to feed livestock. Accordingly, these increased expenses were reflected in the nation's grocery stores as consumers paid more — substantially more — for beef, pork, poultry, eggs and dairy products. [37]

Additionally, the heavy movement of grain to ports, particularly in the Gulf states, for exports to Russia caused disruption in the American freight transportation system and increased the national cost of the sales. Other vital commodities were delayed in shipment, or were not shipped at all.

Dismayed at the abrupt rise in the domestic cost of living index as the United States haemorrhaged grain at subsidized prices, President Nixon, on June 13, 1973, indicated that he would seek new authority from Congress to impose export controls on grains and animal feedstuffs. On June 27, he imposed a temporary embargo on exports of soybeans and soybean products. Nearly a week later it was replaced by an export licensing system that was not as restrictive.

Given the constant rhetoric from the United States, extolling the merits of the free enterprise open market system of price discovery for grains versus what was sometimes branded as "closed socialistic" wheat board systems employed in other countries, it was ironic to find the American government, which for decades had propped up domestic prices by means of export subsidies, now turning to controls and embargoes to deflate the market.

While the Great Grain Robbery had precipitated bitterness and confusion on the American economic and political scene, things had come full circle for the Canadian Wheat Board from the disastrous outlook at the opening of the decade.

Not only were exports booming to the full capacity of the transportation and handling systems with forward sales booked well into the next year, but the depressing factor of the U.S. export subsidy on world grain prices had been removed. The Board's average monthly asking price for No. 1 CWRS wheat, 14 per cent protein, in store Thunder Bay, rose from $1.79 ½ a bushel in August 1972, to $3.56 ¾ in the closing month of the crop year in July 1973. [38] At the outset of the 1972-73 crop year, the initial payment on No. 1 CWRS had been retained at the previous year's level of $1.46 a bushel. However, two-and-a-half months into the crop year, the initial prices on all grades of wheat were increased by 30 cents. A final payment of over 39 cents a bushel brought the total return to the producer to $2.15 a bushel, compared to slightly under $1.60 in the 1971-72 crop year. For durum wheat the price rise was even more abrupt with final payments ranging from $1.10 to $1.16 a bushel. [39]

In addition to the rise in price, Canada's exports of wheat rose dramatically to 577,164,751 bushels and the outward carryover declined to 365 million bushels, the lowest in 21 years. [40] At the start of the new crop year on August 1, 1973, off-farm stocks of wheat in commercial positions, on which carrying charges were payable to the Canadian Wheat Board, dropped below 178 million bushels declining to 165,825,302 bushels. The *Temporary Wheat Reserves Act* was dead. The sunset clause, Section 6 of the Act, came into effect. No carrying charges were payable by the federal Treasury for the 1973-74 or any subsequent crop year. Since its inception in the 1954-55 crop year, the now defunct Act had paid a total of $717,871,258 into the wheat pool accounts of the Board. [41]

Canadian exports of all grains in 1972-73 climbed to a new record of 833 million bushels, indicating a surge in demand despite world production of all grains being the second highest on record at 631 million tonnes. All thoughts of acreage reduction programs were gone. As prices of most grains hit record highs, many people began to question the ability of world resources to meet the accelerating food requirements of an ever-increasing world population. Attention was focused on the situation when the Food and Agriculture Organization of the United Nations recommended international action to assure a minimum level of world security to deal with shortages of grain in the future. [42]

Noting the increasing trend in rising world food production, the Canadian Wheat Board reported:

> Despite this fact, world grain stocks have declined over the past three years. World consumption of grain has increased markedly as a result of not only population growth but also increases in the living standards of people. Countries which in the past cut back on consumption of food during periods of shortages and high prices did not do so in 1972-73. [43]

The Canadian Wheat Board's ability to increase exports to meet this market was now more than ever dependent upon the capacity of the transportation and handling systems. As evidence mounted that continuing retirement of aging box cars without replacement by the railways was seriously hindering the sales efforts of the

Board, the Liberal Cabinet approved the purchase of 2,000 modern railway hopper cars to haul grain. Purchased with funds provided by the government, the new hoppers were to be held in trust for the Crown by the Canadian Wheat Board. Delivery of the badly needed hoppers began in early December 1972, and continued to the end of March 1973. Total costs for the fleet of 100-ton steel hoppers came to $46,091,362.[44] They were allocated to the two major railways, subject to an operating agreement with the Board whereby the cars would be used exclusively for the carriage of grain and could not be used outside of the Western Division without the consent of the Wheat Board.[45]

Studies into the whole system of grain gathering and transportation from the country elevator to export terminals had also been set in motion by the Grains Group in Ottawa. At the start of the 1972-73 crop year, a massive report, covering 11 volumes, on rationalization of the entire system was released in Winnipeg by the Canada Grains Council. After contracting 13 independent studies over a period of two years, the Grains Group carried out costing studies on four alternatives: rationalization of the current system of country elevators and terminals, a high-throughput country elevator system, an inland terminal/satellite system, and a small inland terminal system.

While there were few conclusions drawn in the Grains Group report, the costing studies were based on the removal of 5,500 miles of the 19,500 miles of railway lines in Western Canada by abandonment.[46] It was the first of a long series of studies, commissions and reports that would spur controversy and furious debate in Western Canada into the mid-1980s and beyond.

In the background another emotion charged issue was coming to a head. After first calling for domestic feed grains to be placed under the jurisdiction of the Canadian Wheat Board in the mid-1950s, Eastern Canadian livestock producers had quickly become disillusioned when they found they would have no voice in the pricing of those grains. To counterbalance the domestic feed grains pricing prerogative of the Wheat Board — which chose to use the futures market of the Winnipeg Grain Exchange to set prices, rather than sit as arbiter between the eastern and western factions — the federal government in 1967 established the Canadian Livestock Feed Board. The CLFB was given authority under the *Livestock Feed Assistance Act*, to ensure the availability of feed grain and the "reasonable stability and fair equalization" of feed grain prices outside of the Canadian Wheat Board's designated area.

Institution of the CLFB, which also administered the Feed Freight Equalization Program, failed to quell the discontent. As farm-stored surpluses of grain in Western Canada soared in the late 1960s, rumours of distress selling of barley on the Prairies for as little as three bushels for a dollar began to circulate in the other regions. Fearing a loss of competitive advantage in livestock production to the Prairies, despite continuance of the feed freight subsidy program, which had been put in place during World War II to spur much needed livestock production, Eastern Canadian farmers, backed by British Columbia, began a strident campaign for changes in the domestic feed grains policy. Quebec farmers, while strongly defending retention of the feed freight subsidy, were particularly vociferous in seeking free entry to the Prairie market and bypassing the Canadian Wheat Board.

At the annual meeting of the Canadian Federation of Agriculture, held in Edmonton in February 1972, the politically-charged hot potato exploded. After a Quebec motion to have the federal government make interim payments to Eastern and B.C. farmers to compensate for price differentials on feed grains between the Prairies and other regions was narrowly defeated, the Quebec delegation threatened to withdraw from the CFA. The crisis in the national farm organization was temporarily averted when Albert Allain, President of l'Union Catholique des Cultivateurs, agreed to defer the Quebec withdrawal pending a report by a special committee. Federation Vice-Presidents Roland Pigeon, President of Co-op Fédérée de Quebec, and E.A. Boden, Second Vice-President of Saskatchewan Wheat Pool, were delegated to work out a compromise and bring back the report.[47]

The Pigeon-Boden Committee failed to reach an acceptable compromise between the Prairies and Eastern factions in the fractious dispute. One year later, at the CFA annual meeting, held in Ottawa's Chateau Laurier Hotel in February 1973, a final desperate effort was made to establish a consensus policy to present to the government. On the fourth day of the meeting, the 13-member Quebec delegation rose as a body and left the meeting. Allain, now President of L'Union des Producteurs Agricoles, set up in the previous year to represent all commercial farmers in Quebec, said the delegates would report back to their councils for instructions on whether to remain within the national farm group.[48]

Earlier in the meeting Otto Lang, now Minister of Justice and Attorney-General of Canada while still retaining responsibility for the Canadian Wheat Board, bluntly warned the CFA delegates that he was determined to have a new domestic feed grains policy in place by July 31, at the start of the new crop year. He would do so with or without input from the Federation. However, with the withdrawal of Quebec, the CFA was in disarray. At a closed meeting of the executive, held on the morning following the annual meeting, it was decided that the CFA did not have a feed grains policy as such, and it was up to its individual members to make representations of their own views to government.[49]

That course had already been taken by the Quebec delegates. Immediately after their withdrawal from the meeting, they walked the short distance over to Parliament Hill and began lobbying the government. In the interim between the two explosive CFA confrontations, Pierre Trudeau's Liberal government had gone to the nation on October 30, 1972. The result at the polls was a virtual stalemate with the Liberals winning 109 seats and the Progressive Conservatives 107. In the minority House, the New Democratic Party held the balance of power with 31 seats, while Social Credit held 15 seats, all Créditistes from Quebec, and Independents held two seats.

In the Prairie provinces, the Liberals won in only three ridings. Lang was the sole Liberal returned from Saskatchewan and two Liberals were elected in Metropolitan Winnipeg constituencies. Agriculture Minister H.A. Olson went down to defeat in Alberta. With the Prairie government representation decimated, Eugene Whelan, an Ontario MP, succeeded to the agriculture portfolio in the new Cabinet. The Western farmers' voice was muted in the 109-member government caucus dominated by 58 Quebec representatives. At the opening of the new session of Parliament in early January, notice was given in the Throne Speech that legislation would be introduced on a new domestic feed grains policy:

> The government supports the principle of an equitable relationship of prices of feed grain to livestock feeders in various areas of Canada. It is the intention of the government to implement before the next crop year procedures that will ensure the optimum development of the feed grain industries within Canada. [50]

However, with the minority government performing a delicate balancing act between the Quebec Créditiste splinter and the Western-oriented NDP caucus, Lang was forced to delay his proposed implementation of a new feed grains policy. As reports spread that Wheat Board jurisdiction over domestic feed grains might be removed, the Advisory Committee to the Board, which had been expanded to 10 by appointment of five new members on May 11, 1972, expressed concern. At a meeting in the Wheat Board offices on June 15, 1973, a motion was passed declaring that it was essential that any domestic feed grains policy that was developed must not prevent the Canadian Wheat Board from having complete control of all feed grains that move out of the Wheat Board region: "We therefore strongly oppose any domestic feed grain policy that reduces the marketing function of the Canadian Wheat Board in both domestic and export markets." [51] The motion passed by a margin of five to two, with Lorne Parker, a Ste. Agathe, Manitoba, farmer, and Ivan McMillan, of Craik, Saskatchewan dissenting.

In the face of a gathering storm of protest from the Prairies, Trudeau, Lang and Whelan all gave assurances that no final decision would be made on the feed grains policy until after a Conference on Western Opportunities to be held in late July, 1973, in Calgary. Lang said that press reports stating that domestic feed grains marketing would be removed from the jurisdiction of the Canadian Wheat Board, "do not adequately or fairly represent the thinking of the government." [52]

It proved to be a hollow assurance. Shortly after the Calgary conference, a two-phase program was announced simultaneously on August 3 in Ottawa,

Regina and Quebec City. Under an interim plan, Western feed grains would remain under the Canadian Wheat Board leading up to a "permanent feed grain policy" to become effective August 1, 1974. After that time, Wheat Board control would be removed from the domestic feed grains market. At a Regina news conference Lang stressed that, during the interim period, his proposed future policy would be "subject to intensive rounds of talks between the federal government and the grains and livestock industries and provincial governments." [53]

Since few administrative details of the plan had been spelled out, immediate reaction from the West was mostly cautious. However, Manitoba's NDP Agriculture Minister Sam Uskiw immediately declared the plan to be unacceptable and labelled it as a "sell-out to producers in Eastern Canada." The National Farmers Union was equally incensed, saying that Lang had "placed himself in a dictatorial position in the role of Benedict Arnold to the Western farmers." [54]

Full details of the interim policy did not emerge until late September. It proved to be a complicated and administratively cumbersome nightmare involving four agencies, constant monitoring of prices on the Prairies, and an obligation on the Wheat Board to predict final returns in its barley, oats and feed wheat pools on a monthly basis.

Under the program Western farmers had three options for sale of their grains. They could deliver to the Wheat Board under quota and receive the initial payment and await an anticipated final payment when the pool accounts were closed at the end of the crop year as in the past. Under a new alternative, the farmer could choose to deliver to the Agricultural Products Board under an open quota and receive full payment at a price fixed by the federal Department of Agriculture. That price was calculated midway between the Wheat Board's initial price and its calculated total return after the final payment. The third option involved the sale of "off-board" feed grains within the three Prairie provinces. The previous restriction on movement of feed grains across provincial boundaries within the Wheat Board designated area was removed. Farmers could now make farm-to-farm sales and deliveries to feed mills and feedlots anywhere within the Prairies rather than just within their home province.

It was this last option that raised the most bitter argument since off-board sales on the Prairies dictated the price at which the Canadian Wheat Board was obliged to sell into the eastern and British Columbia markets. Previously, the Board had been selling into these markets at a price competitive to U.S. corn. Under the interim program, the Canadian Wheat Board and the Canadian Livestock Feed Board monitored the prices on Prairie off-board sales. The price at which the Wheat Board sold to Eastern and B.C. markets was fixed by using that monitored price, plus handling and freight costs to the Lakehead.

Purchases by the Agricultural Products Board were stored commercially, or on the farms on the Prairies, and were intended as a guaranteed floor against distress selling. However, in a surging seller's market, it was a clear case of closing the barn door after the horse had gone. Distress selling was over. Even as these cumbersome arrangements were being put into place, the Editor of *The Manitoba Co-operator*, a weekly farm newspaper published by Manitoba Pool Elevators, outlined in mid-August the euphoria of a changing marketplace:

> For a weekly farm newspaper editor it was a week that was almost too much to take. A mind conditioned by years of grain surplus, low prices and dog-eat-dog competition for international markets can absorb just so many shocks resulting from reverses to what have become almost traditional thinking patterns. The intense preoccupation of the urban-dominated newspapers with things agricultural also took some getting used to and the editor's desk top disappeared under a mass of pertinent clippings jostling for space in the paper and in the editor's mind. The inevitable occurred. The mind just boggled.
>
> How does one watch the daily grain price quotations with belief as, towards the end of last week, the price of No. 1 Canadian Western Red Spring 14 per cent wheat crept toward the magic five dollars a bushel mark basis Thunder Bay? Friday it stood at just over $4.93. Returning from the weekend it was found to be $5.44 ¼. Last year on the same date it was $1.81 ½.
>
> There was the jolt when the price of flax on the Winnipeg Commodity Exchange hit $12 a bushel and the board of governors of the Exchange, following an emergency meeting, temporarily suspended trading. Beef livestock prices in Ontario last week shot past the $65 a hundredweight mark. Hogs were selling at $68 a hundredweight in Winnipeg. The Americans revised U.S. crop forecasts downwards by 30 million bushels for wheat and made substantial downward revisions for soybeans and corn. And, despite the fact that the U.S. is still reporting near record crops for all these things, that sent the Japanese out with delegations post-haste in an attempt to obtain stable supplies of grain for the coming year. The European Common Market suspended export licenses for soft wheat and cut off export licenses for durum. Durum surged up $2.05 in a single day at Thunder Bay and stood at the unbelievable price of $8.98 ¼ a bushel early this week. [55]

In an inflation-heated economy, the federal government in Ottawa was watching these same events with apprehension. Following a six-hour Cabinet meeting on August 12, Whelan abruptly announced export controls on beef and pork. This was followed by revisions to the two-price system governing sales of wheat to Canadian millers for domestic consumption. The two-price arrangement originated on July 29, 1971, when an Order-in-Council stipulated that millers would pay the Canadian Wheat Board $1.95 ½ a bushel for wheat, including durum, used for domestic consumption. The price was set on the basis of the minimum price under the International Grains Arrangement. At that time export wheat was selling below the IGA minimum. Then, on January 22, 1972, the federal government set a base price of three dollars a bushel. The price paid by processors remained at $1.95 ½ with the difference of $1.04 ½ being paid directly to the farmers from the federal Treasury based on the number of acres shown in his Wheat Board permit book.

With prices now soaring well above the three dollar base price, Lang announced in Winnipeg on September 11, that a new seven-year program was to be put into effect. Under it, the domestic processors would pay $3.25 a bushel for milling wheat and $5.75 for durum. A consumer subsidy, calculated on the difference between those prices and current export prices, was paid to the Canadian Wheat Board for distribution to producers through the pool account for wheat. The maximum subsidy in each case was to be $1.75 a bushel.[56] In effect, if the export price of milling wheat rose above $5 a bushel during the seven-year period, the producer would be sharing with the government in subsidization of domestic consumer prices. In return he was guaranteed a domestic floor price of $3.25 for the seven-year period.

Against this tumultuous and rapidly changing background on the domestic and international scene at the outset of the 1973-74 crop year, there was a bitter battle being waged by farm organizations across the Prairies. In late October 1973, Lang announced in the Commons that George Turner, a former President and General Manager of Manitoba Pool Elevators, had been appointed to conduct a mail-in vote on the question of placing marketing of rapeseed under the jurisdiction of the Canadian Wheat Board. Factions on both sides mounted a campaign of full-page advertisements in the weekly farm newspapers, with the Prairie Pools and the National Farmers Union as the principal supporters of Board marketing. On the other side, the Winnipeg Commodity Exchange, the Rapeseed Association of Canada and others, called for retention of the open market. As the acrimonious exchange mounted, Saskatchewan Wheat Pool withdrew from membership in the Rapeseed Association and the Manitoba and Alberta Pools followed.

Concurrent with this debate, the late fall annual meetings of the grain handling co-operatives on the Prairies were marked by equally partisan positions on Lang's proposed termination of the Wheat Board's domestic feed grains marketing prerogative at the start of the next crop year. The three Prairie Pools strongly opposed return to the open market. United Grain Growers adopted a policy calling for freedom of choice to allow farmers to sell off-board grain anywhere in Canada while, at the same time, having the option to deliver to the Wheat Board.

The rapeseed marketing battle came to a conclusion when Lang announced on January 15, 1974, that 78.5 per cent of the 32,279 rapeseed producers who mailed back ballots had voted to continue marketing of rapeseed under the open market system. [57] However, debate on the domestic feed grains policy continued to divide western farm organizations. At the Western Agricultural Conference, held in Regina in mid-January to hammer out a consensus policy for presentation to the Canadian Federation of Agriculture, debate was heated. A majority backed retention of the Wheat Board as the sole selling agent for all grains in Canada. [58] There was little chance to debate the Western stand at the national level. When the CFA met in Saskatoon in mid-February, the Quebec delegation had returned to the fold. Delegates were presented with a procedural document, prepared in advance by the executive, which cut off debate and threw the thorny question of the domestic feed grains policy back to government for resolution. [59]

In the vacuum left by the lack of consensus by the nation's most widely representative farm organization, Lang and the Grains Group seized the ball and proceeded to finalize the feed grains policy. When Lang announced the final decision in Regina in late May, the nation was in the midst of a general election. Earlier that month the Trudeau government was defeated when the Conservatives and New Democrats combined forces on a non-confidence vote during the budget debate. The election was set for July 8, 1974.

Lang's Regina policy announcement confirmed the worst fears of pro-Board supporters. An open market policy for sale of domestic feed grains would come into effect on August 1, 1974, if the Liberals were returned to office. While the Wheat Board would remain as the sole purchaser and seller of export grains, the producer would have the option of delivering feed grains to the Board or to the open market for domestic consumption. [60]

On July 8, the Liberals achieved their sought after majority by winning 141 seats to 95 for the Progressive Conservatives in the 264-seat House of Commons. The New Democratic Party splinter was reduced to 16 seats. Social Credit (Créditistes) captured 11 in Quebec, and one Independent was elected. While the Conservatives won the majority of seats on the Prairies, Otto Lang scored an easy victory by over 11,000 votes in his Saskatchewan riding of Saskatoon-Humboldt. He was now free to implement his open market domestic feed grains policy. It went into effect, as scheduled, at the start of the 1974-75 crop year. Its implementation caused continuing controversy in the West, and complications and administrative problems for the Canadian Wheat Board.

While the anomaly of two disparate marketing systems operating side-by-side, decried by the late Jimmy Gardiner in the light of experiences some 40 years earlier, when delivery to the Board was optional, had been reintroduced, the Canadian Wheat Board had more immediate and pressing problems. As controversy swirled around the plethora of political policy initiatives impinging upon its operations, the Board was faced with a growing crisis. The Board's ability to deliver into a booming seller's market was being crippled by deterioration and stoppages in the vital area of transportation to export positions.

Footnotes Chapter Six

1. Appendix, Canadian Wheat Board Advisory Committee Minutes, September 8. 1971.
2. *Ibid.*
3. *Ibid.*
4. *The Manitoba Co-operator*, February 25, 1971, p. 9.
5. Appendix, Canadian Wheat Board Advisory Committee Minutes, October 27, 1971.
6. *Ibid* p. 7.
7. *Ibid.*
8. *Ibid.*
9. *Ibid.*
10. *The Manitoba Co-operator*, June 17, 1971, p. 1.
11. *Dow Jones News Service,* November 5, 1971.
12. Canadian Wheat Board, Central File, USSR 1972.
13. *Ibid.*
14. *Ibid.*
15. *Ibid.*
16. Canadian Wheat Board Press Release, February 28, 1972.
17. Canadian Wheat Board Advisory Committee Minutes, March 8, 1972, p. 6.
18. *Ibid.*
19. *Ibid.*
20. Earl Butz, *Address to Fort Wayne Press Club*, April 21, 1972.
21. Russian Grain Transactions, Report of the Committee on Government Operations, United States Senate, July 29, 1974, p. 5.
22. *Ibid.*
23. Canadian Wheat Board Central File USSR, June 30, 1972.
24. *Ibid.*
25. Report of the Committee on Government Transactions, United States Senate, July 29, 1974, p. 34.
26. *Ibid.*
27. *Ibid*, pp. 18, 19.
28. *Ibid*, p. 36.
29. *Ibid*, p. 39.
30. G.N. Vogel, Memorandum, Canadian Wheat Board Central Files, July 11, 1972.
31. Report of the Committee on Government Operations, United States Senate, July 29, 1974, p. 67.
32. *Ibid.*
33. Canadian Wheat Board Central Files, USSR 1972.
34. Report of the Committee on Government Operations, United States Senate, July 29, 1974, pp. 40, 41.
35. *Ibid.*

36. *Ibid*, p. 32.

37. *Ibid*, p. 57.

38. Report of the Canadian Wheat Board, Crop Year 1972-73, p. 33.

39. *Ibid*, p. 65.

40. *Ibid*, pp. 5, 26.

41. *Ibid*. p. 63.

42. *Ibid*, pp. 5, 6.

43. *Ibid*. p. 6.

44. *Ibid*, Crop Year 1973-74, p. 51.

45. *Ibid*, pp. 48, 49.

46. *The Manitoba Co-operator*, August 24, 1972, pp. 10. 12.

47. *Ibid*, February 17, 1972, p. 2.

48. *Ibid*, February 15, 1973, p. 1.

49. *Ibid*.

50. *Ibid*, January 11, 1973, p. 1.

51. Canadian Wheat Board Advisory Committee Minutes, June 15, 1973, p. 9.

52. *The Manitoba Co-operator*, July 19, 1973, p. 1;

53. *Ibid*, August 9, 1973, p. 1.

54. *Ibid*, p. 8.

55. *Ibid*, August 16, 1973, p. 4.

56. Report of the Canadian Wheat Board, Crop Year 1973-74, p. 53.

57. *The Manitoba Co-operator*, January 17, 1974. p. 1.

58. *Ibid*, January 24, 1974, p. 1.

59. *Ibid*, February 28, 1974, p. 1.

60. *Ibid*, May 30, 1974, p. 1.

CHAPTER 7
OPPORTUNITY LOST

Times go by turns, and chances change by course,
From foul to fair, from better hap to worse.
— Robert Southwell.

Four days before Christmas 1973, the Chief Commissioner of the Canadian Wheat Board announced that he had some good news and some bad news for the Board's Advisory Committee gathered for its 64th meeting in the Board's seventh floor board room.

The good news was that the pricing policy adopted by the Board had paid off handsomely to the tune of an estimated $50 million benefit to the Board's wheat pool over the first four-and-a-half months of the crop year.[1] As prices on the U.S. commodity exchanges fluctuated wildly with no apparent relationship to world supply and demand, due to the uncertain grain situation and speculative pressure and fears of export and price controls, the Board had held the line, keeping Canadian prices at higher and more stable levels.[2]

Referring to the "worrisome period" through which the Board had been passing, Gerry Vogel noted that their analysis of the world's supply and demand picture had led the Board to the belief that Canadian wheat prices, although as much as $1.20 to $1.30 per bushel above U.S. prices, "were more realistic than those of our competitors to the south."[3] Despite this price differential some business had been done, but other buyers were seeking bargains elsewhere and the Board had been accused of unrealistic pricing in some quarters. Conceding that, "try as it may, the Board will not always be right", Vogel said that within the last few days its judgement, in this instance, had been vindicated "as sales in the range of 30 million to 35 million bushels have been concluded at our prices, despite the fact that the supply-demand situation has not changed since the accusations were made."

In the interim U.S. prices had risen and the Board was now fully competitive. At December 18, the American price for Northern Spring 14 per cent, fob

Duluth, stood at $5.64 a bushel, as compared to $5.71 ⅛ for Canada's No. 1 CWRS 14 ½ per cent, fob Thunder Bay, reflecting a normal quality premium for Canada's top grades.[4]

Vogel revealed that:

> During this period the Australians, on two occasions, had approached the point of price collapse, but the Board had been successful in prevailing upon them to hold the line a little longer.[5]

The bad news was that a serious transportation situation was becoming increasingly worse. Explaining the situation, Larry Kristjanson told the Board's advisors that the basic question confronting the Board was whether or not the board's sales should be curtailed because of the very real possibility of being unable to transport the required quantities, or whether sales should continue despite the danger, and at a risk of defaulting on contracts if sales quantities exceeded the transportation facilities.[6]

Opinions among the advisors varied. Roy Atkinson, President of the National Farmers Union, expressed the view that the Board should continue selling and put increased attention on the transportation system to force change. Harold Sneath, President of Manitoba Pool Elevators, and A.M. Runciman, President of United Grain Growers, were more cautious with Sneath pointing out that a continuing sales policy would be "skating on thin ice."[7] Canada's reputation as a reliable supplier might suffer if unfulfilled contracts could not be deferred.

The nagging transportation problems had persisted from before the opening of the 1973-74 crop year. In 1963, the number of six-foot door general purpose boxcars owned by Canadian Pacific and Canadian National railways, was 88,200. By 1973 that had declined to only 48,200. At peak periods 25,000 were needed to handle grain transportation alone.[8] Added to that continuing attrition to the boxcar fleets of the two major railways was an increasingly abrasive labour-management scene in Canada.

At the outset of the crop year it appeared that the legacy of the Operation LIFT program of crop reductions was about to come home to roost, and Canada would be caught with her granaries down. Large export sales in the previous two crop years had reduced the supplies of Canadian cereal grains so significantly that the main limiting factor for sales in 1973-74 appeared to be the volume of grain that would actually be available. But, as it turned out, the limiting factor was not the overall supply of grain, but the volumes of grain which could be moved from the Prairies to export position. Delays in shipments, caused by work stoppages and slowdowns, rail car shortages caused by increasing demand from other segments of the economy and finally, severe snow and spring run-off conditions which caused the closure of a large number of railway branch lines, resulted in export clearances lagging behind the Canadian Wheat Board's sales commitments for the entire year.

Instead of the expected drop in the year-end carryover, closing stocks of wheat and barley on July 31, 1974, were slightly higher than they had been at the beginning of the crop year.

Freed to pursue a more sales-oriented course in a surging world market, and with a more efficient and streamlined administrative structure geared to meet such an eventuality, the Board now faced frustration after frustration from forces outside of its legislated jurisdiction. As fear of shortages among overseas buyers, as well as actual shortages of some grains, drove prices to unprecedented heights during the course of the crop year, Canada's exports of all grains slumped 28 per cent from the previous year to 579 million bushels, including 419 million bushels of wheat and wheat flour. [9]

A portent of things to come was given in the first weeks of the crop year as labour discontent erupted in violence. After four weeks of rotating strikes, 56,000 non-operating railway workers closed down the rail system completely in a 10-day walkout. With the national economy, already beset by a world-wide energy crisis, in paralysis due to the strike, Prime Minister Trudeau called Parliament back from recess. In a national television address on August 27, the Prime Minister declared the strike a national emergency and said the railway workers would be legislated back to work. [10]

As Members of Parliament assembled after the recall, the bitter feelings of the railway workers erupted. About 200 of some 3,000 strikers gathered to protest on Parliament Hill, rushed the Centre Block and burst past security officers at the main door. The mob smashed windows in the Hall of Honour and fought security guards. An RCMP corporal was knocked to the floor and kicked and a television camera crew was turned upon and beaten. However, by Saturday, September 1, the Bill ordering the men back to work under an imposed settlement had been passed. [11]

The strike was over, but it had long-lasting effects during the first part of the crop year. Instead of the expected catch-up effort which had followed similar interruptions in grain shipments during the previous two crop years, the increased transportation demands from other segments of the economy limited the equipment that was put into grain service. By the time navigation closed on the Great Lakes in December, grain shipments from country elevators were running nearly 100 million bushels behind the previous year. [12]

The effects were shattering. At the West Coast, the line-up of waiting grain vessels in English Bay was the longest ever experienced. There were only two occasions, amounting to only 18 out of 248 working days in the entire crop year, that there were no vessels waiting to berth at Vancouver. The results were

Most of the grain exports during the seventies were shipped east. Shown here are two vessels heading through the Welland Canal.

costly. Demurrage charges, paid to vessel owners forced to wait beyond con-tracted loading dates, were estimated at $17 million, the highest ever paid in the 39-year history of the Board. [13]

Grain shipments through Thunder Bay at the head of the Great Lakes never recovered from the effects of the national railway strike. There, the problems were compounded by a shortfall of lake freight resulting from heavy shipments of U.S. grain through the St. Lawrence system. Hopes of an extended naviga-tion season were shattered by severe temperatures, snow and high winds. Shortages of stocks in St. Lawrence ports forced the Wheat Board to defer some export contracts for shipment the following spring, and to borrow stocks from domestic shippers for other export commitments. At Churchill heavy ice con-ditions delayed the arrival of the first vessel by 11 days and the railway strike halted car unloads at the Churchill terminal for a total of 20 days in the first month of the short northern shipping season.

Beside the record demurrage payments, caused by delays in ship loadings, there were other heavy costs and administrative complications imposed on the Board. The Board was forced to undertake an enlarged winter shipping program to move Prairie grain by rail to Eastern ports, at costs ranging up to over 42

cents a bushel for shipments to the Atlantic ports. An extensive trucking program, involving the movement of grain from country points to government
interior terminals, was undertaken in order to speed up shipments to forward
positions. Costs of the trucking program were over 15 cents a bushel for a total
of $3,273,437.[14]

The only bright spot in this dismal picture was the increased final return to
producers. The initial payment, set at $2.25 a bushel for wheat at the start of the
crop year, was increased by $1.50 a bushel on March 1, 1974, and a final pay-
ment of 83.8 cents brought the total price realized by producers to slightly under
$4.58 a bushel for No. 1 CWRS. This compared to $2.87 in the previous year.
For durum wheat the rise was even more spectacular, with final returns jumping
to slightly over $6.61 a bushel, compared to $2.87 in the 1972-73 crop year.[15]

Satisfaction at those increased returns was blunted by the realization that the
opportunity to capitalize on the increasing world demand at record prices had
been lost to limitations and disruptions in the pipeline to export positions. In
March, Vogel estimated that around 50 million bushels in sales had been lost to
Prairie farmers because the Wheat Board had been unable to take advantage of
the potential sales due to uncertainty of delivery to export points.[16] Beside those
lost sales, extra costs of coping with the crisis had also diluted final returns to
the producers.

Worse was yet to come. As the crop year began, so it ended. In May, 1974, a
long-simmering labour contract dispute between Vancouver grain handlers and
the terminal operators flared into slowdowns after the grain companies rejected
a report by a government-appointed conciliator. The federal government implemented Section 81 of the Canada Labour Code, preventing any lockout or strike
action, but slowdowns and disruptions reached crisis proportions by the first
week of August. Grain shipments came to a virtual standstill out of Vancouver.
At the same time, grain shipments out of Thunder Bay were completely shut
down by a strike of deck officers and engineers on 145 Great Lakes ships.

As the Vancouver deadlock dragged on, Lang and the terminal operators
engaged in a heated exchange. The minister urged the members of the farmer-
owned Prairie pools and United Grain Growers, as the operators of the major
terminals, to put pressure on their elected representatives and management, to
accept the recommendations of the conciliation report and end the stalemate.
The grain-handling co-operatives, claiming that the report recommendations by
Dr. Neil Perry were highly inflationary, fought back and refused to bend. The
companies estimated that the Perry recommendations would amount to a 61
per cent increase in pay and benefits to the grain handlers, and would trigger a
new round of inflationary pressures in the economy.

Dismayed at the continued blows to the Canadian Wheat Board's sales effort,
and to Canada's reputation as a reliable supplier on the world market, the Board

forsook its traditional stance of non-involvement in politically explosive issues. In early September, the Chief Commissioner made public a letter to Lang, outlining the costs to Prairie farmers of a strike at Vancouver. The Board urged that every effort be made for a quick settlement, "including, if necessary, the immediate recall of Parliament to legislate a settlement." [17]

It was not until October 10, however, that Parliament passed back-to-work legislation and imposed the recommendations of the Perry report on the Vancouver terminal operators. At the end of the month, West Coast shipments again virtually ground to a halt as 45 of 48 government grain inspectors booked off sick for two days during a labour contract dispute. The action was repeated the next week by inspectors at Thunder Bay, where shipping had resumed following the seamen's strike. On November 25, the grain inspectors at both ports went out on strike, again choking off export shipments. The strike lasted nine days and ended with only seven days left in the shipping season out of Thunder Bay. [18]

The crippling strikes and stoppages appeared to be endless. Entering 1975, CNR engineers booked off work for five to six days. In February and early March, federal grain weighmen and samplers went on a strike lasting 25 days. That strike overlapped another by West Coast longshoremen which lasted 19 days. In April and May, and again in early June, longshoremen at Montreal, Trois Rivières and Quebec City went out on strike for a total of 33 days. As the 1974-75 crop year drew to a close in July, pilots on ships plying the St. Lawrence went on strike at Baie Comeau for five days. [19]

When the appalling toll of strikes was totted up, labour-management disputes in various parts of the system had affected grain shipments on 143 out of 220 working days in the crop year, representing 65 per cent of the time based on a five-day work week and excluding holidays. [20] In a world market of unlimited opportunity and high prices, Canada's wheat exports slid back to a slim 394,559,463 bushels, [21] for an all-time low of 17.1 per cent of the world trade in 1974-75.

Meanwhile the long-awaited window of opportunity was closing. The Board's average monthly asking price for No. 1 CWRS, in store Thunder Bay, had hit a high of $6.07 ⅛ in November and December 1974. After that, it slid progressively down and stood at $4.70 ¼ in the closing month of the crop year in July. [22]

Costs of the sorry two years of lost opportunity for the Western Canadian economy may never be fully calculated. While the flaring nation-wide labour-management confrontations were the principal culprit, the damage was exacerbated by the shortage of transportation facilities to make up the shortfalls following the work stoppages. The damage went beyond the immediate financial losses. Canada's reputation as a reliable source of supply, built up so painstakingly in the past, suffered a severe blow.

Some of the repercussions were outlined to the first farmer-elected Advisory Committee to the Wheat Board when they held their inaugural meeting on June

20, 1975. On May 15, Lang had acceded to requests from the farm organizations for an elected, rather than government appointed, Advisory Committee. The Canadian Wheat Board's designated area was divided into 11 electoral districts, and mail-in ballots were sent out to all Wheat Board permit holders. A total of 67 farmers filed nomination papers in the election, supervised by George Turner, who had conducted the earlier rapeseed marketing plebiscite. Among the 11 successful candidates were five former members of the previous appointed Committee including: Roy Atkinson, President of the National Farmers Union; Gordon Harrold, President of Alberta Wheat Pool; W. Dobson Lea, President of Unifarm, Alberta's affiliate to the CFA; Lorne Parker of Ste. Agathe, Manitoba; and E.K. Turner, President of Saskatchewan Wheat Pool.

New members to the Committee were: Donn Mitchell, Douglas, Manitoba; Everett Murphy, Estevan, Saskatchewan; Victor Althouse, Kelvington, Saskatchewan; Avery Sahl, Mossbank, Saskatchewan; Ted Strain, North Battleford, Saskatchewan; and Orville Reber, Burdett, Alberta. Pending amendment to the Canadian Wheat Board Act, the elected members were appointed to the Advisory Committee for four-year terms.

Lang was at the inaugural meeting to congratulate the new Committee as some of the grim tidings were outlined. Doug Treleaven revealed that the strikes had cost the Board three months of sales to Japan at about five million bushels per month for a loss of some $50 million to $55 million. Of more concern was that Japan had lost patience with Canada's ability to deliver, and had indicated that any future agreements would be 25 per cent less than they would have been. Worse still, Canada lost the Japanese school lunch program which amounted to 300,000 tonnes a year. The Japanese were now using less expensive American wheat in the school lunch program, and the chances of Canada regaining the program were remote. [23]

Charlie Gibbings, who had just returned from China, had further bad news. Shipping delays in 1974 reduced the amount shipped to China by 300,000 tonnes, and the carryover of shipping delays into 1975 postponed negotiations on a new contract with the Chinese. Overall, Gibbings estimated that Canada's shipping performance had resulted in a loss of sales to China of 800,000 tonnes. Vogel noted that, not only had the sales been lost, but the sales the Board lost were at a time when they could have secured a higher price. [24]

The disruptions and inadequacies of the transportation system were not the only problems to plague the Wheat Board in the 1974-75 crop year. Even though transportation problems had crippled Canada's potential on the booming world market, the Canadian Wheat Board was about to run out of a sufficient carry over and suitable grades to service that market. In the spring of 1974, new troubles loomed. The Prairie grain crop suffered from adverse weather conditions in virtually every stage of development from seeding to harvest. A late wet spring delayed seeding and cut back on seeded acreages. This was followed by drought in the summer, and an early September frost arrived before the late sown crop had matured. Finally, cool wet weather delayed completion of harvest in many areas until late October. As a result the Prairie crop fell 18 per cent below the 1973 level. Wheat production dropped 109 million bushels to 465 million bushels. Barley fell to 379 million bushels and oats to 198 million bushels from 444 million and 273 million bushels respectively in 1973.[25]

Of equal concern to the reduced yields was the poor quality of the crop. Only about 38 per cent of wheat deliveries fell into the two top grades, compared to 82 per cent in the previous year, while 31 per cent fell into the lowest grade, No. 3 Canada Utility. Barley and oats suffered the same losses in grades.[26] In addition, due to the late wet autumn, the largest portion of the Prairie crop was harvested as tough or damp.

Early in the year, the movement of tough and damp grain had to be limited to prevent plugging terminal drying facilities and interfering with the movement of other grain. Later in the year, producer deliveries were so low there were times when the Board's selling ability to meet contract commitments was being threatened. This was particularly the case with high-grade wheat. Special programs had to be undertaken to free up all available stocks of high-grade wheat, and to move dwindling supplies in the country into forward position. Special arrangements were made with the Canadian milling industry to free all stocks of high-grade wheat which were not immediately required, in order to assist the Board in its export commitments. In addition, Canadian mills were required to utilize No. 3 CW, at a rate of 10 per cent of their total milled product, until the shortage of top grades could be alleviated.

The shortage of malting quality grades of barley meant that the malting companies had to use 18.6 million bushels of selected No. 1 Feed barley for malting purposes. Breakfast cereal manufacturers faced even greater shortages of high-grade oats. The situation became so critical in the early months of 1975, that the Wheat Board authorized imports of additional supplies of oats from the United States.[27]

Even in the face of all these woes, and the disastrously low strike-plagued exports, the carry over of grains was declining. Total stocks of wheat fell from 370 million bushels at the start of the 1974-75 crop year to 295 million bushels at the close. This was the lowest wheat carry over in 23 years. On the farms there was only 55 million bushels of low-grade wheat in the bins to tide over until the new crop was taken off. Barley stocks fell to 188.5 million bushels from 208.4 million at the start of the crop year, and closing oat stocks fell to 73.4 million bushels from 77.4 million at the opening of the year.[28]

Tomorrow had arrived and the inventory was indeed lower. It had all but disappeared. What remained was far below Canada's traditionally high grades. Total farm-held stocks of all grains and oilseeds on the Canadian Prairies was 145 million bushels at the end of the 1974-75 crop year.[29]

In addition to the frustrations of the reduced low-quality crop, and the constant disruptions in the transportation pipeline during the year, the Board's problems were further compounded by implementation of the domestic feed grains policy on August 1, 1974. With sales of Western Canada feed grains removed from the jurisdiction of the Board and placed on the open market, the Board took the position from the start of Lang's new policy that the open market should be allowed to function without interference or price influence from the Board through utilization of any stocks held by the Board for export purposes.[30]

The Wheat Board was not, however, allowed to withdraw completely from the domestic feed market. It was recognized that, as the sole holder of stocks at the outset of the year, the Wheat Board would have to supply enough grain to meet domestic needs until the open market had become self-sustaining. It had been expected that this point would be reached by October, but because of the extended work stoppages, it was not possible to maintain an adequate movement of domestic feed grains until the end of the calendar year. As a result, the Board continued to participate in the domestic feed grains market on an exchange of futures basis until that time. The Board was also obliged to provide the grain companies with stocks at Thunder Bay on a switch basis against domestic feed grains held in country positions, as well as between delivery points in the country.

After withdrawing active participation in the domestic market in January 1975, the Board was again drawn in toward the end of the crop year when open market prices fell below the Board's initial payment for feed wheat and the open market did not generate enough supplies on its own. The Board then made sales to the domestic feed market on a flat basis with the price related directly to the export price. The Board was obliged to maintain domestic stocks at Thunder Bay as an assurance of supply to Eastern Canada.

The government philosophy, as far as the domestic market was concerned, appeared to be: A Canadian Wheat Board if necessary, but not necessarily a Canadian Wheat Board.

The 1975-76 crop year opened with hopeful prospects for the sale of Canadian grain. World grain production in 1975 was the second highest on record, but crops in the Soviet Union had once again suffered a setback. A dry fall and winter combined with a hot summer to reduce the Soviet wheat crop 21.2 per cent to 66.1 million tonnes, the lowest level since 1965.[31] Traditionally, the Russians first approached Canada to meet their needs, but the Board's ability to meet those needs was sorely limited. On June 17, 1975, in Winnipeg, the Board negotiated a sale of two million tonnes of wheat to Exportkhleb. However, given the poor quality of Canada's rapidly declining stocks of grain, shipments could not be scheduled until October and November when the new crop came off. This was followed, on July 22, by the sale of one million tonnes of durum to the Soviet Union, with shipments to start in November through to 1976. With the Russian need urgent, a contract for 750,000 tonnes of wheat and 50,000 tonnes of barley for immediate delivery was entered into in mid-August. Due to Canada's now non-existent inventory of high-quality wheat, the Soviet Union contracted for No. 3 Canada Utility, normally considered as feed.

The United States was now virtually the only source of supply available to the Soviet Union to meet the shortfall. As in 1972, Exportkhleb teams began negotiations with the international grain traders. But the disastrous fallout from those 1972 sales had resulted in a tightening of regulations by Washington. Each time prices climbed too fast, the Administration intervened directly to dampen the rise. In late 1972-73, a ceiling was placed on further U.S. sales to the Russians and a temporary embargo was imposed on soybean exports. In 1973-74, American sales reporting procedures were tightened and the Administration imposed limits on the quantities that could be sold in specified periods. In 1974-75, Washington stopped a major sale to the Soviet Union and exporters were required to obtain government approval before completing sales to another country.

Responding to reports of deteriorating crop conditions in the Soviet Union, American producers began withholding their wheat from the market, and prices on U.S. exchanges rose steadily in July 1975. In August, the White House again intervened. President Gerald Ford, fearing another round of inflationary pressure, imposed a temporary moratorium on sales to the Soviet Union. Prices immediately began to decline.

As these events were taking place on the American market, the Canadian Wheat Board had virtually withdrawn from the market and was unable to take advantage of the strengthening prices at the start of the crop year. Carry over stocks from the disastrous 1974 crop had all been committed. Any new sales would have to come from the 1975 crop, where the outcome was once again in serious doubt. A heat wave in July had been followed by a cold and drizzly August, and some frost damage occurred. The cold wet weather continued through September until late October, and the first snow came in mid-October.

Thus, from mid-August to late October, the volume and quality of the Prairie crop remained a large question mark. With no reserves to fall back on, the Canadian Wheat Board was forced to be cautious and hold back on sales. By the time the results of the 1975 crop were known, and the Board was able to resume its all-out sales effort, the higher prices at the start of the crop year had already gone into decline due to Washington's intervention in the marketplace. Monthly average asking prices for No. 1 CWRS at Thunder Bay, which stood at $5.16 ⅛ a bushel in September 1975, declined to $3.65 ⅜ in August 1976.[32] The world price boom was over. Another window of opportunity had passed.

In the United States, the Administration, after ensuring that further sales to the Russians would not jeopardize supplies within the U.S. and bring another price spiral, entered into a five-year sales agreement with the Soviet Union. It provided for the sale of six million to eight million tonnes of grain annually, and cleared the way for the Soviets to buy a total of 17 million tonnes of grain and oilseeds for shipment from July 1975, to September 1976. However, signing of the agreement in October and lifting of the export moratorium, did not bolster prices as expected. Instead, prices slid even faster. The reason appeared to be that the Russians, anticipating the outcome of the agreement negotiations, had quietly covered their needs with the international traders before the actual signing took place. With this business out of the way, there were not enough buyers waiting in the wings to hold the line on prices.[33]

In spite of being withdrawn from the market during the period of higher prices, the Wheat Board exported 450 million bushels of wheat and flour during the crop year with a final return to producers of $3.98 a bushel for the top grade.[34] Exports of barley also rose to 199,376,464 bushels from the transportation plagued total of 138,392,728 bushels in 1974-75. And, for the first time, a separate pool was set up for designated barley sold to purchasers, including selected pot, pearling and malting barley. Previously selected barley had been combined into a single pool with the lower priced feed barley.

The late 1975 crop, while not up to average quality standards, was improved in quality and quantity from the previous year. With a wheat crop of 600 million bushels, and a relatively smooth transportation year, the Board was able to press the delayed sales. As a result carry over stocks in Canada again fell. Total wheat stocks in Canada, including farm stocks in Eastern Canada and British Columbia, fell to 293.2 million bushels at the close of the 1975-76 crop year.[35]

As the Canadian Wheat Board struggled through the crop and transportation plagued years of the first half of the seventies, a number of initiatives were underway, both at the Board and at the political level. As the transportation noose tightened on the Board's efforts to move grain into a world in which fears were being expressed that the Malthusian theory — that world population increases would outstrip the global capacity for food production — had come to pass, there were calls for action.

When the second session of Canada's 29th Parliament opened in early March 1974, the government came under heavy fire from the opposition for the failure of the railways to move grain to export. Shortages of railway rolling stock and motive power dominated the question period. Lang promised creation of an emergency transportation committee to see what steps could be taken to move grain more rapidly to the ports. He also announced that the federal government had reached agreement on the rehabilitation of 2,400 boxcars at a cost of $6.85 million. Under terms of the agreement, the boxcars would be used exclusively for the shipment of Western grain for a period of five years.[36]

Lang's announcement came in the wake of press releases from the Wheat Board in which Vogel estimated that 50 million bushels of sales had been lost to

Prairie farmers, and that shipments had fallen 35 million bushels behind schedule in the previous 10 weeks.[37] During the debate on the Speech from the Throne, Transport Minister Jean Marchand candidly agreed with former Prime Minister John Diefenbaker on the grain transportation problem:

> He is right. Railway companies are indeed not interested in carrying wheat. It is not profitable; they have been shaken by the present situation and do not want to buy cars to carry wheat. Even if they were paid, I doubt they would do it.[38]

The Transport Minister just as candidly admitted that the government did not have the authority to force the railways to purchase rolling stock to carry grain:

> Honourable members may say "you are the minister, you do it." I have a few answers to that. It is true that honourable members gave responsibilities to the minister, but they forgot to give him any authority at all in many instances.[39]

As the pressure mounted, Lang, during a visit to Estevan, Saskatchewan in late May, announced that Ottawa was immediately ordering 4,000 more grain hopper cars at a cost in excess of $100 million to add to the 2,000 already purchased by the government.[40] In order to cope with load limitations on secondary main lines and branch lines, 1,600 of the cars would be lighter aluminium models while the remaining 2,400 would be 100-ton steel hoppers. While the announcement was welcomed by the Board, the Chief Commissioner continued to press for more massive action to meet the crisis. At a National Transportation Conference, held in Ottawa on April 10, Vogel noted that the Board had put smaller demands on the railways during the year because of grain supply limitations. Yet the railways were 26,515 boxcars behind in their own minimum targets.[41]

Declaring that it was not a short-term problem, Vogel called for long-term solutions. To assist in that long-term solution, the Board, with producer funds, was prepared to purchase 4,000 hopper cars, provided certain conditions were met. The railways would guarantee that there would be 14,000 boxcars over and above the anticipated 10,000 hopper car fleet for grain transportation and the fixed Crowsnest statutory rate for moving grain would remain. Additionally, the railways would upgrade the viable lines to carry the hopper cars, and would provide necessary power to ensure the speedy and dependable movement of grain.[42]

Vogel also called for the priority implementation of modernization of the country elevator system, improvement in the rail facilities through the mountains and improvement in the facilities at the West Coast, including the construction of larger elevator facilities.

There was no response from the railways. With the prospect of a Crowsnest Rate reform firmly in hand, the railways were not about to co-operate in easing the pressures which brought about the calls for a review.

As early as 1972, while outlining his domestic feed grains policy, Otto Lang had been intimating that the "Holy Crow" might be reviewed. Then, in Regina in January 1974, at the annual meeting of the Palliser Wheat Growers Association , a militant commodity group founded in 1970, Lang declared outright that, "legislation setting artificially low rates for grain movement must be reconsidered."[43] Lang made the statement in response to a call for relaxation of the rates from the president of the Palliser Wheat Growers (now the Western Canadian Wheat Growers Association).

By September of that year, Lang had a blueprint for reform of the Crow. He presented a concise proposal for changing the freight rate system to Cabinet entitled: "The Bold Approach: The Freight Rate Freeze, the Branch Line Freeze, Grain Handling and Transportation." The politically explosive document proposed, among other things, elimination of the Crow Rate and creation of a "Crow benefit" fund to compensate farmers indefinitely for higher freight rates. However, the government was not ready to guarantee expenditures on the program unless it won popularity for the Liberals on the Prairies. Lang was told he would have to sell the program in the West first.

Sakatchewan Wheat Pool, as the largest and most powerful farm organization in the West, was the key to the success of the plan, since Saskatchewan was the province most affected by any change in the Crow. Relations between Lang and Saskatchewan Pool were, however, less than cordial. There was bitterness over Lang's Operation LIFT program, and the Pool had strongly opposed the removal of the jurisdiction of the Canadian Wheat Board from the domestic feed grains market. Also, Lang's criticism of Pool management in the West Coast grain handlers strike led to a resolution being passed at Saskatchewan Pool's 1974 annual meeting, calling for Lang's replacement as Minister Responsible to Parliament for the Wheat Board.

Given the political reality of the need for Pool support, Lang chose a strange forum to launch his campaign for Crow reform. On October 29, 1974, in an address to the semi-annual meeting of the Canada Grains Council in Edmonton, Lang stirred the hornet's nest. Although noted for speaking extemporaneously, or from scant notes, Lang read a carefully worded speech in which he stressed that he was putting forth a topic for discussion and not government policy. It was clear, however, that Lang's aim was a complete reform of the Crow. In his briefcase that night was the specific plan for that reform, but it was not to be implemented during Lang's tenure in office.

The Crow debate was to rage across the Prairies over the next decade and more. The bitterness of the debate split and shattered Western affiliates of the Canadian Federation of Agriculture and spread into Eastern Canada. While vitally concerned with the outcome, and the implications of the final solution, the Canadian Wheat Board, as a Crown Corporation, was forced to sit on the sidelines and watch.

In mid-April 1975, Lang and Marchand jointly announced the establishment of two commissions to enquire into separate aspects of the Prairie rail network. A former Supreme Court Judge, Mr. Justice Emmett Hall, was named to head up a five-member commission to examine on a thorough regional basis all social and economic aspects of railway branch lines on the Prairies. In a separate enquiry, a Washington, D.C. consultant, Carl M. Snavely, was appointed to determine the costs and revenues of grain traffic in Canada and their relationship to the general operations of the railways. [44]

While recommendations with respect to the Crow Rate were specifically excluded from the terms of reference of the two commissions, it was clear that the emotionally charged issue was inextricably entwined in the outcome of the enquiries, either explicitly or by inference. When the Hall Commission report on Grain and Rail in Western Canada was delivered to the government two years later on April 18, 1977, Otto Lang had succeeded Marchand as Minister of Transport. That portfolio, along with continued responsibility for the Canadian Wheat Board, made the former law professor the most powerful figure in Western Canada's immediate destiny.

The final report, forwarded to Lang, was a 545-page volume, backed by another volume of major research projects and a third volume of relevant statistical material. Few of the wide-ranging recommendations were implemented directly, and many of the issues on which the Hall Commission came down firmly were still the subject of hot debate when this history was written.

Apparently finding the task of conducting a study into rationalization of the Prairie grain handling and transportation network, without reference to the Holy Crow, akin to presenting a treatise on hell without mentioning the Devil, the Hall Commissioners ignored its deletion from their terms of reference. In their final recommendation, they called for retention of the Crow Rate and said the difference between the statutory rate and the actual cost of transporting grain should be paid directly to the railways. [45]

The Commissioners found little merit in the concept of inland terminals serviced by unit trains:

> The unit train concept would not be of much economic value to the producers unless a new and marked departure in the freight rate structure for the carriage of grain was adopt-

ed by Parliament in which the mileage related statutory rate principle is discarded.

The commission is firmly of the view that variable tariffs which would give plants, capable of loading unit trains now or in the future any preferential rate treatment, must not be introduced. [46]

Recommending that the Canadian Wheat Board be given a more prominent role in the total co-ordination function of grain transportation, the Commission noted strong support for the board in most of 1,408 briefs and submissions made at 99 meetings held across the Prairies and in Vancouver:

> Throughout the hearings there was almost universal support for the Canadian Wheat Board. There is probably no single institution in western Canada which affects the daily lives of farmers more than the Canadian Wheat Board. In some cases, there was mild criticism of some Board practices in the area of selling, car allocation, application of quotas, etc. However, there is no doubt that the Board is accepted as the producers' friend. [47]

A total of 12,414.3 miles of the 18,736 miles of the Prairie rail lines had previously been guaranteed to remain in operation by the federal government to the year 2000. Called on to decide the future of the remaining 6,229.3 miles of trackage, the Hall Commission recommended that 1,812.6 miles be added to the basic network and that 2,165.5 miles of branch lines be abandoned over a period of five years. The remaining 2,343.6 miles were to be placed under the jurisdiction of a "Prairie Rail Authority" for continuing assessment. [48]

The key recommendation for a Prairie Rail Authority, which would have broad powers to manage the rail lines in the west and keep them in a state of repair and decide upon future abandonments, was not acted upon. Lang chose rather to act upon the recommended abandonments to 1981, and to place the fate of the lines remaining in limbo in the hands of the Prairie Rail Action Committee for further study.

The final configuration of the Prairie rail network was of vital concern to the elevator companies, which had already begun a program of modernization of the primary elevator system and were turning to construction of larger high-throughput elevators at more widely dispersed points. The number of primary elevators on the Prairies reached its high point in 1935, with 5,728 elevators in operation having a total storage capacity of 189.9 million bushels. By 1955 the number of primary elevators had declined slightly to 5,403 at 2,083 delivery points. Storage capacity, however, had climbed to 334.3 million bushels. From then on, rationalization of the system went forward at a fairly rapid pace and accelerated at the start of the 70s. By 1976 the number of primary elevators had declined to 3,964 at 1,496 delivery points with a combined storage capacity of 343.8 million bushels.[49]

These closures of low volume elevators, combined with mergers between companies and consolidation of facilities at a reduced number of delivery points, made the operation of a refined Block Shipping System by the Canadian Wheat Board more manageable and efficient. Through amalgamation the number of elevator companies had also declined to 19. The largest takeover in this consolidation occurred in 1972, when the Prairie pools acquired 1,092 elevators from the Federal Grain Company. Also, in 1974, one of the large multinationals, Cargill Grain, became one of the major participants on the Prairies with the acquisition of 286 primary elevators from National Grain. The entry of Cargill, as a competitive factor in the grain handling industry was attributed to Lang's open market domestic feed grains policy and occasioned some bitterness on the part of the pools and the National Farmers Union.

As these events were going forward, there were changes and adaptations to meet the new environment at the Canadian Wheat Board. In February, 1970, acting on an initiative by the Wheat Board to capture part of a market development fund established by Lang, the Canadian Wheat Board and the Board of Grain Commissioners put forward a proposal for a Canadian International Grains Institute. The Institute would supplant the incoming foreign missions previously sponsored by the Wheat Board. The federal government supported the concept and provided one million dollars to cover the capital costs of equipping the Institute. This educational facility, embracing such areas as marketing, processing, technology, handling, storage and transportation, was opened in 1972. Occupying 1,860 square metres of space in a new Canadian Grain Commission building, located just south of Winnipeg's Portage Avenue and Main Street, the CIGI includes class and conference rooms, a library, laboratories, and a flour mill and pilot bakery capable of running tests in commercial quantities.

Incorporated on a non-profit basis, CIGI is governed by a five-member Board of Directors on which the Canadian Wheat Board, Canadian Grain Commission and the Department of Industry, Trade and Commerce are represented. Operating costs of the Institute are shared on a 60-40 basis by the federal government and the Wheat Board. Since its inception, courses have been attended by incoming groups from all over the world.

As the impact of world weather patterns on market conditions became more apparent, the Canadian Wheat Board, in March 1975, set up a Weather and Crop Surveillance Section to assimilate and analyze meteorological data available from all the important agricultural areas throughout the world. The data was provided by the World Meteorological Organization on an instantaneous basis via a direct computer hook-up and from other sources. Provision was also made for future incorporation of satellite imagery in the Board's overall crop surveillance.[50]

In the same year, Doug Treleaven and Bob Esdale retired from the Board. Treleaven began his career with the Board in 1954 as Director of Statistics and Economics and served successively as Secretary, Executive Assistant to the Board, and Manager of the Board's London office, before being appointed a Commissioner in 1965. Esdale came to the Board in 1971 after serving with the Grains Group in Ottawa. Treleaven's place as Assistant Chief Commissioner was taken by Larry Kristjanson, and Dr. J.L. Leibfried and F.M. Hetland were appointed as Commissioners on December 24, 1975. Leibfried, an American farm boy, who graduated from an American university with a Ph.D. in economics, joined the staff of the Board in 1954 as Economist and Executive Assistant to the Board. In 1974 he became Co-ordinator of the International Policy and Planning Division. Hetland, a Saskatchewan farmer, who had been active as a Liberal party organizer in that province, served for five years as a Commissioner of the Canadian Grain Commission before his appointment to the Canadian Wheat Board.[51]

The Board was now deeply concerned at the frequent delays in shipments from the West Coast, caused by a variety of problems, and an erosion of confidence in Canada as a reliable supplier by overseas customers, resulting in increased demurrage charges and lost sales opportunities. On April 12, 1976, the Board announced an incentive program designed to encourage the construction of up to 14 million bushels of additional terminal capacity at West Coast ports. Grain companies building additional terminal capacity were guaranteed storage payments on 90 to 100 per cent of their total licensed capacity, less 10 per cent which they had to reserve for non-board grains. The payments were to start the day the facility became operational and to continue to July 31, 1985. In response, the Board received commitments for the building of 10.4 million bushels of additional capacity at Vancouver, including: Alberta Pool, 2.8 million bushels; Saskatchewan Pool, three million bushels; United Grain Growers, two million bushels; and Pioneer Grain, 2.6 million bushels.[52]

In another area, the Board was expanding the activities of its market analysis and development involving the testing of new varieties by end users at home and abroad. Some Western farmers were challenging Canada's dependence on Hard Red Spring wheats and looking to the south where higher-yielding, but lower quality,* varieties were being grown. The danger of these American varieties being illegally imported and grown posed a potential danger that, being visually indistinguishable from licensed Hard wheat varieties in Canada, they might be mixed in the system thereby degrading the quality, and high reputation, of Canadian milling wheat.

Two distinct programs evolved: one aimed at enhancing Canada's position as a supplier of high quality durum wheats and the other at exploring market opportunities as food and feed for newly developed Utility wheat varieties which would be visually distinguishable from Canada's high-quality wheats to prevent mixing. The first durum variety tested was Wakooma and, in the high-yielding wheat category, Pitic 62 and Glenlea were tested.

By 1975-76, two varieties of barley had been added to the Marketing Analysis and Development Program. In 1976, grower contract programs were instituted on Glenlea wheat, Wakooma and Macoun durum, an unlicensed purple wheat, and Beacon and Klages barley. Under these programs, the Wheat Board contracted with producers on fixed acreages of the varieties of grains to be tested. The grains, sometimes unlicensed, were then tested in overseas markets to ascertain their acceptability. Livestock feeding trials were also instituted at Canadian universities to test new varieties of Utility wheat and barley.

In spite of the new and expanded activities, the number of people employed by the Wheat Board had declined. From a high of 808 employees, including 724 permanent and 84 temporary at July 31, 1972, the number was reduced to 677 in 1976, made up of 574 permanent employees and 103 temporary.[53]

On the political scene, Otto Lang finally piloted his long-sought *Western Grains Stabilization Act* through the House of Commons, and it was proclaimed on April 1, 1976, with its effective provisions retroactive to January 1, 1976.[54] Designed to even out the boom and bust years common to the Western grain industry, the program was set up under a separate and independent administration. The Canadian Wheat Board was to sell aggressively into world markets without being saddled, as it sometimes had been in its early years, in levelling or stabilization of the farmer's income.

At its inception all Canadian Wheat Board permit holders were enroled in the stabilization program, but those not wishing to participate were given the option of withdrawing up to December 31, 1978. At the end of its first year of operation, 77 per cent of producers eligible to participate in the program were recorded as full participants.[55] Under the plan, a stabilization fund was established on the basis that it would be self-sustaining over a period of 20 years. Participating farmers contributed to the fund through a levy of two per cent on their sales of the six major grains; wheat, oats, barley, rye, flax and rapeseed, which was deducted at the time of delivery. The federal government matched these payments on a two-for-one basis, contributing two dollars for each one dollar paid in by the producer.

Stabilization payments were to be made when the net cash flow to farmers in the Canadian Wheat Board designated area fell below the average of the previous five years. Net cash flow was determined by calculating the difference between overall cash receipts for the grain sold and the related costs of producing it. While there were no payments from the fund in the first year of operation, a total of $368 million was paid out to participants in 1977 and 1978.

If, as noted, establishment of the stabilization fund was tacit affirmation of the Wheat Board's role to sell aggressively, that prerogative was thoroughly exercised in 1976, as the next chapter reveals.

Footnotes Chapter Seven

1. Canadian Wheat Board Advisory Committee Minutes, December 21, 1973, p. 2.
2. *Report of the Canadian Wheat Board, Crop Year 1973-74*, p. 24.
3. Canadian Wheat Board Advisory Committee Minutes, December 21, 1973, pp. 1, 2.
4. *Ibid*, Appendix.
5. *Ibid*, p. 2.
6. *Ibid*, p. 7.
7. *Ibid*.
8. *The Manitoba Co-operator*, January 3, 1974, p. 4.
9. *Report of the Canadian Wheat Board, Crop Year 1973-74*, p. 1.
10. *The Manitoba Co-operator*, August 30, 1973, p. 1.
11. *Ibid*, September 6, 1973, p. 1.
12. *Report of the Canadian Wheat Board, Crop Year 1973-74*, p. 35.
13. *Ibid*, p. 39.
14. *Ibid*, p. 41.
15. *Ibid*, p. 54.
16. *The Manitoba Co-operator*, March 14, 1974, p. 1.
17. *Ibid*, September 5, 1974, p. 1.
18. *Ibid*, December 12, 1974, p. 1.
19. *Report of the Canadian Wheat Board, Crop Year 1974-75*, p. 35.
20. *Ibid*, pp. 35, 36.
21. *Ibid*, p. 23.
22. *Ibid*, p. 25.
23. Canadian Wheat Board Advisory Committee Minutes, June 20, 1975, p. 6.
24. *Ibid*, pp. 6, 7.
25. *Report of the Canadian Wheat Board, Crop Year 1974-75*, p. 37.
26. *Ibid*.
27. *Ibid*, p. 18.
28. *Ibid*. p. 38.
29. *Ibid*.
30. *Ibid*, p. 33.
31. *Ibid*, p. 5.
32. *Ibid*, Crop Year 1975-76, p. 27.
33. *Ibid*, p. 19.
34. *Ibid*, p. 57.
35. *Ibid*, p. 38.
36. *The Manitoba Co-operator*, March 4, 1974, p. 1.
37. *Ibid*.
38. *Ibid*, p. 12.
39. *Ibid*.

40. *Ibid,* April 4, 1974, p. 1.
41. Canadian Wheat Board, Press Release, April 10, 1974.
42. *Ibid.*
43. *The Manitoba Co-operator,* January 17, 1974, p. 1.
44. *Ibid,* April 24, 1975, p. 1.
45. *Report of the Grain Handling and Transportation Commission, Volume 1,* April 18, 1977, p. 545.
46. *Ibid,* p. 186.
47. *Ibid,* p. 538.
48. *Ibid,* pp. 503, 504.
49. *Ibid,* p. 134.
50. *Report of the Canadian Wheat Board, Crop Year 1975-76,* p. 48.
51. *Ibid,* p. 50.
52. *Ibid,* p. 42.
53. *Ibid,* p. 51.
54. Western Grains Stabilization Administration, Annual Report 1976, p. 1.
55. *Ibid.* p. 2.

CHAPTER 8

OPPORTUNITY TAKEN

Present circumstances make heroes or scapegoats, depending on the clouded future, but with an 800 million bushel crop overhanging us it is too dangerous to endeavour to hold the price line.
— *G.N. Vogel, September 20, 1976.*

Chief Commissioner Gerry Vogel returned from holidays in late July 1976, to find a rapidly changing world grain situation. During his absence, the world price of wheat, previously buoyed up by uncertain crop prospects in almost every major grain producing corner of the world, had begun to soften. It was time to assess a complex situation and take a calculated risk.

Earlier prospects had been that the Western Canadian crop might be the only one on a global basis to emerge successfully. Up to mid-June, and in some cases mid-July, there were reports of serious drought in almost every major grain growing area except Canada, with the U.S. winter wheat area appearing to be the most seriously affected. Below normal moisture conditions also threatened crops in the Soviet Union, and drought was reported in Eastern and Western Europe. Similar conditions were reported in India, Australia and Argentina.

Responding to these reports, the price of wheat climbed slowly but steadily with No. 1 CWRS 13 ½ per cent, basis Thunder Bay, reaching a high of $4.78 ¼ on June 5, 1976. After that it began a slow descent to $4.29 by the end of the month. [1]

In the board room at the Canadian Wheat Board building it was decision time for the Commissioners, as they gathered to plot strategy for the newly opened crop year at the start of August. Marketing intelligence reports showed clearly that the world crop situation was turning. Beginning in mid-June, reports of more favourable crop conditions had begun to come in as rain fell in the previously drought stressed areas of the world. Would that more optimistic outlook continue through to harvest time? The first cautious price decline on U.S. markets indicated that the commodity traders were becoming nervous.

Adding to their caution was the fact that it was a presidential election year in the United States, and uncertainty prevailed over the grain policies that might be implemented by a new administration.

Having lived from hand-to-mouth over the previous two years, due to supply and quality limitations in the 1974 and 1975 crops, the Board was faced with a dilemma. Only 55 million bushels of wheat of dubious quality was stored on Western farms entering August and the new crop year.[2] All of the limited supplies of high-grade wheat available in commercial positions had been committed for domestic use and for export to traditional customers overseas. If the decision was taken to sell, and sell hard, the contracts would have to be for grain

Esmond Jarvis was Chief Commissioner of the CWB from 1977 to 1990. It was a period marked by growth in world wheat production, record Canadian exports and the advent of trade wars and export subsidies.

that was still in the fields, and grades and quantities were not yet fully known. However, even the most conservative crop estimates showed that a possible record crop was in the making, and grades promised to be high. Seeding on the Prairies got off to an early start and the area sown to wheat was up 18 per cent at 27,165,000 acres. An early dry spell had been followed by much needed rains in June and, under ideal conditions, harvesting started as early as late July in some southern regions.

The commissioners weighed all aspects of the situation and decided they would take the risk that harvesting conditions would remain favourable over the next month and more, and that the improved outlook would continue in the rest of the major grain producing countries. Offers would be made to the private trade at discounted prices for grain to be shipped at forward dates during the 1976-77 crop year and beyond.

Selling to the trade on cargo-by-cargo basis began on August 4. By August 23, a total of 28 contracts had been entered into covering 832,943 tonnes of wheat for shipments from October, 1976, as far ahead as December, 1977.[3] Over the next six days, a further 28 contracts were entered into covering 1.28 million tonnes of wheat.[4] From August 30 to September 3, sales to the trade snowballed with 49 contracts being signed for a further 1.22 million tonnes of wheat.[5]

In a period of one month, the Canadian Wheat Board sold 3,332,943 tonnes (122,465,650 bushels) of wheat for shipment at forward dates. Speculation as to the discounts, offered by the Board to the trade, have emerged in a number of sources since that time. Dan Morgan, in *Merchants of Grain*, declared that: "American spring planted wheat comparable to Canada's wheat was selling in Minneapolis for $148 a ton; the Board offered it at $135 a ton."[6] In Washington, Assistant Secretary of Agriculture Richard Bell angrily charged that the Board was undercutting prices by 20 cents a bushel.

The record does not bear out those assertions. The August sales were at discounts of three to five cents a bushel from the Board's posted prices.[7] The first sale of 30,000 tonnes of No. 1 CWRS, 13.5 per cent, to one of the large multinational companies on August 4, for October shipment, was at $4.22 ½ a bushel ($155 a tonne), from St. Lawrence ports.[8] (Since the Canadian dollar was then at a premium of six per cent over the American dollar, the equivalent price in U.S. funds was approximately $164.55 a tonne.) On that same date, U.S. No. 2 Dark Northern Spring 14 per cent was quoted at $3.94 a bushel ($144 a tonne), basis Duluth.[9] Although freight from Duluth to the St. Lawrence has to be taken into that equation, Canadian wheat was still obviously selling at a premium to U.S. spring wheats of similar quality.

After signing the contracts, the private traders promptly hedged their cash positions (their purchases of Board wheat) on the Chicago Board of Trade. Since futures prices in forward months on U.S. exchanges were as much as 20 cents a bushel higher than the nearby, the traders were able to protect themselves against any drop in prices. As indications of the Canadian Wheat Board's aggressive ploy into the market emerged south of the border, there were angry cries of protest. In September, the USDA began to receive reports that the multinational traders were offering Canadian wheat into export markets in Europe, South America and the Caribbean at discounts from the American price. A rumour emerged that Louis Dreyfus had sold some of the Canadian wheat to American millers in Buffalo, New York. With the presidential election set for November 2, the U.S. Administration was furious. A formal note of protest was sent to the Canadian government in Ottawa, declaring that the price cutting could lead "to unnecessary weakening of the general level of world wheat prices."[10]

The Canadian Wheat Board had no intention of revealing its negotiated prices, and the reply from Ottawa merely stated that the Board "would be happy to meet with U.S. officials."[11]

Critics, who had assailed the Board for allegedly pricing Canada out of the market in 1973, by holding the price line in the face of fluctuating markets, were now charging the Board with underpricing and weakening the market. At a meeting of the farmer Advisory Committee to the Board on September 20, 1976, Vogel set the record straight. By that time it had become obvious that the Soviet Union, despite early predictions of a diminished harvest, would bring in a large grain crop and would not be in the market to any large degree. Vogel explained that the industry was now faced with a totally new set of circumstances. He did not anticipate any more than minimum purchases by Russia, and China remained a question mark. For two years, limited supplies had created a hand-to-mouth situation which required restrictive sales in order to protect traditional markets. "Now we find ourselves faced with large quantities and the name of the game is sell."[12] The final reckoning some months later, found a record Western Canadian grain crop of 1.627 billion bushels, including 838.2 million bushels of wheat.

Noting Bell's charges that the Board was selling at a 20 cent a bushel discount, Vogel commented that Bell "really doesn't know" what the Board was selling at. "Sales have been made cargo by cargo, at a premium over the U.S. equivalent — but less of a premium than heretofore."[13] He noted that the U.S. system had been "unable to cope with the changing circumstances because it lacks the flexibility to 'horse trade' in a horse trading market."[14]

During the recent period of restricted Board sales, many had been lulled into the belief that directly negotiated agency-to-agency contracts were the only weapon in the Board's sales arsenal whereas, in fact, it was a mixed private-public system. Referring to recent editorial comment, lauding the Board's increased sales activity with the trade as a new and desirable policy, Larry Kristjanson commented, "In reality it is not new. It is a reversion to practices of the past in periods when supplies were sufficient to make unnecessary the Board's monitoring and supply control policies of the recent past."[15]

While critics continued to insist that the Board sales to the trade, and the subsequent protection taken on the Chicago Board of Trade, had depressed the price at a loss to the Board's current and potential sales, the ultimate world crop results and trade in 1976-77 clearly validated the Board's move. The world wheat harvest totalled a record 417.4 million tonnes, 11 per cent above the previous record of 377.3 million tonnes in 1973-74, and up 18 per cent from 1975-76. In the U.S., the wheat crop soared to 2.14 billion bushels and Soviet grain production was a record 224 million tonnes. As a result, world trade in wheat slumped eight per cent to 61.3 million tonnes from 66.5 million tonnes in 1975-76. [16]

Canada's share of that reduced market increased to 22 per cent from 18 per cent in the previous year at 13.4 million tonnes, while the U.S. share of the market fell from 47 per cent in 1975-76 to 41 per cent in 1976-77. American wheat sales dropped 19 per cent from the previous year to 25.9 million tonnes. At the same time the U.S. wheat carry over at the end of the crop year rose 67 per cent to 30.2 million tonnes. [17]

Clearly, the abrupt downturn in the market in September, 1976, was caused by revised assessments of world crops and trade prospects, rather than the Board's aggressive sales stance in its offers to the trade. Further, the Canadian farmer had profited substantially by the decision. Had the Board delayed sales to the date of the shipments the sales prices would have been substantially lower. For example, the noted sale on August 4, at $4.11 ½ would have returned around $3.50 a bushel at the time of the shipment in October. Similar, and even higher, windfalls were returned on sales shipped up to late 1977.

Further sales of 1,178,485 tonnes of wheat were made to the trade from September 7 to October 15, 1976, but these were contracted after the price break and were delivered for shipment when roughly similar prices prevailed.

A more literal assessment of the Canadian Wheat Board's coup was given early in 1977 by the Australian *Primary Industry Newsletter*:

> The Canadians caught Australia, Argentina and the U.S. with their pants downs by offering a substantial portion of its record stocks to the trade. The Canadians reasoned that prices would not hold with a world record crop and another big crop predicted next year...The Canadian Wheat Board is still happily counting its money, content that it has gained for its growers more from the marketplace than seemed likely considering the world stocks situation. [18]

The sales to the trade also resulted in exports to countries which Canada had not been able to supply in two or three years. Altogether 12 countries were added to the list of Canadian customers in 1976-77. [19] By the close of the crop year on July 31, 1977, the price of No. 1 CWRS 13.5 per cent, had declined to $2.86½, basis Thunder Bay. Despite that, the total realized payment to Western Canadian farmers on Board deliveries for that grade in the 1976-77 crop year was slightly under $3.19 a bushel, basis Thunder Bay or Vancouver.[20]

Outlining its sales and pricing policy for the year in the annual report, the Board could be forgiven for taking a slight bow:

> The decision turned out to be a good one. The large sales to the trade in July and August, along with other sales the board made directly, contributed substantially to 1976-77 pool accounts for wheat and the size of the final payments farmers received early in 1978.[21]

It was a fitting climax to the career of Gerry Vogel as Chief Commissioner. In the closing weeks of the crop year, Vogel was approached to assume the position of executive director of the World Food Programme. He accepted the appointment and retired from the Board on September 30, 1977, to take up his new duties in Rome.

Vogel's six-year tenure as Chief Commissioner of the Board spanned a tumultuous period during which Western Canadian agriculture moved from record surplus through a series of difficult crop years and shortages of grain exacerbated by the onset of a growing transportation crisis and labour strife and stoppages. A soft-spoken, dedicated man who carried his responsibilities heavily, Vogel had a history of coronary problems. There can be little doubt that the stresses of the period contributed to a further strain on his health. Vogel was not destined to complete his five-year assignment in Rome. In early May, 1981, he suffered another heart attack and died in a Rome hospital at the age of 62.

His position as Chief Commissioner of the Canadian Wheat Board was filled by the appointment of W. Esmond Jarvis on October 3, 1977. Born on a Manitoba farm at Gladstone, Jarvis graduated from the University of Manitoba as an agrologist. A former Deputy Minister of Agriculture in Manitoba, he served later as Associate Deputy Minister of Agriculture Canada in Ottawa and was Co-ordinator of the Ottawa Grains Group before his appointment as Chief Commissioner of the Board.

The appointment was looked upon as a sharp break with tradition since, with the exception of the early formative years of the Canadian Wheat Board, an outsider had never before been appointed to the top position on the Board. It aroused some controversy and was branded by some critics as a "political appointment." The facts behind the appointment were that Jarvis had been groomed to assume the position of Deputy Minister of Agriculture in Ottawa. When that position became vacant, Jarvis was by-passed by an Executive

Assistant to Prime Minister Trudeau, Dennis Hudon, who was appointed Deputy Minister from outside of the Department of Agriculture. Having been "bumped," Jarvis was reconciled with the Canadian Wheat Board top job.

After holding a press conference in Winnipeg in mid-September to announce the appointment of Jarvis, Lang continued on to Saskatoon in the same week to initiate a major step in the rehabilitation of Western Canada's rail network. There, an agreement was signed between the federal government and the two major railways to commence work on upgrading of 2,099 miles of rail in Western Canada. [22] Long years of neglect had left much of the Prairie rail network inadequate to handle the increasing fleet of heavier hopper cars and it was expected that the total program might take up to eight years to complete. That, and other transportation constraints, were to be the major preoccupations of the Board well into the next decade.

Before the end of the 1977-78 crop year, there were several more developments aimed at improving Canada's ability to meet the anticipated increase in world markets for wheat and feed grains. The Canadian Wheat Board had been pressing for expanded facilities on the West Coast to service the growing markets on the Pacific Rim. While expansion of terminal facilities were underway at Vancouver, it was evident that there were restraints on the vulnerable lines through the mountains which limited future expansion. To the north, however, was the underutilized CNR line to Prince Rupert, B.C., which presented an excellent opportunity for development.

The first shipments out of the mountain-ringed all-season port at Prince Rupert had been made by George McIvor in the mid-1920s when he was Western Sales Manager of the Central Selling Agency of the Prairie pools in Calgary. McIvor was to later become the longest serving Chief Commissioner of the Canadian Wheat Board. Sir Henry Thornton, President of the CNR, rented the new and yet unused elevator at the northern B.C. port to the pool for one dollar a year. Deciding to take a risk on the port, which was then unknown in shipping circles, McIvor, along with Henry Wise Wood, President of Alberta Wheat Pool, proceeded to London where they booked 120,000 tons of Japanese shipping on the Baltic Exchange, with an option on Vancouver "in case the thing went sour." [23]

The shipping rate out of Prince Rupert was only nine pence a ton higher than Vancouver for the grain to be shipped to Europe via the Panama Canal, amounting to a trivial half-cent a bushel. The space was booked at 32 shillings and sixpence a ton. When the time for shipment came, a coal strike in Britain caused an abrupt rise in rates to 50 shillings a ton on the coal-fired shipping of the day. "We booked at 32 and six and sold at 50. We made about three-quarters of a million dollars on the deal," McIvor recalled. [24]

Now, over 50 years later, the aging government-owned terminal at Prince Rupert was considered inadequate to meet the surging demand out of the West

Coast, and the Wheat Board was pressing for a new facility. Thus, in mid-March, 1978, projects totalling $27.8 million to upgrade the port facilities at Prince Rupert were announced in Ottawa. Agriculture Minister Eugene Whelan announced the commitment of $11.5 million toward the upgrading of the old terminal elevator, and Lang announced that the federal government would contribute $16.3 million toward development of a new shipping site on Ridley Island in the harbour. [25]

The start on improvements to the ailing grain handling and transportation system came none too soon. Later that same month, Commissioner Charlie Gibbings announced that the Canadian Wheat Board could not take on any additional sales commitments until the coming August, some three months hence. While the supply of grain was more than adequate, Canada's transportation and handling system was fully committed to the end of the crop year. [26]

The full impact of the drastic restriction in the pipeline into an expanded world grain trade was now coming home to Prairie farmers and their organizations as they watched market opportunities slip away and grain inventories on their farms rise. By July 31, 1978, stocks of all grains on Western farms had climbed to 9.044 million tonnes and was rising rapidly. [27] In early May 1978, Allan McPherson, President of Alberta Pool, announced that Alberta Pool would immediately organize a consortium of western grain companies with the objective of building and operating a modern 100 million bushel a year grain terminal on Prince Rupert's Ridley Island. [28]

Organization of the project brought together a strange consortium of bedfellows with differing policy objectives, but united in the need to upgrade Canada's faltering ability to deliver wheat the Canadian Wheat Board could obviously sell. The co-operatively owned Prairie pools and United Grain Growers joined with the private trade, represented by Pioneer Grain and Cargill Canada, in the huge Prince Rupert project.

However, the rail line and port upgrading would not bear fruit until well into the future and the Wheat Board, looking into that future, foresaw a need for even more initiatives to meet its potential. The frustrations and problems facing the Board were being compounded as the 1978-79 crop year began. The 1978 crop in Western Canada was seeded on the largest acreage on record, and produced the second highest grain harvest ever at 37.893 million tonnes. [29] Farm stocks were growing. Labour problems were again hampering the already inadequate delivery system. In September, a three-week illegal strike by 180 railway workers at Thunder Bay began and extended into October. It was followed by a strike of Great Lakes marine officers and deck hands later in the month which was quickly ended by a back-to-work order by Parliament.

In August, the Chinese turned to the United States for one million tonnes of wheat, which American authorities frankly admitted was forced by Canada's West Coast shipping delays. [30] Japan was becoming increasingly critical of the delays in shipping, and demurrage was piling up as long lines of ships were again waiting for cargo.

To add to these woes, sluggish grain prices that began with the large world grain crop of 1976 were still prevailing. Faced with rapidly escalating input costs, impelled in large part by a world energy crisis and rising fuel prices, many Western farmers were becoming increasingly bellicose and there appeared to be a growing alienation toward established institutions. A new generation of farmers, who had not experienced the exploitation by the private grain companies in the 1920s, the Depression and hardship of the 1930s and World War II, were openly challenging long sought for rights held sacred by farmers of the previous generation. The Canadian Wheat Board, along with the Pools, the Canadian Grain Commission and others, were now seen as the "establishment," to be questioned rather than as a "cause" to be championed.

While this new breed, many of them college educated, was knowledgeable, aggressive, impatient and pragmatic in most cases, they were also highly leveraged with high capital debt obligations. Their economic survival was dependent on cash flow, and anything that affected it was open to questioning. In this new environment, it was almost a foregone conclusion that the question of centralized marketing, vis-a-vis the "free market" alternative, would become the focus of renewed debate. Imposition by the government of the domestic feed grains policy had added fuel to that debate, and traditional opponents of the Wheat Board system were taking every opportunity to exploit the situation.

The strain of two disparate systems, operating side-by-side on the relatively limited domestic market, was now exacerbated by the transportation crisis. The Board, in spite of exercising impartiality to the point of detriment to its own export program in its role of co-ordination and allocation of the scarce supply of rolling stock, was charged with withholding cars for off-board and non-board shipments. At the annual late fall farm organization meetings in 1978, the Board forsook its previously low public profile in the domestic feed policy debate and spoke out forcefully.

Esmond Jarvis led off the attack on the domestic feed grains policy at the annual meeting of Manitoba Pool Elevators in early November. Questioning whether two marketing systems could be accommodated in a single transportation and handling system without one seriously undermining the other, the Chief Commissioner declared: "The answer is no, unless a way can be found to achieve much greater discipline in the delivery of grains to the off-board market."[31]

Several blocks away at the concurrent meeting of United Grain Growers delegates in Winnipeg's Marlborough Hotel, Jim Leibfried was delivering a similar message:

> It is truly a vicious circle. Because when the export movement of feed grains is hampered, then board quotas don't

open and more farmers come under pressure to deliver at dis-
tressed price levels on the limited domestic market. That, in
turn, pressures elevator managers to ship more open market
stocks to terminals which either congests the system or forces
the board to use off-board grains to meet export commitments. The latter, in turn, keeps board quotas low or non-
existent and forces more farmers toward the open market and
even lower prices. [32]

One week later, at the annual meeting of the Saskatchewan Wheat Pool in
Regina, Charlie Gibbings put the case against the policy in blunt terms.
Pointing out the difficulties of operating the Board system in parallel with the
domestic open market system, Gibbings declared:

We can start immediately by building up our handling and
transportation facilities to enable farmers to achieve their
growth potential or we can revert to the philosophy of the pig
at the trough where those with the biggest snout get the
biggest share. [33]

The Board's open attack, on the politically sensitive feed grains policy, was
followed almost immediately by another controversial move. In late November,
it was announced that the Canadian Wheat Board would place tenders for 500
to 2,000 grain hopper cars. Expected to cost up to $90 million, the hoppers
would be the first to be purchased directly with Western grain producers' pooled
earnings. Declining to be quoted, Board officials suggested that the federal
Cabinet's refusal to buy 4,000 more hoppers and repair 1,500 boxcars earlier in
the year was the "turning point" in Board thinking. They said the decision
would be fully explained when tender quotations were finalized. [34]

While controversy erupted over the use of producers' funds to acquire the hoppers, the move was unanimously supported by the farmer-elected Advisory
Committee to the Board. [35] Conscious of the need to accelerated change in areas
outside of its immediate jurisdiction to meet those goals, the Board kept up the
pressure. Even as the Board's hopper car acquisition was being debated, another
move was revealed. The Wheat Board had offered to bankroll half of the estimated $200 million cost of the terminal project at Prince Rupert if the consortium of
six grain companies would agree to have the new facility operational by 1981.

While the Board declined to discuss the offer, made shortly before Christmas
1978, to match the consortium dollar for dollar by means of a repayable loan,
published reports by members of the Board's Advisory Committee revealed
that the matter had been discussed at the December 19, 1978, meeting of the

Committee and a motion approving the Board's actions had been passed unanimously.[36]

The offer was not taken up, but the urgency of the project, the largest ever undertaken by the grain industry, had been brought home. At a two-day conference on grain transportation problems, convened by Manitoba's Premier Sterling Lyon in Winnipeg on January 8 and 9, 1979, Alberta's Premier Peter Lougheed announced that his province would provide $100 million financing to the Prince Rupert consortium from Alberta's oil-based Heritage Fund.[37]

Events moved quickly. Shortly afterwards the Canadian Wheat Board confirmed that, at a separate meeting held during the Winnipeg conference and attended by the Prairie premiers and Otto Lang, the Board had called for a "hopper task force." Under the proposal, the federal government and the three Prairie Provinces were asked to share the cost of purchasing 10,000 hopper cars over the next six years at a cost of $450 million. The Board warned that: "If positive action were not forthcoming from the provinces and the federal government, the Board would be forced to make additional purchases of its own."[38] Pointing up the cost, if action was not taken, the Board said that, unless additions were made to the grain fleet, Western grain exports could be expected to decline by about one million tonnes a year. "At a nominal value of $150 per tonne, this would represent a loss of more than $4.2 billion to Prairie farmers and to the Western economy by 1985."[39]

The Board warned further that the loss in income would be even greater if potential increases in grain exports were taken into account:

> By maintaining its current share of expanding world grain trade, Canada could be exporting an average of 30 million tonnes of grain each year by 1985, an increase of 8.8 million tonnes over 1977-78. This additional volume, again at a nominal $150 per tonne, would represent an increase in revenue of $5.3 billion to the economy of Western Canada by 1985.[40]

In the interim, the Board exercised its earlier announced intention of acquiring hopper cars by placing orders for 2,000 steel hopper cars in mid-January. The move to purchase the cars was almost immediately challenged by the Palliser Wheat Growers Association. Seeking a restraining injunction in a Regina court, the Saskatchewan-based commodity organization claimed that the Wheat Board's enabling legislation did not give it authority to purchase equipment, such as hopper cars, with producers' funds. They asked for a full court hearing on whether the Board could borrow money to buy the cars, charge interest as an expense to producers, or subsidize rail transportation. Mr. Justice P.H. Maguire ruled that an injunction could not be granted for an act already done, but steered clear of deciding whether the Board could make future purchases, leaving the legal question undecided.[41]

Meanwhile Lang, after announcing that the government would reimburse the CPR for half the costs of rehabilitating a further 1,000 boxcars, had made settlement of the Crow Rate issue a condition of any further hopper car purchases. Speaking at a news conference, following a meeting of the Senior Grain Transportation Committee in Regina in late January, Lang said neither the federal government nor the Canadian Wheat Board would purchase any further cars until the statutory freight rate issue was settled.[42]

The Minister's hopes for a revision of the inflation eroded statutory rate had been buoyed at the round of farmer organization meetings in the previous November. The Prairie pools, as the largest constituency of grain farmer representation in the West, had maintained a united front against any change to the Crow Rate, long regarded as the birthright of the Prairie farmer. However, at a press conference preceding the opening of Manitoba Pool Elevators annual meeting in November 1978, Jim Deveson, a blunt outspoken farmer from Arden, Manitoba, and President of Manitoba Pool, took the bull by the horns. Noting a growing discrepancy between the Crow Rate and real transportation costs, Deveson called for immediate discussion on the statutory rate and suggested the possibility of farmers paying a larger share of the cost. Aware of the sensitive ground he was breaking, Deveson asked farmers to consider the consequence if nothing were done in the face of deteriorating rail service.[43]

At the concurrent meeting of United Grain Growers, A.M. "Mac" Runciman, President of U.G.G., suggested that transportation of grain from the Prairies could be speeded up if a review of the Crow were undertaken. While calling for

CWB Grain Transportation staff at one of their regular car allocation meetings with the railways.

the statutory rate to remain on export grain shipments, Runciman called for its removal on domestic movement, "and let the chips fall where they may."[44]

The ball was rolling, and in the same week that Lang made purchase of further hopper cars conditional on settlement of the Crow issue, bitter debate broke out at the annual meeting of the Western Agricultural Conference in Regina as Prairie delegates to the Canadian Federation of Agriculture sought to reach a consensus position on the emotional issue to present to the forthcoming CFA annual meeting. When the dust settled, the WAC had adopted a policy statement declaring that Western farmers were ready to negotiate a new formula on the historic Crow Rate. But Saskatchewan Pool, spearheaded by its President, E.K. "Ted" Turner, remained adamantly opposed to initiating any negotiations. Divorcing itself from the policy, the powerful Saskatchewan Pool indicated it would carry its own "stand fast" resolution to the annual meeting of the CFA, and expressed strong reservations on remaining a member of the Western Agricultural Conference.[45]

It was a precursor of things to come. In the long, emotional and convoluted debate to follow, the Crow issue was to sunder the farm organizational structure on the Prairies and threaten the viability of the Canadian Federation of Agriculture on the national scene. The Manitoba Farm Bureau and the Saskatchewan Federation of Agriculture, as provincial representatives to CFA, foundered on the rocks of the Crow debate, and the Western Agricultural Conference sank with them. The Prairie pools and United Grain Growers withdrew from active participation in the provincial general farm organizations and charted separate lobbying courses at the national level.

In this divisive splintering of the Prairie farm voice, the Canadian Wheat Board, while vitally concerned with the outcome, was obliged to publicly stand aside and privately spur on as best it could the immediate need for capacity to deliver into a growing world potential.

For Lang, it was the end of a political career that had spanned a turbulent decade of accelerating change on the Prairies. On May 22, 1979, Canadian voters went to the polls to once again elect a minority government in Ottawa. The Trudeau government fell to the Progressive Conservatives under their new leader, Joe Clark. Final results showed 136 seats for the Conservatives, 114 for the Liberals, 26 New Democrats, and six Créditistes from Quebec. For the Liberals, the Prairies were a wasteland. Among the casualties was Otto Lang who placed third in his riding of Saskatoon-Humboldt. The Lang era was over. A 44-year-old Vegreville, Alberta, farmer, Don Mazankowski, became Transport Minister with responsibility for reporting to Parliament for the Canadian Wheat Board.

Lang was to shortly reappear in a new role on the private grain trade scene. On August 15, 1979, he was appointed Executive Vice-President of Pioneer Grain Co. Ltd. in Winnipeg.

In the same week that Lang's new appointment was announced, an extensive report on a study that he had initiated 11 months earlier was released in Ottawa by Mazankowski. Carried out by the American consulting firm of Booz-Allen and Hamilton, Inc., the study recommended changes over a wide spectrum of the Prairie grain industry. The report estimated that expenditures of between $1.3 billion and two billion dollars might be required up to 1985-86 to meet grain export demands in the near future. [46]

The Booz-Allen report called for the expenditure of $400 million on 9,300 more hopper cars, immediate negotiations on the expansion of facilities at Prince Rupert, and acquisition of 125 new locomotives at an estimated cost of $106 million. It said a further $700 million would be required for branch line rehabilitation, $100 million for the Prince Rupert facility, $160 million to improve CNR main line capacity, $100 million to improve CPR main line capacity, and $148 million on joint operations to facilitate rail movement through the Fraser Canyon on the vulnerable route to the West Coast.

In addition to these recommendations for massive expenditures, the report covered a large number of administrative and regulatory functions within the trade. Among them was a controversial recommendation that the block shipping staff of the Canadian Wheat Board be removed to a "neutral home." Noting a "perceived potential conflict of interest" in the Board's allocation of cars between Board and private trade grains, the report favoured relocation of the block shipping staff to report to a managing director of a proposed Grain Transportation Improvement Task Force. [47]

Little noted at the time was a recommendation that consideration be given to replacing the Canadian Wheat Board's quota system with a system under which the Board would buy all Board grain stored on farms following on-farm inspection. The farm-stored grain would then be called forward to primary elevators as required to meet export commitments some weeks later at the ports. "This could facilitate drawing down all elevators on a given set of rail lines each week in a manner designed to increase rail operating efficiency as well as increasing the responsiveness of the system and maintaining an eventual basis of equity in the system." [48] That proposal was to surface later in the form of a "Market Assurance Plan," and generate yet another debate.

For the present another dispute flared over the Board's delivery quota system. In August 1978, the Advisory Committee to the Board had appointed a committee to undertake a review of the quota system, the first since 1970. Chaired by Dobson Lea, the committee consisted of Bob Moffat, former General Manager of Manitoba Pool, George Bradley, former Country Operations Manager of Saskatchewan Pool, and Mike Martin, Director of Western Grain Transportation for the Wheat Board. Their report, delivered to the Advisory Committee on January 22, 1979, was a 41-page document suggesting more than 20 changes in the quota system.

A major recommendation for a return to seeded acreages of the principal grains as the basis for assignment of quotas, and elimination of summerfallow, forage crops and specialty crops from the formula, was rejected by the Advisory Committee. They recommended, however, that the most controversial aspect of the report — delivery quotas for off-board domestic feed grains — be adopted by the Board.

When the Board announced that it would act on the recommendation of the Producer Advisory Committee and institute delivery quotas on off-board grains, there was an immediate outcry from the Winnipeg Commodity Exchange and from the Palliser Wheat Growers Association. In a resolution, passed at a meeting held in St. Andrews, New Brunswick, in late July, Canada's provincial agriculture ministers, with the exception of Saskatchewan, called on the federal government to postpone implementation of the domestic feed grain delivery quotas. Prior to the meeting, the Clark government, in a press release, reaffirmed the principles of the open-market policy as laid down by its Liberal predecessors. However, the government declined to act on the request by the provincial ministers and off-board quotas went into effect on August 1, 1979.

Even as this new controversy was splitting Western farm organizations into separate camps, the Conservative government had established yet another task force. Headed by Manitoba MP Jack Murta, the three-man committee was asked to make recommendations for implementing an emergency program on grain movement in Western Canada.

Alarmed at one of the terms of reference for the new task force, that of appointment of a Grain Transportation Co-ordinator to oversee grain movement and allocation of cars between Board, non-board and off-board domestic feed grains, the Advisory Committee to the Wheat Board forwarded a unanimous resolution to the government asking that, in the event of such an appointment, the Wheat Board retain its existing transportation responsibilities under the Block Shipping System.[49]

Events at the political level were now moving swiftly. Two weeks after releasing the Booz-Allen report, a memorandum of understanding was signed between the federal government and the Prince Rupert consortium on July 31, 1979. In addition to the building of a new terminal with a minimum capacity of eight million bushels, the agreement provided for transfer to the consortium of the existing government terminal for a token sum of one dollar, and for the federal government to purchase an additional 5,000 grain hopper cars.[50]

In late August, the Murta task force recommended appointment of a Grain Transportation Co-ordinator within the next two-and-a-half months and immediate assumption of transportation co-ordination duties by an interim ad-hoc committee. Shortly thereafter, Mazankowski announced the terms of reference for a co-ordinator as a "middle-ground" between extreme opinions within the grains industry. One week later, on September 24, Dr. Hugh Horner, Alberta's Minister of Economic Development and Deputy Premier of the province, announced at a press conference in Edmonton that he was resigning from the Alberta government on October 1 to accept the post of Co-ordinator effective October 15.[51]

By early December, Horner had announced the appointment of his senior staff members and the Grain Transportation Authority established a permanent office in the heart of Winnipeg's grain trade. Under enabling federal legislation, the GTA became operational on March 17, 1980, and assumed responsibility for procurement and allocation of grain cars between the Board and the private trade.[52] Following the allocation, the block shipping staff, which remained at the Canadian Wheat Board, worked out the detailed shipping plans to move the grain from specific Prairie points to specific port areas.

Despite the acrimonious charges from the trade on rail car allocations, which led to the establishment of the GTA, evidence as to the Board's more than even-handed procedures came from the Canadian Livestock Feed Board. In mid-August 1979, the Secretary of the CLFB, A. Douglas Mutch, charged that some participants trading Western grains into eastern Canada appeared to have been attempting to "manipulate rail car movement to their own personal advantage." At the same time Mutch said the Wheat Board had "met the test" in the allocation of sufficient grain cars to service the domestic feed grains market, "sometimes to the detriment of it own export marketing program."[53]

In a later review of the 1978-79 crop year, released the following December, the CLFB, as the federally appointed watchdog for feed grain users outside of the Wheat Board designated area, declared that transportation capacity short-falls had placed a severe strain on the domestic feed grains price structure and threatened to fragment the market. While producer marketings fell 15 per cent during the year, domestic feed grain deliveries (off-board) rose 25 per cent and rapeseed marketings (non-board) jumped 66 per cent. The CLFB said the priority for non-board grains and oilseeds resulted in the Wheat Board becoming a "residual receiver of rail cars."[54]

A changing world marketplace had also injected a new element into the disruptive domestic feed grains debate. The long period of sluggish grain prices, that began with the big world grain crop in 1976, finally came to an end in the late spring of 1979. The largest increases were in wheat. The price of No. 1 CWRS 13.5 per cent at Thunder Bay rose over $66 a tonne ($1.80 a bushel) from May 1, to a peak of $236 a tonne ($6.42 a bushel) on June 22.[55]

The strongest impetus on prices once again came from the Soviet Union as result of another major setback in its 1979 crop. Grain production in the Soviet Union fell to 179 million tonnes, some 46 million tonnes below target and 56 million tonnes below the record output in the previous year.[56] Excitement gripped the markets as the United States indicated that it was prepared to offer up to 25 million tonnes of wheat and corn to the Soviets. China had also entered the market heavily. Thus, in late 1979, export prices for Canadian feed grains were well above domestic prices. The domestic feed grains policy was now not only disrupting the tight transportation system, but the Western farmer was losing money on each bushel diverted from the export market.

In these circumstances, the Board commissioners kept up their pressure on the domestic feed grains policy. At the November meeting of Manitoba Pool Elevators, Gibbings bluntly told delegates that Western Canadian grain producers had "continually been shafted by Canada's domestic feed grains policy." [57] Two weeks later in Calgary, Leibfried told Alberta Wheat Pool delegates that the corn competitive formula, at which the Board was obliged to sell and maintain stocks in Eastern Canada, had "worked as a kind of heads-you-win, tails-we-lose arrangement for Western Canadian farmers." The policy, he said, had tied the hands of the Board in attempting to maximize returns to producers. [58]

Another result of the surging world price found Western farmers subsidizing consumers of bread on the domestic scene. The federal government's two-price wheat policy was modified effective December 8, 1978. Under the new policy, the government subsidy was removed. The Board was directed to charge domestic millers the export price between a range of four dollars and five dollars a bushel. Should the export price drop below four dollars, the Board continued to sell at the four dollar minimum into the domestic market. However, should the export price rise above five dollars, the Board was obliged to sell at the five dollar maximum to domestic millers. With export prices now well over six dollars a bushel, it meant that the farmers were subsidizing consumers by over one dollar a bushel. Based on purchases by Canadian mills and the actual value of exports at the time those purchases were made, that consumer subsidization by farmers reached an estimated $54.6 million in the 1979-80 crop year. [59]

The closing years of the 1970s were difficult and frustrating for the Canadian Wheat Board. Faced with steeply rising input costs, Prairie farmers were at the same time confronted with a series of traumatic changes. An aging and dilapidated rail system denied them the ability to deliver to their productive potential into a clearly expanding world market. For many of them the unthinkable had happened: their once inviolable heritage of the Crow Rate was being questioned, splitting their organizations into warring factions. There were rail line abandonments, strikes and work stoppages, controversy over the domestic feed grains policy, and divisions between commodity groups. In this atmosphere, it was inevitable that the Canadian Wheat Board would be drawn into the vortex of discontent.

Throughout the 70s new splinter groups emerged to add their voices to the clamour of varying farm policy proposals on the Prairies. Minority groups, such as the Western Barley Growers Association, funded by a grant from the Alberta

A large snowstorm hit the Prairies in February 1978, blocking the CP Rail main line near Gull Lake, Saskatchewan for five and a half days, with drifts up to 12 feet deep.

provincial government, the Flax Growers Western Canada, the Palliser Wheat Growers Association (later to become the Western Canadian Wheat Growers Association) and others adopted policies critical of the Canadian Wheat Board and called for marketing choice for the farmers. In the livestock-oriented province of Alberta, the provincial government set up its own Alberta Feed Grains Commission, which pursued a course for independent marketing.

On the other side of the equation, the Prairie Pools, in which the majority of Western farmers had a voice, and the National Farmers Union strongly supported the Board, seeking extension of its powers to other grains and elimination of the domestic feed grains policy of dual marketing. United Grain Growers, while supporting the export role of the Board, clashed with the Pools on the domestic feed grains issue. Added to this diversity were a growing number of commodity marketing boards and associations in the livestock and poultry sector.

It was against this divisive backdrop that the Canadian Wheat Board approached the promise and the challenge of the 1980s. And, as the decade of the 70s drew to a close, there were growing indications that the export target of 30 million tonnes of grain by 1985 could be met. The transportation outlook was improving with the 2,000 hopper cars ordered by the Board coming into service. Additionally, in the fall of 1979, the Alberta and Saskatchewan provin-

cial governments had each ordered 1,000 hopper cars to be added to the grain
fleet. The federal government had agreed to lease another 2,000 hoppers and a
total of 5,000 boxcars were in the process of rehabilitation. The province of
Manitoba had also agreed to lease 400 to 600 hopper cars on a temporary basis,
to help relieve the transportation crisis.

Active planning for construction of the new Prince Rupert terminal was
underway, and upgrading of the permanent rail network was proceeding. Across
the face of the Prairies rationalization and consolidation of the country elevator
systems were reaching a new impetus. In spite of a widely popular view that the
country elevator system was still in the "horse and wagon" era, accelerated
changes had taken place over the previous decade. Between 1971 and 1978, the
number of primary elevators in the Prairie Provinces declined by almost 30 per
cent — from 3,423 to 2,423 — and future projections were for a further reduction to 1,750.[60] At many of the consolidated delivery points, new and modern-
ized high-throughput elevators were being constructed or old installations
upgraded to handle higher volumes.

On the international scene, world grain trade had been increasing at an accelerated rate over the previous ten years. Trade in wheat was up 70 per cent; that
in coarse grains by 156 per cent; oilseeds 81 per cent and rice 65 per cent. Taken
together, world trade in all grains in 1979, amounting to 245 million tonnes,
was more than double the level of ten years previous.[61] Despite a near record
world grain crop in 1979, there was an unprecedented import demand, and
world wheat and coarse grain trade increased by 16 per cent. World trade in
wheat reached a record 85 million tonnes and world trade in coarse grains was
a record 97 million tonnes.[62]

Impelled by that demand, prices remained strong throughout the summer
and fall of 1979, and by December showed signs of moving to higher levels.
Then, in late December, Russian troops moved into Afghanistan. The entry into
the 1980s was to be marked by an unprecedented use of grain exports as a tool
of foreign policy, injecting a new element onto the world stage.

Footnotes Chapter Eight

1. Appendix to the Canadian Wheat Board Advisory Committee Minutes, December 20, 1976.
2. *Report of the Canadian Wheat Board, Crop Year 1976-77*, p. 26.
3. Personal File, R.L. Kristjanson, Memorandum D.J. Hoyes to J.L. Leibfried, August 23, 1976.
4. *Ibid*, Memorandum to the Board, August 30, 1976.
5. *Ibid,* September 7, 1976.
6. Dan Morgan, *Merchants of Grain*, p.331.
7. Personal File, R.L. Kristjanson, Memorandum to the Board, August 30, 1976.
8. *Ibid*.
9. Appendix to the Canadian Wheat Board Advisory Committee Minutes, December 20, 1976.
10. Dan Morgan, *Merchants of Grain*, p. 331.

11. Canadian Wheat Board Advisory Committee Minutes, September 20, 1976, pp. 7, 8.

12. *Ibid*, p. 6.

13. *Ibid*, p. 7.

14. *Ibid*.

15. *Ibid*.

16. *Report of the Canadian Wheat Board, Crop Year 1976-77,* pp. 3 -8.

17. *Ibid*, p. 7.

18. Appendix Canadian Wheat Board Advisory Committee Meeting, February 1, 1977.

19. *Report of the Canadian Wheat Board, Crop Year 1976-77,* p. 15.

20. *Ibid*, p. 47.

21. *Ibid*, p. 15.

22. *The Manitoba Co-operator*, September 22, 1977, p. 1.

23. Taped Interview George McIvor.

24. *Ibid*.

25. *The Manitoba Co-operator*, March 16, 1978, p. 1.

26. *Ibid*, March 30, 1978, p. 1.

27. Report of the Canadian Wheat Board, Crop Year 1978-79, p. 23.

28. *The Manitoba Co-operator*, May 11, 1978. p. 1.

29. *Report of the Canadian Wheat Board, Crop Year 1978-79,* p. 21.

30. *The Manitoba Co-operator*, September 7, 1978, p. 1.

31. *Ibid*, November 16, 1978, p. 4.

32. *Ibid*.

33. *Ibid*, November 23, 1978, p. 1.

34. *Ibid*, November 30, 1978, p. 1.

35. *Ibid*, January 4, 1979, p. 9.

36. *Ibid*, pp. 1, 9.

37. *Ibid*, January 11, 1979, p. 1.

38. *Ibid*, February 15, 1979, p. 1.

39. *Ibid*, p. 8.

40. *Ibid*.

41. *Ibid*, March 8, 1979, p. 1.

42. *Ibid*, February 7, 1979, p. 1.

43. *Ibid*, November 9, 1978, p. 1.

44. *Ibid*, p. 13.

45. *Ibid*, February 1, 1979, p. 1.

46. *Ibid*, July 19, 1979, p. 1.

47. *Ibid*, p. 11.

48. *Ibid*, July 26, 1979, p. 13.

49. *Ibid*, August 16, 1979, p. 1.

50. *Ibid*, August 2, 1979, p. 1.

51. *Ibid*, September 27, 1979, p. 1.

52. *Report of the Canadian Wheat Board, Crop Year 1979-80,* p. 18.

53. Grain Facts, Canadian Livestock Feed Board, August 3, 1979.

54. *The Manitoba Co-operator*, January 3, 1980, p. 1.

55. *Report of the Canadian Wheat Board, Crop Year 1978-79,* p. 15.

56. *Ibid*.

57. *The Manitoba Co-operator*, November 15, 1979, p. 1.

58. *Ibid*, December 6, 1979, p. 1.

59. *Report of the Canadian Wheat Board, Crop Year 1979-80,* p. 16.

60. *The Western Producer*, June 28, 1979.

61. W.E. Jarvis, *Address to the Prairie Production Symposium, Saskatoon*, October 29, 1980.

62. Report of the Canadian Wheat Board, Crop Year 1979-80, pp. 3 -9.

CHAPTER 9

THE PHANTOM FOOD WEAPON

If war is the extension of a nation's foreign policy, so too, is the conduct of its international grain trade.
— *Richard Gilmore: A Poor Harvest.*

In the closing months of 1979, a wave of marketing euphoria was sweeping across the wide breadth of the American Central Plain. At the annual Agricultural Outlook Conference in Washington there were optimistic predictions that the upcoming decade of the 1980s would tax the capacity of U.S. farmers to meet unlimited opportunities in a burgeoning world market. The American farmer, although buffeted by climbing production costs and soaring interest rates, could take solace in strengthening prices and sales opportunities, limited only by the capacity of the storage, transportation and port facilities to cope with the demand.

Howard Hjort, the U.S. Department of Agriculture's Chief Economist, told the Outlook Conference that the prospect for near capacity production in the 1980s meant that most of the readily available cropland would be used, and demand for production inputs — especially fertilizer, fuels and machinery — would remain strong.[1]

The indications that spurred the optimism emerged when the Soviet Union entered the market early after again experiencing heavy winterkill of its fall sown crop and then hot, dry "Sukhovey" winds shrivelled the spring sown crop. Not even a large U.S. wheat harvest and the expectation of a bumper U.S. corn crop could defuse the excitement of the market over the massive Russian purchases, which exceeded by far anything ever before seen on the world grain scene.

Appearing before a Senate Agriculture Subcommittee, Thomas Saylor, Associate Administrator of the USDA's Foreign Agricultural Service, defined the magnitude of the possible Soviet incursion into the market. The Russians, he said, would take up to 25 million tonnes of U.S. grain in the fourth year of a grain supply agreement which began on October 1. In the years ahead, Saylor said, the USSR was expected to be a "constant, permanent" buyer, instead of the "erratic, variable" purchaser that characterized the 1970s.[2]

In the same week, Charles Pence, another official of the Foreign Agricultural Service, confidently assured the annual convention of the Washington Association of Wheat Growers, gathered in Spokane, Washington, that the Russians "should be good customers for U.S. grain, probably forever."[3]

In this heady atmosphere, the American farmer required little urging. The late November 1979, USDA crop survey estimated American winter wheat acreage up 10 per cent at 71 million acres and commented: "The new crop futures provide a favourable price structure and the lack of set-aside requirements will encourage farmers to expand winter wheat acreage."[4]

Wheat plantings in Colorado, New Mexico, Oklahoma and Texas were reported to be the largest since 1953, and new and expanded technology assured yields that would far exceed those of earlier record acreage. For the American it was "all systems go," and the euphoria of the marketplace spread onto the international scene. In mid-December, Sir Leslie Price, Chairman of the Australian Wheat Board, declared the outlook to be "bullish," and told a press conference in Sydney that he expected to see world wheat prices reach record levels in the coming year.[5]

At the November Washington meeting, William Miner, Co-ordinator of the Ottawa Grains Group, outlined Canada's intention to upgrade the nation's grain

From left to right: Andy Stephen, CN Rail, Esmond Jarvis (Chief Commissioner) and Jim Liebfried (Commissioner) witness delivery of the CWB hopper cars.

handling capacity to reach an export goal of 30 million tonnes by the mid 1980s. That goal was met with some scepticism by the Americans. An agricultural attaché's report from Ottawa declared that Canada would probably be unable to increase grains and oilseeds production to a level required to sustain exports of 30 million tonnes by 1985-86. "There will have to be sustained evidence that significantly more grain and oilseeds are moving from the farms though the system into export channels before an appreciable rise in agricultural production takes place," said the report.[6]

For the Americans the situation was clear. In the expanding global grain markets, only the immense potential of the U.S. Great Central Plain could meet the demand of an expanding world population. The after-shock of the 1972 "Great Grain Robbery" had resulted in the Nixon Administration's 1973 embargo on soybean exports and the 1974 and 1975 Ford Administration grain embargoes. Those embargoes had roused the ire of American farmers, who saw the use of their productivity as an unwarranted weapon of foreign diplomacy. Now, a new Democratic Administration was in power, and President Jimmy Carter, himself a farmer, had vowed during the 1976 election campaign that he would never initiate another embargo. It appeared that the massive American penetration into markets of the Soviet Union and China was secure.

Those expectations were shattered and the dream died on Friday evening, January 4, 1980. President Carter appeared on the nation's television screens to announce that, despite his earlier promises, he was invoking an embargo on all outstanding wheat, corn and soybean contracts with the Soviet Union. On December 24, 1979, 40,000 Soviet troops had poured across the border into Afghanistan to aid in toppling the government and installing a new leader, Abrak Karmal.

Under the terms of the five-year U.S.-USSR agreement, entered into in October 1975, the Soviets would be allowed to take eight million tonnes of wheat and corn, but the additional 17 million tonnes, agreed to for the 1979-80 crop year, would not be delivered. The embargo would remain until Soviet troops withdrew from Afghanistan. Based on consultation with other grain exporting nations, Carter expressed confidence that those countries would not replace U.S. grain by making additional shipments to the Soviet Union.

The withdrawal of the Soviet forces did not materialize. In the aftermath of the use of the "food weapon," world markets were thrown into confusion. The entry into the 1980s was chaotic.

In Canada, as in the United States, it was an election year. On Tuesday, December 11, 1979, the New Democratic Party had combined with the Liberals to defeat the shaky minority government of Prime Minister Clark in a non-confidence motion during the budget debate. Only weeks before, on November 21, Pierre Trudeau announced in the Commons that he was stepping down as the Leader of the Liberal Party. Now, with a general election called for February 18, and no time to choose a successor, Trudeau had, in effect, been recalled to again head the Liberals in the campaign.

With that election campaign already underway, Prime Minister Clark announced that Canada would support the U.S. embargo and limit Soviet purchases from the Canadian Wheat Board to about three million tonnes. Ottawa would reimburse farmers for any losses resulting from the Canadian or U.S. government actions. Other major exporting nations, with the exception of Argentina, undertook to supply no more than "normal and traditional" quantities to the Soviet Union.

For Canada, the agreement to limit shipments to traditional levels during the 1979-80 crop year, raised a major question. Over the previous 10 years, Canada's yearly exports of grain to the Soviet Union had varied widely; from a low of 300,000 tonnes in 1970-71 to a high of five million tonnes in 1972-73.[7] Beside that variability, the only traditional aspect of sales to Russia was their verbal commitment to always come to Canada first when in need of grain. The Soviet Union had lived up to that agreement since 1971.

On February 18, the minority Conservative government was swept away after only nine months in office. The issue had been decided in the vote-heavy provinces of Quebec and Ontario even before the polls closed in the later time zones across Western Canada. The Liberals, under Trudeau, had won a majority of 147 seats with the Progressive Conservatives winning in 103 ridings and the New Democrats in 32. West of Winnipeg, all the way to the Pacific, not one Liberal was elected.

Senator Hazen Argue (right) was Minister of State Responsible for the Canadian Wheat Board in Pierre Trudeau's (next left) Liberal government in the late seventies and early eighties.

Once again the Prairie Provinces were in the political wilderness. Trudeau was forced to turn to the Senate to appoint a Westerner as Minister Responsible for the Board. Hazen Argue, a Saskatchewan farmer and chairman of the Senate Agriculture Committee, had been the national leader of the CCF, the forerunner of the NDP. He resigned from the NDP in 1962 and won a seat as a Liberal candidate the same year. Defeated in the general election of 1963, Argue was appointed to the Senate in February. 1966. When the final figure on Canadian exports was established at 3.8 million tonnes for the 1979-80 crop year, it was announced by Senator Hazen Argue as Minister of State responsible to Parliament for the Canadian Wheat Board.

An ardent supporter of the Wheat Board marketing system, Argue, as Chairman of the Senate Agriculture Committee, had spearheaded a drive to encourage pricing co-operation between the principal exporting countries following the precipitous drop in grain prices in 1978-79. His initiative led to meetings in Winnipeg and Washington between members of the Canadian Senate and ranking U.S. senators from the large grain producing states in the summers of 1978 and 1979. Seen in many quarters as a counter "agripower cartel" to the Organization of Petroleum Exporting Countries (OPEC), whose pricing policies had imposed an energy crisis and spurred world-wide inflationary pressure, the proposal gained a measure of acceptance.

Under the popular slogans of "food for crude" or "a bushel for a barrel," pressure from the farm state Senators, and the American farm community, forced a somewhat reluctant Secretary of Agriculture Robert Bergland to meet with Australian, Argentinian and Canadian Agriculture Ministers in the spring of 1979. An informal agreement was reached to co-ordinate marketing and productivity in their respective countries. However, in the heady atmosphere of rising prices and previously unsurpassed purchasing by the Soviet Union and China in late 1979, such proposals evaporated.

Now, in early 1980, the draconian implementation of food as a weapon of international diplomacy, had thrown the markets into confusion. Despite efforts by the American government to forestall a major price decline in the aftermath of Carter's partial embargo, grain prices dropped steadily over the next four months. By mid-April, U.S. corn prices had dropped nine dollars a tonne from the early January level while export prices for U.S. Hard Winter Ordinary wheat were down $30 a tonne. Since the embargo limitation affected the price of high-quality wheat more severely, Canadian wheat prices were down about $35 a tonne.[8]

For the United States, the fallout from the partial embargo was costly. In its attempts to lessen the domestic impact and shore up prices, the government took over open market contracts on 4.1 million tonnes of corn and 4.2 million tonnes of wheat. At the same time the loan rate and storage payments to U.S. farmers were raised. Even more costly than that drain on the Treasury was the dramatic realignment of export and import relationships, in which the Soviet

Union relegated the United States to the position of a residual supplier and turned to other sources for its needs.

Even in the short term, the effect of the embargo on Soviet purchasing was minimal. Exportkhleb's heaviest buying of American grains through the international traders actually took place during the fall of 1979, allowing enough time to ship roughly 13 million tonnes before the embargo was announced in January and another 2.5 million tonnes thereafter. Figures from the International Wheat Council and the Food and Agriculture Organization of the United Nations, showed that the Soviet Union imported 30.9 million tonnes of grain in the 1979-80 crop year. The grain came from the following countries: Australia, four million tonnes, Argentina, 5.1 million tonnes, Canada, 3.8 million tonnes, European Economic Community, 900,000 tonnes, and the U.S., 15.2 million tonnes. [9]

For the Argentinians, who declined to pay even lip service to the U.S. request for a co-operative embargo, it proved to be a windfall. The fob prices for Argentine Trigo Pan (bread wheat) averaged $218 a tonne in February, 1980, about $30 a tonne above comparable wheats from other exporters. [10]

That disparity, between Argentine and American prices, also produced windfall profits for some of the international traders holding Argentinian contracts for sales to countries other than the USSR. The traders simply switched wheat from those contracts to the Russians for sale at the higher price. They then replaced the wheat to the other countries by purchasing on what was now a buyer's market in the U.S. The observation by Congressman Mark Andrews, of North Dakota, in 1975, that the grain trade was "an international barony that operates under no one country's rules," was fully borne out.

For President Carter, it was a blow to his aspirations for a second term. With the ineffectiveness of the embargo becoming apparent, Republican candidate Ronald Reagan grasped the growing discontent with the policy and hammered away at the issue, calling for the lifting of the embargo during the 1980 presidential campaign. As the opening year of the decade that had held such bright promise progressed, there was growing disenchantment among the other exporting nations that had promised to support the U.S. embargo. By November 1980, their support for the embargo was almost completely eroded by the signing of a long-term agreement between the United States and the People's Republic of China.

Under that pact, signed in October 1980, China agreed to take from six million to eight million tonnes of U.S. grain in each of the four years of the agreement. A rankling feature of the agreement to the other exporters, particularly Canada, was a clause that appeared to impose a pro-rata sharing of the China market in the event that the Chinese cut back on exports during the term of the agreement.

Article II, subsection 2, of the agreement provided that, if by virtue of exceptional circumstances, China should reduce her total imports:

> Any such reduction of imports of U.S. wheat and corn to the People's Republic of China which shall be applied to imports from the U.S. shall be carried out on a basis no less favourable than to imports from other foreign suppliers.

In Washington, Thomas Saylor, Associate Administrator of the USA Foreign Agricultural Service, in defending the clause, bluntly declared; "The U.S. does not intend to become a residual supplier to that market." [11]

Two weeks later the Canadian Wheat Board announced the sale of 2.1 million tonnes of grain to the Soviet Union, to be shipped in the 1981 calendar year. Added to previous contracts, the new sale brought total Canadian grain exports to the Russians to 5.729 million tonnes, including 4.219 million tonnes wheat and 1.573 million bushels of barley. At the same time, Secretary of State for External Affairs Mark McGuigan announced in Ottawa that the federal government "has decided to move to resume the export of grain to the USSR along normal lines and not to agree to volume restraints on grain exports to that market in 1980-81." [12]

For Canada, the Soviet embargo was over. There only remained settlement of the government's promise to reimburse farmers for any effects occasioned by Canadian participation. In many quarters it had been argued that Canada had only given lip service to co-operating with the American embargo, and had continued to ship grain to the Soviets to the limit imposed by Canada's restricted handling and transportation capacity. When the final settlement of the government promise for reimbursement was announced in mid-June 1981, Argue appeared to confirm that contention. The compensation plan did not consider sales volume, "since the Wheat Board has confirmed that the volume of their exports was not reduced by the embargo," said the Senator. He added that the embargo strengthened Canada's trading position with Russia, since the U.S. had lost the confidence of the Soviet Union. [13]

In spite of those assertions, the government recognized that announcement of the embargo had depressed grain prices when the market reacted negatively to the expectation that the Russians would be denied substantial quantities of grain. Based on that decline, payments totalling $81 million were disbursed by the federal Treasury to Canadian farmers. Western farmers received $68 million and Eastern farmers $13 million. Distribution of the western payments was carried out through the Western Grains Stabilization Administration. [14]

Clearly Canada's grain exports in 1979-80 were to the limit of the logistical restraints to tidewater. With the Canadian Wheat Board hopper cars, and others,

CWB's Peebles Kelly, Treasurer/Comptroller, and Gordon Machej, General Director of Grain Transportation (l to r kneeling), survey the production of 2,000 hopper cars, built in 1979. The CWB make this purchase because farmers were losing export sales as a result of a rail car shortage. The federal government had stopped buying rail cars because of government cutbacks and the railways had refused to invest money in grain transportation due to low rail freight rates for grain.

coming on stream, and increasing surge capacity at the West Coast, a new record for Canadian grain exports was set at 23.5 million tonnes. Achievement of the new export record was aided by milder weather during the winter, allowing the railways easier operating conditions, and by an early start for shipping on the Great Lakes. Even with the negative price impact of the embargo, final realized prices to Western Canadian farmers were also at a record high. With the initial payment set at $4.25 a bushel, and final payment of slightly over $1.09, the final return for No. 1 CWRS wheat rose to slightly over $5.34 a bushel. [15]

Exports of Canadian grain in the 1980-81 crop year, at 23.1 million tonnes, were only a shade under the previous year's record, but the sales value of grains delivered into the Canadian Wheat Board pools reached a new high, it soared to $5.6 billion as compared to the record in 1979-80 of just under $3.9 billion. [16]

That abrupt rise in returns was occasioned by a sudden increase in world prices at the start of the 1980-81 crop year, which unfortunately turned out to be a temporary aberration. World production of grains, including rice, had climbed steadily over the 1970s, rising from 1.314 billion tonnes in 1971 to 1.565 billion tonnes in 1980. In spite of that rise of over 250 million tonnes, fears were being openly expressed that it was not keeping pace with world consumption. World population growth and the demand for more diverse diets in some of the more affluent nations, resulted in more livestock feeding, causing an even more abrupt rise in demand for stocks from the surplus producing nations. In 1976, when the Canadian Wheat Board originally prepared export targets, it estimated that, by 1985, world trade in wheat would reach 85 million tonnes, and in coarse grains 94 million tonnes. By 1980 those estimates were already being exceeded. World trade in wheat hit 93 million tonnes and the coarse grain trade totalled 101 million tonnes.[17]

It was a world far removed from that 45 years previous when the Canadian Wheat Board came into being. In 1935-36, the world's grain trade was almost entirely in wheat at approximately 514.3 million bushels, a scant 14 million tonnes. On the import side Europe, and particularly Great Britain, dominated purchasing. But, while the volume of world grain trade had expanded dramatically by almost 14 times to nearly 200 million tonnes, the number of players had been drastically reduced. The people controlling 75 per cent of the world trade could now fit into one room. In 1980, 42 per cent of the wheat traded in the world went to only five countries. Eighty per cent of the wheat traded on world markets went to 25 countries, and of those 23 had centralized government purchasing agencies.

Within that reduced number of buyers were two key players; the steady, but growing purchases by China's Ceroil food agency and the sometimes erratic, but massive, purchases by the Soviet Union through Exportkhleb. With Asia accounting for 36 per cent of the world wheat trade, China at 13.7 million tonnes was the largest purchaser in 1980-81. The Soviet Union, with purchases of 15 million tonnes, accounted for 16 per cent of the world wheat trade in the same year. Two government agencies accounting for over 30 per cent of the total world wheat purchases. In this expanded, but at the same time concentrated market, a single sales agreement could equal the total world trade of the previous 45 years.

As that buying pattern developed in the fall of 1980, the Rome-based United Nations Food and Agriculture Organization sounded an alarmist note when it declared that a state of global alert for world food security existed, with production failing to keep pace with world population growth. The World Food Council, also based in Rome, noted that food reserves had halved over the past two years, removing the cushion against crop failures.[18] In the United States corn belt, a comparative crop failure had occurred. A searing July heat wave reduced the U.S. corn crop by 33 million tonnes from the previous year. The total coarse grains crop in the United States, including corn, sorghum, and barley dropped by 40 million tonnes.

Combined with that dramatic drop was a poor spring wheat crop in Canada and smaller crops in Argentina and Australia. Thus, despite a record U.S. wheat crop of 64.5 million tonnes, impelled by a pre-embargo 11 per cent increase in winter wheat acreage, prices rose to all-time high levels. Led by a sharp jump in U.S. corn prices, which rose from $112 a tonne in July to as high as $160 a tonne, basis the Gulf, in January 1981, wheat prices followed. Top grade Canadian wheat jumped to an all time high of around $290 a tonne ($7.90 a bushel), basis Thunder Bay, by December 1980. [19]

For the Canadian Wheat Board, sales opportunities were again limited only by the ready availability of supplies. About 4,000 new hopper cars were added to the grain fleet during 1980-81, bringing the total in service to 14,000. Altogether, hopper cars moved 13.7 million tonnes of Prairie grain in 1980-81, or 52.5 per cent of total shipments during that period. The additional storage capacity at Vancouver also proved an asset. The extra grain in store came in handy several times during the crop year when a surge of vessels arrived at West Coast ports, or when rail car arrivals were disrupted. [20]

Prairie farmers were able to deliver all the Board grain they wished in 1980-81, and the farm carry over fell to the lowest level in years with only 1.36 million tonnes left in farmers' bins at the end of the crop year. However, as the crop year progressed, a number of forces were building on the international scene. In January of 1981, mid-way through the crop year, prices began a long slide. By the end of the crop year, the price of No. 1 CWRS, 13.5 per cent, fob St. Lawrence, had dropped to $240 a tonne from the high of around $290; a slump of $1.36 a bushel.

Western farmers had, however, received record total returns on their output. In mid-January, Argue announced that initial payments were being raised and $450 million in adjustment payments were sent out to farmers who had made deliveries to the board. The initial payment on No 1. CWRS wheat rose from $4.25 to $5.35 a bushel, while feed barley initial payments rose 15 cents to $2.85 a bushel. A final payment of 69.7 cents a bushel on the top grade wheat brought total returns to over $6.04 a bushel.

At the start of the 1980-81 crop year, the range under which wheat was sold to domestic Canadian millers — previously set between a four dollar minimum and a five dollar a bushel maximum — was raised to a minimum of five dollars and a maximum of seven dollars. Even with that increase in the maximum, the farmers actually subsidized Canadian consumers by about $4.7 million, since the export price rose above seven dollars in the fall of 1980 and early 1981, before falling back. [21] In effect, the board was obliged to sell into the domestic market below the export price during that period.

Behind the mid-year slump in prices lay shifting patterns in the world's grain trade. Interwoven into that new, and subdued pattern, were the threads of political and economic forces. Hit hardest in that watershed year in the history of the grain trade was the United States.

Throughout the decade of the seventies, as previously stated, global grain trade expanded dramatically, particularly for coarse grains. Then the rise came to a sudden halt. World wheat trade levelled off. It rose to 100.88 million tonnes in 1981-82, then dropped to slightly over 97 million tonnes the next year, but rose again to over 100.6 million tonnes in 1983-84. However, coarse grain trade, having peaked at 108.8 million tonnes in 1980-81, began a dramatic decline, dropping 18.1 million tonnes in three years to 90.7 million tonnes in 1983-84.

It was a trend that precipitated a decade of financial problems, and bankruptcies for both American and Canadian farmers. In the heady period of the 1970s, the massive productive capacity of the United States had been unleashed. The impetus to meet the confidently expected demand of the 1980s could not easily be slowed. In the relative prosperity of the 1970s, American and Canadian farmers invested heavily in machinery, chemicals and fertilizers. Soaring land values were pledged as security against high interest loans to finance the rapidly inflating inputs for all-out production. The necessity of many highly-leveraged farmers to produce to meet financial commitments, acted as a ratchet locking the wheels of production in place.

In August 1982, the American publication *Business Week* summarized the situation: "The law of supply and demand says falling prices should lead to more demand and less supply. But, farmers have turned that axiom upside down."[22] Farming was being driven by fixed costs, rather than by variable ones. As costs rose sharply, putting a tight squeeze on cash flows, farmers responded by planting from fence-post-to-fence-post to stay solvent, making up for operating losses with paper gains from inflated real estate values.

The roots of this disruptive turnaround — which was to lead to all-out export subsidy wars — were complex. In early 1981, there was uncertainty on the U.S. commodity exchanges. Ronald Reagan, having pledged the lifting of the U.S.embargo on grain sales to the Soviet Union, was sworn in as President on January 20, 1981. But, with turmoil breaking out in Poland following imposition of martial law and the prospect of Russian intervention, the decision was delayed. In the background, the Organisation of Economic Co-operation and Development (OECD) in Paris predicted a continuing rise in world grain prices. At the same time, the International Wheat Council in London predicted a rise of at least 100 million bushels in world wheat consumption for the coming year.[23]

When, on Friday, April 24, Reagan finally acted on his campaign pledge to lift the American embargo, there was little reaction from Moscow. The United

States had been relegated as a residual supplier to the Soviet Union in a declining world market. But, in the uncertainty of early 1981, American farmers were still producing full out. The harvested wheat area in the United States, which averaged around 50 million acres in the early seventies, had risen dramatically. In the 1981-82 crop year it had swollen to a record of close to 81 million acres with production of 2.8 billion bushels.[24]

American coarse grains acreage, while remaining relatively constant at around 100 million acres through the seventies, was increasing in yields. Following the drought-reduced crop in 1980, coarse grains were harvested on 107.6 million acres in 1980-81, with a bin-busting production of 248.9 million tonnes (approximately 9.8 billion bushels.)[25] Meanwhile, the dominant U.S. share of the world's coarse grain markets, which stood at 72 per cent in 1979-80, had declined to 64 per cent in the 1980-81 embargo year. It now slid to less than 60 per cent of a drastically curtailed market.

U.S. carry over crops, entering into the 1982-83 crop year, burgeoned to over 64 million tonnes (2.5 billion bushels) of coarse grains and 30.4 million tonnes (1.1 billion bushels) of wheat.[26] At the same time the European Economic Community was aggressively moving subsidized grain into the world markets in increasing volume. Entering the 1980s, the EEC became a net exporter of grains, taking over third position among world wheat exporters with 13.9 per cent of the trade in 1980-81 and 14.5 per cent the next year. Spurred by subsidized price guarantees, wheat production in the EEC jumped from 36.6 million tonnes in 1970-71 to over 55 million tonnes one decade later in 1980-81.[27]

In the EEC, land which had not seen a plough for hundreds of years was brought into production by the subsidy incentives. At the same time in the United States a similar spate of "sod-busting" had been precipitated by the illusory promise of limitless markets in the 1980s. Environmentally sensitive lower quality pasture land was sown to cereal crops. When Washington instituted incentives to reduce acreage in the face of rising carry overs, it was this relatively unproductive land that was idled. Meanwhile, the cash incentives paid out to idle the land were used by farmers to increase production on their higher quality land by use of fertilizers and other technology. Production sometimes increased rather than declined. Thus, the land idling programs became self defeating.

Against this backdrop of buildups in the U.S. and the EEC, the world grain market was stabilizing as the world recession deepened. The energy crisis imposed by a steep rise in oil prices by the OPEC cartel, saw the price of crude rise from $2.20 a barrel in 1973 to $11.50 by 1976, and to a benchmark of $34 in early 1982. The energy-deficient developed nations, whose industries had been fuelled by cheap imports, faced steadily rising inflation as fuel costs soared and their international balance of payments sank into deficit. The impact on the developing and Third World nations was even more severe as they turned to the

World Bank for ever increasing loans at record interest rates in an effort to keep their inflation stricken economies afloat.

Faced with this recessionary and highly competitive atmosphere, the Canadian Wheat Board was still optimistic it could reach its target of of 30 million tonnes of grain exports by 1985. There was major scepticism that production on the Prairies could be expanded to meet that challenge, and in October, 1980, the Advisory Committee of the Wheat Board sponsored a Prairie Production Symposium. Held at the University of Saskatchewan in Saskatoon, the three-day symposium brought together farmers and academics to explore that challenge.

Dr. Leo F. Kristjanson, President of the host university, summed up the mood of the delegates:

> The conference seemed almost unanimous in its view that the farmers would adopt the new technologies, would change their farming practices and, by doing so, would meet the target of a 16 million tonne increase in average production by 1990 if some market and income stability, and guarantees are put in place. A number of speakers suggested some type of Market Assurance Plan for producers. Indeed a guaranteed delivery opportunity for each year's production is probably the most important incentive producers need to make an all-out continuous production effort. A commitment in this regard by the federal government and/or the Canadian Wheat Board is essential. [28]

A suggestion for such a Market Assurance Plan had emerged earlier in a joint statement issued following a meeting of the Advisory Committees to the Canadian Wheat Board and the Canadian Livestock Feed Board. The suggestion came in an effort to reconcile differences on the still troublesome domestic feed grains policy. The Producer Advisory Committee to the Wheat Board now seized upon the MAP proposal and delegated a sub-committee to work out details. The plan basically proposed that the Board would contract with producers to purchase their output of Board grains and pay storage charges on the grain until it was called forward for delivery.

Delegates to the January 1981, meeting of the Western Agricultural Conference gave the concept their basic approval pending finalization of the details. The Advisory Committee then decided to air the MAP proposal at the annual round of farmer meetings sponsored by the Canadian Wheat Board in each of the 11 Advisory Committee electoral districts from mid-February into March.

Proponents of the plan argued that MAP would encourage increased production by providing income assurance in two ways: first, by guaranteeing farmers payment on any grain committed for delivery to the Board and carried over on their farms at the end of the crop year; secondly, by providing farmers with storage payments on carried-over grain until its delivery was called for at a later date. The plan, they said, would improve utilization of the expanding grain transportation facilities, and would also incorporate a factor in the Wheat Board's delivery quota system to give farmers with higher yields improved delivery opportunities. It would also eliminate the need for the cash advance program.

Even before details of the proposal were presented for discussion at the farmer advisory meetings, there was an outburst of condemnation from supporters of the open market concept on the Prairies. Alberta's Agriculture Minister Dallas Schmidt declared that his province would pull out of the Canadian Wheat Board jurisdiction if the plan were adopted. Both he and Manitoba's Agriculture Minister Jim Downey charged that the federal government was imposing the MAP proposal without consulting the provinces.[29]

Debate at the regional advisory meetings was heated, particularly in Alberta where there was heavy opposition to the plan. At a meeting held in Miami, Manitoba, Esmond Jarvis assured some 600 farmers that MAP was not being pushed from Ottawa, or from the Wheat Board, "It's up to the producer committee and you."[30]

A number of the elected Committee members were dismayed that the intent behind the MAP proposal had been misconstrued in many quarters, and that it had acted as a "lightning rod" to rally anti-Board forces behind a vituperative campaign across the Prairies. At a meeting of the Advisory Committee on March 31, 1981, there was unanimous agreement that the plan would be shelved. A press release was drawn up:

> The Advisory Committee to the Canadian Wheat Board announced today that it will not proceed with further development of a Market Assurance Plan for Western farmers until there is a clear indication of widespread support for the proposal from grain farmers and farm organizations.

At a news conference, Roy Atkinson, Chairman of the Advisory Committee, declared the chief architects of the defeat of the MAP proposal to be "open market promoters like Agriculture Ministers Dallas Schmidt of Alberta and Jim Downey of Manitoba."[31] At the April 1981 annual meeting of the Canada Grains Council, Glen Flaten, President of the Canadian Federation of Agriculture, and Dobson Lea, Vice-Chairman of the Council, said the concept should be reviewed as part of larger production questions. Senator Argue and federal Agriculture Minister Eugene Whelan also indicated support for further discussion of the MAP proposal.[32] However, it has remained in limbo.

The Canadian Wheat Board meanwhile continued to press toward the export goals in the increasingly competitive market. In April, the Board announced the signing of long-term contracts with three shipping companies to ensure additional lake freight would be available to move Board grain through the Great Lakes and St. Lawrence Seaway over the next several years. Under terms of the contract, the three companies were able to each acquire one new lake vessel to expand export capacity through the Great Lakes.

The next month the Wheat Board announced signing of the largest single long-term agreement for the sale of wheat and feed grains in its history. The agreement, between the Board and Exportkhleb, under which the Russians agreed to take 25 million tonnes of wheat and feed grains over a five-year period, followed an exchange of letters in Ottawa on a new Canada-Soviet trade pact.

Late in the 1980-81 crop year, there were further signs that the logistical restraint on Canada's grain exports might be loosened. CP Rail filed an application with the Canadian Transport Commission to undertake the largest rail building project since the transcontinental railway was completed almost 100 years previous. The $500 million project involved the driving of two tunnels with a total length of about 10 miles, building 11 bridges and laying 21 miles of new main line track through the Rogers Pass area of the Selkirk Mountains in British Columbia. The four-year project was designed to eliminate the most restrictive bottleneck on the main line between Calgary and Vancouver. CP President W.W. Stinson hinged the start of the massive project on a solution of the Crow Rate controversy. He declared that CP would "only proceed with the project if a way can be found for the railway to be compensated for multi-million-dollar losses it incurs moving export grain traffic."[33]

Entering the 1981-82 crop year, generally poor economic conditions around the world, combined with a heavy buildup of grain stocks in the United States, began to weigh heavily on prices. The slide in grain prices, that began in the previous crop year, continued throughout the year. The price of No. 1 CWRS 13 ½ per cent, fob St. Lawrence, fell from about $248 a tonne to $212 a tonne when the Board pools were closed at the end of October 1982.[34] High interest rates restricted forward purchases by importers, and there were strong concerns over the ability of some countries, especially those with large foreign debts, to pay for their grain purchases.

With a record 1981 crop in prospect on the Prairies, the need for an aggressive sales effort by the Canadian Wheat Board became apparent. In late September, an export target of 26 million tonnes was announced. Once again there was scepticism that level could be sold or moved. However, by the end of the crop year, 27 million tonnes of grains and oilseeds had been exported.

Ironically, the impact of the recession on the domestic scene aided in the achievement of that new record. The general downturn in the economy reduced rail shipments of other commodities and more railway-owned cars and main line capacity were available for grain.

The importance of the sales and transport success were summarized in the annual report of the Board:

> Fortunately, the large increase in exports did partly offset a sharp decline in prices from the previous year. The total value of wheat board sales for the year was $5.1 billion compared to 5.6 billion in 1980-81. Had sales volume not increased, the farm income picture in Western Canada would have been very bleak. [35]

In spite of the stagnating world markets in the following year, the Board's push toward its mid-1980 export target continued. At the close of the 1981-82 crop year, total Canadian grain and oilseed exports had surged close to the 1985 target at 29.4 million tonnes. The new record was achieved in an increasingly acrimonious subsidization battle between the U.S. and the EEC, and bitter competition for markets. Prices slipped even further, averaging around $205 a tonne, basis Thunder Bay for top grade wheat throughout the crop year. However, with the increased exports, net returns to Western farmers, basis in store Thunder Bay or Vancouver, from the sales of Board grains was $5.3 billion, or nine per cent above the previous year. [36]

The export target of 30 million tonnes was surpassed the next year, one year ahead of schedule. A total of 30.7 million tonnes of Canadian grain and oilseeds went to world markets in 1983-84, representing an increase of 50 per cent in just five years. The success of the export record was tempered however by disappointing grain prices in a highly competitive world market.

As a result of the aggressive sales drive by the Board, carry over stocks in Western Canada dropped sharply during the 1983-84 crop year. Total carry over fell from 16.5 million tonnes at July 31, 1983, to only 12.1 million tonnes by July 31, 1984. On-farm stocks of all grains and oilseeds fell by over three million tonnes to a near record low of 3.2 million tonnes. [37] As the Canadian Wheat Board moved toward its fiftieth anniversary year, maintenance of the export drive was now totally dependent on continued and expanding production.

Then, in 1984, drought struck the Western plains. Prairie grain production dropped drastically to 35.6 million tonnes. With about 15 million tonnes required for domestic consumption, 20.65 million tonnes were left for export purposes. Total exports of Western grains slumped back to 23 million tonnes in 1984-85. Even with these curtailed exports, the carry over of grain into the

1985-86 crop year was again reduced. At an estimated 11 million tonnes, it was the lowest since the 1951-52 crop year.

Beset by inflationary input costs, Western Canadian farmers found themselves in the worst possible scenario; reduced volume and deflated prices. Major crop setbacks in Canada, Australia or Argentina no longer exerted any perceptible market influence. Carry overs in those three major exporting countries represented a mere 16 per cent of world stocks entering into the 1985-86 crop year, but prices remained stagnant.[38]

Overhanging the world market were massive mountains of grain in the United States and the European Economic Community. The Americans held the lion's share at 88 million tonnes — almost 66 per cent of the world carry over. It consisted of 39 million tonnes of wheat and 49 million tonnes of coarse grains. At 24.3 million tonnes, the ten member states of the EEC held approximately 18 per cent of the world stocks. Both the United States and the EEC were projecting bumper crops in 1985 assuring a further buildup in world stocks. Behind this ominous and destabilizing stockpile was that multi-billion subsidy and credit war that had escalated to new heights in 1982.

As the growing surplus in the EEC captured an increasing share of the world grain market by means of high export subsidies, and U.S. stocks climbed following the ill-fated 1980 embargo on sales to the Soviet Union, the Americans and Europeans locked horns. High support prices to farmers in the EEC propelled wheat production close to 60 million tonnes in 1982-83 and, aided by increasing export subsidies, the EEC increased its share of the world market to 14.5 per cent. Meanwhile, the United States, with an all-time record crop of 75.25 million tonnes of wheat, saw its share of the market drop to 41.2 per cent from 48.4 per cent the previous year.

Early in April 1982, Richard Lyng, U.S. Deputy Secretary of Agriculture, warned in Paris that the U.S. and EEC were on a collision course and that increased subsidized U.S. exports were possible if American farmers continued to lose markets to the Europeans. Later that same month, at an Ottawa meeting of the exporting nations, called by Senator Argue to explore "ideas that may assist in adopting policies that would tend to improve world grain prices," open warfare broke out. While the meeting was behind closed doors, there was an exchange of recriminations and threats in statements to the press outside the committee rooms.

Sir Leslie Price, Chairman of the Australian Wheat Board, issued a statement noting increased concern over the aggressive approach by the U.S. on wheat exports. U.S. spokesman Donald Novotny declared that "the central marketing boards (of other countries) put us at a disadvantage," and warned that the U.S. was prepared to take new actions, including the possible use of export subsidies, if other nations continued to increase production and exports. Claude Villain, head of the EEC Commission on Marketing, declared that the EEC export sub-sidies were authorized under the General Agreement on Tariffs and Trade (GATT), and they were not prepared to end them.[39]

The bitter rhetoric continued at a European grain trade conference held in Zurich, Switzerland, in early June 1982. Allan Tracy, U.S. Deputy Under-Secretary of Agriculture, vowed that Washington would step up its attack against the EEC grain export subsidies. Villain responded by telling the confer-ence that the Americans "were living in cloud-cuckoo land if they thought the EEC was going to withdraw from the market."[40]

The American retaliation was not long in coming. In mid-October, 1982, President Reagan announced a $1.5 billion "Blended Credit" Program. Under it, Washington was to provide $400 million in direct credit guarantees for agri-cultural exports in each of the three years of the program. These direct credit guarantees would be "blended" with $100 million in interest-free credit each year. This subsidization of interest provided a discount of about 20 per cent in rates. In early January, 1983, a further $250 million in direct interest-free cred-it was authorized to expand the program. Secretary of Agriculture John Block said the extra funds would be blended with at least one billion dollars in Commodity Credit Corporation export credit guarantees to produce interest rates below commercial levels.

An illustration of the use of subsidization and the Blended Credit Program was given on January 17, 1983, in an agreement signed in Cairo. Under the agreement, the Americans delivered one million tonnes of flour at $155 a tonne, bagged, freight paid and landed on the dock in Egypt, a wheat to flour equiva-lent of $3.08 U.S. a bushel. The price for similar flour at the mill in Kansas was quoted at around $200 a tonne. Beside that deep discount, the Egyptians were given blended credit terms, equating approximately eight per cent interest over a three-year period.[41] There were howls of outrage and threats of retaliation from the EEC, particularly from the French who considered Egypt to be their tradi-tional market.

In this cut-throat atmosphere, not even a crop disaster in Australia served to bolster prices. A burning drought cut Australia's wheat production in 1982 to 8.9 million tonnes. It was the lowest level in 10 years and consideration was given to importing feed wheat from Canada at one point.

The 1982 crop in Western Canada also posed problems for the Canadian Wheat Board. Many areas of the Prairies experienced heavy frost in the last week of August. As a result 21 per cent of the wheat crop failed to meet the visual specifications of the top three grades. Analysis by the Canadian Grain Commission indicated the frost-damaged wheat still had a number of desirable milling and baking characteristics, and a special sales effort was launched in order to maximize returns for Western farmers.

Under the plan, worked out by the Board's sales and market development staff, the Canadian Grain Commission made extensive laboratory tests of milling and baking quality and provided advice to the Board to help in assessing marketability in different areas of the world. Under strict monitoring, the frost-damaged wheat was identified and binned in terminals as "Wheat — Special Bin." Samples, along with letters describing the Special Bin wheat, were sent to 81 prospective customers in Canada and overseas. Commissioners and Board sales staff travelled to 16 countries on trade missions to discuss the wheat with buyers and millers. Accredited export agents of the Board in the private trade also worked closely with the Board in developing markets for the Special Bin wheat and in making significant sales.

As a result of that unique program, the entire crop of frost-damaged wheat delivered by growers had been sold by the end of the crop year. Sales of over 2.5 million tonnes, involving 21 countries were made during 1982-83. [42]

With U.S. grain carry over climbing steadily from 40 per cent of the world total in 1980-81 to 60 per cent at the close of the 1982-83 crop year, the Reagan Administration announced a new crop reduction plan. Known as PIK (payment-in-kind) the program offered American farmers government-held commodities in return for idling their land. Farmers were allowed to sign up to divert 10 to 30 per cent of their base crop acreage, or to bid to divert their whole crop base. Participating wheat farmers received in return 95 per cent of the normal yield on the diverted land from government held stocks. Producers of other commodities received 80 per cent of normal yields.

Since the massive fall planted U.S. winter wheat crop was already in the ground, PIK had little impact on wheat production, but the program did have an impact on U.S. corn and soybean production. However, a severe drought in the U.S. corn belt during a critical stage of development made an even greater contribution to reduced output of those crops. American corn production was cut almost in half to 4.2 billion bushels. Coarse grain prices rose as a result, bringing some strength to wheat which realized an increase in demand for livestock feeding.

The price increase was short-lived. With PIK behind them, American farmers resumed all-out production in 1984. U.S. corn production climbed back to 7.65 billion bushels and the American coarse grain crop climbed to 9.3 billion bushels. In the face of rebuilding U.S. stocks, world prices slid back once more.

Appearing before the House of Commons Standing Committee on Transport on August 18, 1983, Esmond Jarvis outlined the problems facing the Canadian Wheat Board on world markets:

> Maintaining Canada's share of the export grain market is
> not going to be easy. Subsidized competition always presents

a severe problem for our Western producers. Exporters, such as the USA and EEC, provide immense funding to their grain producers, directly through public expenditures or indirectly through price mechanisms. We could spend days debating which of those two has the higher subsidies. But there is no doubt that Canada, even with the Crow Rate and the cash advance programs, is far behind that of our two major competitors.

Figures presented by the Board for the 1982-83 crop year, indicated a net subsidy of roughly two dollars a bushel in the EEC and $1.12 a bushel to wheat producers in the United States. The U.S. figures included all direct payments to farmers, PIK payments, farmer owned reserve storage and interest payments, inland waterways subsidies, blended credit subsidies and the Egyptian flour deal. In comparison to this, subsidies to Western Canadian farmers, including federal payments into the Western Grain Stabilization Fund, interest on advance payments and the Crow Rate transportation subsidy, were shown at 37 cents a bushel.

A measure of the government supported competition faced by the Canadian Wheat Board was given in a Reuters despatch from Washington:

> U.S. agricultural spending on domestic price support programs soared to a record $19 billion in the 1983 fiscal year that ended September 30, up from just $4 billion when Reagan took office.
>
> The domestic farm price support budget in the current year is expected to drop to $6 billion or $7 billion, but that does not include the cost of about $11 billion in government-owned commodities given to farmers under the payment-in-kind (PIK) program, the officials said. [43]

In the European Community, the budget allocated $14 billion for farm subsidies in 1983 as surplus food stocks built up and world commodity prices slumped. The farm subsidy spending amounted to two-thirds of the total Common Market budget. [44]

Almost 50 years before, in the depths of the Great Depression, John I. McFarland, the first Chief Commissioner of the Canadian Wheat Board, echoed a strangely similar world as he defended his stabilization efforts on behalf of the Western Canadian farmers:

> The only effect of a free and open market in Winnipeg, would be elimination of Canadian farmers, while the pro-

duction efforts of farmers in other countries would continue unabated because of subsidies, high tariff protection, quotas, milling restrictions, currency inflation, etc. I therefore again affirm there can be no such thing as a world price in a world where production is controlled by subsidies and not by price.[45]

McFarland's strategy had been to accumulate wheat in the federal government's stabilization account, effectively removing it from the world market. That device was effective to an extent because Canada was then the largest single player in an infinitely more limited world market. In the war of the national Treasuries of the 1980s, the Canadian Wheat Board had only one alternative. That was to sell aggressively by meeting the subsidized prices in the hope that volume would deflect the impact on the Western Canadian grain economy of lower prices.

Footnotes Chapter Nine

1. *The Manitoba Co-operator*, November 15, 1979, p. 17.
2. *Ibid*, December 6, 1979, p. 6.
3. *Ibid*, p. 6.
4. *Ibid*, November 29, 1979, p. 6.
5. *Ibid*, December 20, 1979, p. 11.
6. *Ibid*, p. 3.
7. *Report of the Canadian Wheat Board, Crop Year 1979-80*, p. 3.
8. *Ibid*, p. 13.
9. *Ibid*, p. 3.
10. *Ibid*, p. 14.
11. *The Manitoba Co-operator*, November 20, 1980, p. 4.
12. *Ibid*, December 4, 1980, p. 1.
13. *Ibid*, June 25, 1981, p. 10.
14. *Ibid*, p. 1.
15. *Report of the Canadian Wheat Board, Crop Year 1979-80*, p.35.
16. *Ibid*, Crop Year 1980-81, p. 14.
17. *Ibid*, p. 5.
18. *The Manitoba Co-operator*, December 4, 1980, p. 8.
19. Report of the Canadian Wheat Board, Crop Year 1980-81, p. 15.
20. *Ibid*, p. 19.
21. *Ibid*, p. 17.
22. *The Manitoba Co-operator*, September 9, 1982, p.4.
23. *Ibid*, February 5, 1981, p. 1.
24. USDA Foreign Agriculture Circular, Cereal Grains, April 26, 1982, p. 115.
25. *Ibid*.
26. *Ibid*.
27. *Report of the Canadian Wheat Board, Crop Year 1983-84*, p. 19.

28. Dr. L.F. Kristjanson, *Some Elements of an Action Program to Increase Grain Production in Western Canada*, pp. 9, 10.

29. *The Manitoba Co-operator*, February 12, 1981, p. 1.

30. *Ibid*, February 19, 1981, p. 12.

31. *Ibid*, April 2, 1981, p. 1.

32. *Ibid*, April 16, 1981, p. 1.

33. *Ibid*, July 2, 1981, p. 1.

34. *Report of the Canadian Wheat Board, Crop Year 1981-82,* p. 14.

35. *Ibid*, p. 13.

36. *Ibid*, Crop Year 1982-83, p. 14.

37. *Ibid*, Crop Year 1983-84, p. 20.

38. Grain Matters, Canadian Wheat Board, Sept./Oct. 1985, p. 5.

39. *The Manitoba Co-operator*, April 29, 1982, pp. 1, 13.

40. *Ibid*, June 17, 1982, p. 9.

41. *Ibid*, March 10, 1983, p. 4.

42. *Report of the Canadian Wheat Board, Crop Year 1982-83,* p. 29.

43. *The Manitoba Co-operator*, December 15, 1983, p. 9.

44. *Ibid*, March 10, 1983, p. 1.

45. Address by John I McFarland, Winnipeg Canadian Club, April 11, 1935, p. 10.

CHAPTER 10

HALF A CENTURY

He that will not apply new remedies must expect new evils; for time is the greatest innovator. — Francis Bacon

On July 7, 1985, the Canadian Wheat Board celebrated half a century as the principal seller of Canadian grain. As the Board entered upon its 50th year of marketing at the close of the month, it had compiled an impressive record of contribution to the national economy. Over the previous 49 years, sales into export and domestic markets totalled over 727.6 million tonnes of wheat, barley and oats. From those sales over $72 billion ($72,216,961,494)[1] had poured from around the world into Western Canada.

As the chosen instrument of the federal government to meet intense, and more often than not subsidized, competition in a volatile world market, that impressive record had been achieved at what was probably the lowest drain on public coffers than in any other major grain exporting nation. Sales of wheat, as the major export grain, amounted to 590,130,486 tonnes (almost 21 billion bushels) for a return of over $60 billion ($60,590,409,368). For that huge input into the Canadian economy, the federal Treasury was called upon only once, after the Canadian Wheat Board assumed monopoly control of wheat sales in 1943, to make up a deficit in the wheat pool.

Previous to 1943, deficits were almost a foregone conclusion since, under a dual marketing system, farmers delivered to the board only when the guaranteed initial payment was above the open market alternative.

In the 1968-69 crop year the Canadian government, in a vain attempt to bolster prices and shore up the faltering International Grains Arrangement, held the price line. The result was a massive carry over that strained Canada's storage capacity to the limit, and resulted in a deficit of $39,787,979 in the Canadian Wheat Board pool for wheat.

By comparison to the continuing multi-billion dollar farm support programs in other major exporting countries, particularly the United States and those of

The CWB regularly offers tours of its head office in Winnipeg. In the spring of 1988, King Carl Gustaf XVI and Queen Sylvia visited the CWB. Shown here talking to Chief Commissioner Esmond Jarvis (left).

the European Economic Community, that deficit must be viewed as infinitesimal. It amounted to only six per cent of the $668,625,682 in wheat sales in the crop year in which it was paid out, and less than seven one-hundredths of one per cent (0.0697 per cent) of total wheat sales since 1935 when the Wheat Board came into being.

Deficits in the Canadian Wheat Board's barley pool, at $30,115,034 over the years, were higher on a percentage basis, but still amounted to only three-tenths of one per cent on sales totalling over $10.2 billion ($10,213,828,350). Once again those deficits were consciously inspired by the federal government in an effort to diversify Western Canadian crop production and break into the expanding world feed grains market in the late 1960s and early 1970s. In order to do so, initial prices for barley were set at a premium to encourage production.

Taken together with several small deficits in the oats pool over the first half century, Canadians had benefitted by that immense $72 billion plus contribution to the nation's balance of payments at a cost to the national Treasury of only approximately one-tenth of one per cent of total sales. The remainder of the costs of the operation of the Canadian Wheat Board — 99.9 per cent — were borne by the farmers of Western Canada, through deductions on their sales. It is an enviable record matched by few, if any, of the other grain exporting nations.

It is true that Western Canadian farmers have benefitted from time to time from other subsidies such as federal payments into the Western Grain Stabilization Fund, interest on advance payments and the Crow's Nest Rate transportation subsidy. However, the Canadian Wheat Board cannot, as the record shows, be considered as a subsidized contender on the world grain markets as claimed in the continuing rhetoric from the United States.

That enviable record was achieved in an erratic world of boom and bust during which the Board's system was progressively adapted to meet changing circumstances. It will be for future historians to record the outcome of the challenges faced by the Board in the mid-80s and onwards. That challenge came in a world vastly changed, but in some ways strangely reminiscent of that in which the Canadian Wheat Board began its first faltering and uncertain steps fifty years earlier.

Once again the world economy was gripped in a recession, matched only by the bitter Depression of the 1930s, which precipitated the birth of the Board. Across the Prairies many areas were again facing drought and grasshopper infestations for the second consecutive year. Inflated input costs, low commodity prices, and high interest rates reaching into the 18 to 20 per cent range, had intensified the cost-price squeeze on many farmers. Particularly hard hit were those who had entered farming in the late 1970s when land prices soared in relatively buoyant markets. Now, land prices, as the principal equity base for financing, were declining and farm bankruptcies reached levels not seen since the "dirty thirties."

On the international scene, the previously noted price-supported mountains of grain in the United States and the EEC overhung the market exerting increased downward pressure on prices. The dramatic surge in the world's wheat and feed grains markets, that erupted in the late seventies and early eighties, had levelled off despite a continuing climb in world population.

Sadly, the lesson, outlined five decades earlier by John I. McFarland, that cut-throat selling would not expand demand in a world bent on food self-sufficiency

In 1987, the CWB presented COFCO, China's importing agency, with an advertisement and grain art acknowledging their 35th anniversary of association in the grain trade. Shown from left to right are: Back Row - E. Suen (CWB), A. Man (CWB), Wang Jiongbao (COFCO), F. Hetland (CWB), Yuan Zianghong (COFCO), L. Kristjanson (CWB), Lian Yongang (COFCO). Front Row - Li Fyu (COFCO), W. Smith (CWB), Cao Wantong (COFCO), E. Jarvis (CWB).

at any cost, and where price consequently was not a regulator of production, had yet to be learned by a number of the major exporters. Referring to the disastrous price decline of 1932, when Canada's top grade of wheat dropped to a low of 38 ½ cents a bushel on the Winnipeg Grain Exchange, McFarland noted:

> The prices in that crop year were the lowest in 400 years and more, and yet the Stanford University Statistical Service shows in that year of record low prices, world's consumption was less than in either of the two preceding years, and only a few million bushels more than that of last year. [2]

Fifty years after that observation, Argentina, with her economy in tatters, explosive inflation rampant, and lacking ability to extend credit terms which had evolved into a major feature of the world's grain trade, was selling at whatever price would move the crops. It was a historic pattern which saw Argentina, having no storage facilities of consequence, dumping wheat on foreign markets shortly after harvest. In September 1985, the USDA reported an Argentine sale of 75,000 tonnes of wheat to Lebanon at $117.85 U.S. a tonne ($3.21 U.S., or $4.48 Canadian, a bushel) landed in Lebanon. [3]

In Winnipeg, the Canadian Wheat Board was keeping an anxious eye on Washington, where a new five-year farm policy bill was making its tortuous way through the legislative process. The Wheat Board's Report to Producers on the 1983-84 crop year warned:

> As you receive this report, proposals for a new U.S. Farm Bill will be under intense debate. The main thrust will be toward lower export prices, based on the premise that sales of U.S. farm products, and U.S. market share, will then be increased substantially. However, Canada and other competing countries will have no choice but to follow suit, leaving market prices lower and market shares unchanged. [4]

American farm state representatives in the Congress, obsessed by a steadily growing share of the world market falling to the European Community, engaged in a long, rancorous and divisive debate with the federal Administration, by vowing to cut agricultural spending by reducing price supports unless strong action was taken. For the 1985-86 crop year, the USDA forecast that American exports of wheat would drop to their lowest level in 10 years at 27.2 million tonnes, or 33.5 per cent of the world trade, compared to over 50 per cent in the late 1970s and early 1980s. At the same time the EEC's share of world trade was forecast to rise to 18.2 per cent. The November 1985 Foreign Agricultural Service Circular of the USDA commented:

> In spite of recent setbacks in world demand, the record shows sustained growth in the EC market share of world trade and a closely corresponding decline in U.S. export market share. This apparent cause-effect relationship is particularly important when viewed against the fact that the Community uses export subsidies which at times are as high as $60-$70 per ton and had not acted directly to curtail surplus production, whereas the United States has sought to avoid export subsidies and provides income and loan rate protection only to producers who cut back production.

Throughout the summer and fall of 1985, American legislators struggled to complete the new Farm Bill with the main thrust being aimed at reducing the loan rate to offset the strong U.S. dollar which had risen to a substantial premium over other world currencies. By November, American wheat exports were lagging 50 per cent below the previous year at 15 million tonnes, compared to 31 million tonnes a year earlier, and the farm price for wheat had fallen below the $3.30 a bushel loan level to $2.95 a bushel. Under these circumstances, American farmers were increasingly placing their crops under loan and forfeiting wheat to the Commodity Credit Corporation.

Noting the growing carry over in the United States, Jarvis expressed the Canadian Wheat Board's concern at the 1985 Saskatchewan Agriculture Conference in Saskatoon:

> Current trends in world markets depend not so much on the presence and size of unsold grain mountains in the United States and the European Economic Community, but on people's reaction to them. I don't know exactly how high a 38 million tonne pile of wheat is, but I am afraid it may be high enough to block out the light of clear thinking from some American policy makers.[5]

Two days after Christmas 1985, Washington lowered the boom. The fears of the Board were realized. President Reagan signed into law a new Farm Bill which was expected to cost the U.S. treasury $52 billion over the following three years. The loan rate, which effectively set a floor price on which U.S. grain traded on world markets, was initially reduced to three dollars a bushel for 1986 ($4.19 Canadian). However, under competitive circumstances, Secretary of Agriculture John Block was empowered to reduce the loan rate in 10 per cent increments to as low as $2.40 a bushel ($3.35 Canadian).

To protect American farmers against the expected drop in world prices, the support target price to U.S. farmers was retained at $4.38 a bushel ($6.12 Canadian). In order to obtain this guaranteed price, American farmers were obliged to reduce their wheat acreage by 25 per cent. In addition, the USDA was required to offer farmers who had already planted the 1986 winter wheat crop, a 10 per cent paid diversion at two dollars a bushel, bringing the maximum possible wheat acreage reduction in 1986 to 35 per cent.[6]

To back up this export-oriented pricing action, the Reagan Administration approved continuation of the two billion dollar export Payment-in-Kind bonus programs, which offered commodity stocks to exporters as a subsidy to make U.S. grains more competitive on world markets. Additionally, the legislation launched a new program of three to five-year export credit guarantees under which at least $500 million in new guarantees must be allocated each fiscal year. On top of that, the existing one to three-year GSM-102 export credit guarantee was to be mandatorily funded by $5 billion annually.

In Winnipeg, the Canadian Wheat Board was prepared to weather the gathering storm. In contrast to its earliest conception, the Board was no longer an emergency instrument of price stabilization. Nor, as in the late sixties, was it constrained by the political fiat of attempting to bolster world prices in support of a faltering International Grains Agreement. In that latter period the cost had been high, with Canada holding a 27 million tonne carry over of wheat, a proportionately worse condition than that faced by the United States in the mid-eighties. On the transportation and handling scene, the restrictive bottlenecks of years of neglect were rapidly being rectified.

Jim Leibfried, who retired on January 31, 1985, at the close of the 50th anniversary year, encapsulated the new mood as he reviewed the latter stages of his 21 years with the Board — 10 of them as a Commissioner: "It's been a hell of a lot more fun being on an offensive team rather than on a defensive one."

The necessity of an aggressive stance was underlined by the realization that Western Canadian grain farmers, in relation to their more highly subsidized European and American counterparts, were forced to export to survive. Making that point, Esmond Jarvis noted:

> This may seem self-evident, but I mention it because this might not be true in other countries. For instance, consider what would happen if the export market for American grain disappeared tomorrow. This would no doubt be a terrible blow, but I suggest that grain farming would survive without fundamental changes. This is because about 50 per cent of wheat and 75 per cent of feed grains go to the domestic market. The same is true of the EEC.
>
> In Canada, with our relatively small population, total loss of the export market would have very severe repercussions. There would be a market for only about one-third of the recent annual Prairie production. I believe that Canada produces more grain surplus to per capita domestic requirements than any other country in the world…Therefore, our perspective as your marketing agency is one in which we assume we must live or die with the export market. [7]

Clearly Canada could not, and would not, give up its established place in the face of intensifying competition. A measure of the Board's ability to meet that competition was given by Ronald G. Fraase, Vice-President of U.S. Wheat Associates, in a despatch from Rotterdam. He reported that "aggressive pricing practices, along with continued cleanliness of grain has yielded success for the Canadian effort as reflected in the large share of the European market captured in the last few years." Fraase noted that the Canadian Wheat Board had increased its market share in the EEC from 43 per cent in 1981-82 to 57 per cent in 1982-83 and 1983-84. He commented:

> While Canada has been aggressively supplying the quality needed by the buyer, developing innovative arrangements to

reduce shipping costs, aggressively pricing its product, and extending favourable credit where useful, the U.S. has ignored or antagonized the European market...The aggressive Canadian effort has been responsive to the needs of the buyers. [8]

Viewing the Canadian success, Mel Maier, Administrator of the North Dakota Wheat Commission, called on American farmers to upgrade the quality of their crops: "We are rapidly approaching the point when too high a portion of the total acreage planted to spring wheat is seeded with varieties of less than desirable or unacceptable milling and baking performance." [9]

Introduction of some of those same American varieties into Western Canada caused problems for the Canadian Wheat Board. Some western farmers, seeking higher-yielding varieties to offset inflating input costs, imported seed for the unlicensed, lower quality, semi-dwarf wheats which were visually indistinguishable from Canada's traditional high-protein Western Red Spring wheats. Fearing that the inferior varieties might be mixed with top-grade bread wheats, the Board warned growers against their production and the Canadian Grain Commission was forced to take rigorous inspection measures to safeguard Canada's reputation for quality.

Concerned about the proliferation of the American varieties, Jarvis told the 1985 annual meeting of Palliser Wheat Growers in Winnipeg that Canada had an effective market development tool that her competitors did not have:

Shipments of our wheat, regardless of class, are cleaner and more consistent from cargo to cargo than those of our competitors. The best market development producers can do is to grow the products their customers want. [10]

To offset the threat, the Board accelerated development and promotion of a higher yielding, medium quality wheat variety designated as HY 320, which was visually distinguishable from the higher quality bread wheats. A test marketing program, conducted jointly by the Wheat Board and the Canadian Grain Commission, was announced in February 1983, to evaluate the quality and market acceptability of HY 320. Developed at Agriculture Canada's Swift Current Research Station in Saskatchewan, the new variety was grown on 159,000 acres according to 1984 Wheat Board contract records. Preliminary tests, using the supplies grown under contract the previous year, were carried out in the Canadian Grain Commission's Grain Research Laboratory to evaluate milling quality and determine its dough strength, loaf volume and other baking qualities.

As a second stage, HY 320 was tested under commercial milling and baking conditions at a number of Canadian mills, bakeries and processing plants.

Robert Boyson, a local Winnipeg artist, uses a variety of grains and oilseeds to create rural scenes. This picture hangs in the CWB head office. His work has also been given by the CWB to foreign customers.

Finally, commercial-sized milling and baking tests, using container shipments of 90 to 300 tonnes, were carried out in Mexico, Brazil, Egypt and Malaysia. Laboratory tests on smaller samples were also carried out in Singapore, Sri Lanka, Indonesia, Poland, Japan, India and the United Kingdom.

The test results indicated that HY 320 could be acceptable in most countries where flat breads, French (hearth) breads, noodles and steamed breads are consumed. Results of the 1984 evaluation program showed that, on dry land, HY 320 outyielded Hard Red Spring varieties by an average of 26.4 per cent. [11] In January 1985, the new variety was licensed by Agriculture Canada, and the Canadian Wheat Board had another weapon in its arsenal to compete in countries where the specialized breads were consumed and where buyers were price-conscious. At the same time, acceptance of HY 320 by farmers promised to remove the threat posed by the unlicensed American varieties.

Also, in its anniversary year, the Wheat Board's freedom to call forward varieties of grain to meet the sales demand, and to meet the increasingly competitive pricing, was enhanced by amendments to the *Prairie Grains Advance Payments Act* and the *Western Grain Price Stabilization Act*. The amendments further relieved the Board of the implied responsibility to act as an instrument of price support. In late April 1984, Senator Argue announced Cabinet approval for doubling the interest-free cash advances to farmers on farm-stored grain pending delivery to the Board. Under the amendments passed by Parliament and in effect at the start of the 1984-85 crop year, the maximum advance to an individual farmer was increased from $15,000 to $30,000, while two partners could draw $60,000 in advances and three or more partners up to $90,000. At the same time, the provision requiring that spousal partnerships be treated as individuals was revoked.

Amendments to the voluntary Western Grain Stabilization Program, in which 77 per cent of Western farmers were enrolled, had raised the limits for farmers' contributions. After paying out $115 million for 1977 and $223 million for 1978, disbursements from the fund, jointly financed by participating farmers and the government, had lagged. Payouts from the fund were triggered when the net cash flow from grain sales fell below that of the previous five years. However, despite declining world prices and a tightening cost-price squeeze on hard-pressed Prairie farmers, record sales by the Canadian Wheat Board made up in volume what was lost from cash flow in per bushel value. Thus, by mid-1984, over $900 million had built up in the fund with no further payments having been triggered.

In July 1984, Parliament amended the Act by changing the calculation on a payout from the calendar year to the crop year. At the same time, the payout trigger was made more sensitive to declining farm incomes in calculating the cash flow on the margin between the money received for grain and total production costs. The result was an interim payment from the Stabilization Fund in April 1985. Cheques totalling $450 million were sent out to 131,900 Western farmers by the Western Grains Stabilization Administration in Winnipeg. A further payment of some $100 million was mailed in late 1985.

Improvements to the *Canada Crop Insurance Act* of 1959, under which contributions and loans out of the federal Consolidated Revenue Fund were made to the provinces for the operation of provincial crop insurance programs, provided a further source of stabilization by minimizing fluctuations resulting from crop production losses due to unavoidable natural hazards.

Refinements in the Block Shipping System were also instituted at the start of the 1984-85 crop year, adding new efficiencies to the Board's administration of the grain gathering complex. The western rail network was divided into 196 "train runs," which were simply a railway line connecting a number of delivery points. Under the previous system, elevator companies had been able to request cars at points along any one of three or four train runs within each shipping block. The Board now announced delivery quotas by train runs, rather than block, and allocated cars to the elevator companies on the same basis. The grain companies were free to distribute rail cars along the train run as they saw fit.

Modernization of the elevator system also added to the increased efficiency of the delivery system. By the start of the 1985-86 crop year, consolidation by the grain companies had reduced the number of licensed primary elevators in Western

Canada to 1,940 units with a capacity of 7,994,680 tonnes. [12] It was a far cry from the peak number of 5,728 primary elevators in 1935 with a capacity of 5,168,900 tonnes. [13] That scarcely supported the popular media myth of a Prairie elevator system still based on the horse and wagon configuration of the past.

Continuing attrition of the farm population on the Prairies had also resulted in a dramatic reduction in the number of farmers with delivery permits from the early days of the Board. In 1940-41, when the Board's quota delivery system was first instituted, permit books were sent out to 229,844 farmers. At the start of the 1984-85 crop year that number had been reduced by 37 per cent to 145,469 permit holders. [14] Over that same period the farm population in Western Canada, which stood at 1,148,200, or 47.2 per cent of the total population in 1941, was reduced by over 50 per cent to 485,800 in 1976, or 12.8 per cent of the population. [15]

To service that leaner, more streamlined grain gathering system, the modern hopper car fleet, administered by the Board, had swelled to 19,023 at the start of the 1985-86 crop year. The federal government had purchased or leased 15,192 hoppers, of which 147 had been destroyed. The Wheat Board purchased fleet of 2,000 had been reduced to 1,978 by the wreckage of 22 cars, and the provinces of Saskatchewan and Alberta had each supplied 1,000 cars.

At the Canadian Wheat Board building, the Management and Information Services Division, which pioneered the use of computerization in the grains industry, was engaged in a number of projects aimed at speeding up the flow of the mountains of paperwork that has always been associated with handling grain. Computer technology created immense possibilities in an industry generating over three million cash tickets at primary elevators, half a million rail bills of lading to cover loading of grain, and approximately the same number of terminal receipts each year.

International Business Machines marked the Board's anniversary with a reception in Winnipeg in recognition of a 50-year relationship dating back to 1935 when the Board acquired an automated punch-card system. The salesman who worked with the Board on the 1935 system later became President of IBM. The Board's first main-frame computer was acquired in 1963 and by the mid-80s there had been several major equipment upgrades. Use of the computer proved invaluable in the setting up of the Block Shipping System in the late sixties.

By the mid-1980s, virtually every grain company in Canada had installed, or was experimenting with, computers at the country elevator level. Mini-computers at an increasing number of primary elevators were issuing receipts at the time of delivery, storing the information, updating inventories and recording details of the cars into which grain was loaded as well as performing other functions. All of the information was fed each night into the grain company head office which, in turn, fed the pertinent information to the Wheat Board, the Grain Transportation Agency, and the railways.

The Canadian grain industry's entry into the computer age was accelerated by the Canadian Wheat Board's establishment in 1980 of the Country Information Project Committee to assist grain companies in establishing their systems. The CIP Committee and grain companies worked together to refine current and future information needs, and to establish standards for data transmission.

Alberta Wheat Pool was the first company to send grain purchase data via computer directly to the Canadian Wheat Board in 1982, cutting out some six to seven days in reporting the supplies of grain available for shipment. By the start of the 1985-86 crop year, 73 per cent of the tonnages being handled by the Board were on a computer-to-computer link with the primary elevators. With computers slated for installation at more country elevators, that percentage was expected to rise to 85 per cent by the end of the year. The only country points excluded from the computer network at that stage were expected to be small independent primary elevators, and those slated for future abandonment by the major grain handling companies.

Electronic transmission of information was proving to be a formidable tool for accuracy, timeliness and efficiency, providing faster data on stocks and faster response times on quotas and shipping. The largest payoff promised to be man-

The new Prince Rupert Grain terminal opened for business in the spring of 1985, greatly expanding Canada's West Coast shipping capacity to growing markets in the Asia Pacific Rim. The first vessel was the World Prize, *shown loading a cargo of wheat bound for China.*

agement of grain cars. With timely information, delays were minimized, backlogs were prevented, and costly demurrage charges were reduced. By 1985, turnaround times for grain cars between country points and port terminals had been reduced to an overall fleet average of 14 days, as compared to the 18 to 21 days in the 1970s. Car turnarounds between Manitoba and Thunder Bay had been reduced to as low as seven to eight days in peak periods.

The growing number of modern hopper cars not only increased the size of the car fleet available to the Board, but also increased the average load capacity substantially. By 1985, the Board's Grain Transportation Division was administering a fleet of 26,000 to 27,000 cars with an average capacity of 75 tonnes, as compared to a fleet of 22,000 to 24,000 cars in the 1970s which averaged 60 tonnes. Mike Martin, Director of Grain Transportation Western, calculated that, with increased capacity and efficiencies generated by computerization, the Board had gained six days a month on a cycle basis.

Computerization was also extending into other work areas such as weather reporting, tracking of railway cars, automatic weighing and inspection data at terminals, and crop reporting. Speaking at the annual meeting of the National Farmers Union in Charlottetown in December 1984, Harold Bjarnason, Director of Planning for the Board, predicted that, eventually, Wheat Board delivery permits would become like credit cards. He suggested that the time might come when the Board was linked directly with farmers through computers, and that the Board would know precisely how much grain the producer had to deliver into the system. Aiming toward that day, the Board initiated a study in 1985 to determine the feasibility of computerizing the permit books.

At the University of Manitoba a three-year study, supported by the Science and Engineering Council, was underway to assess the possibility of grading grain by computer. That research, largely funded by United Grain Growers, was later abandoned after little progress was made.

On May 16, 1985, two hopper cars, one with Government of Canada and the other with Alberta Government emblazoned on their sides, snapped a 30-foot ribbon across the track leading into the loading bay of the newly completed Prince Rupert Grain Terminal. It marked the official opening of the most highly computerized export grain terminal in the world. The $275 million state-of-the-art structure could clean grain to export standards as fast as it could be unloaded, and grain movement and selection of bins was computer controlled. With the highest throughput rate of any Canadian terminal, the new structure was 700 kilometres closer than Vancouver to the Pacific Rim. It was expected to increase West Coast export capability by 20 per cent. Prior to the official opening, the *World Prize* took the first shipment of grain out of the port on March 18, 1985. The ship carried a cargo of 25,199 tonnes of Nos. 1, 2, and 3 CWRS wheat destined for China.

Other initiatives to unlock Canada's previously restricted pipeline to world markets were underway in the Board's anniversary year. Across the Prairies a $520.1 million federal Government program to upgrade 3,426 miles of grain branch-lines was in progress. Announced in May, 1984 by Transport Minister Lloyd Axworthy, the program was expected to take five years to complete. Axworthy, a Winnipeg MP and the only Liberal member in Western Canada, replaced Jean-Luc Pepin in the transport portfolio on August 12, 1984.

The rail line upgrading program was one of the policy initiatives promised by the Liberal government as part of the Western Grain Transportation Act, passed by Parliament on November, 14, 1983. Passage of that Act, which terminated the once sacred Crow's Nest Pass Rate, unleashed a flurry of activity by the railways who were now guaranteed compensatory rates for hauling grain. The bitterly fought legislation had barely cleared the floor of the House of Commons when a Montreal spokesman announced that CP Rail was pulling out all stops on its proposed multi-million dollar rail expansion in the West.

Thus, in the spring of 1985, drilling crews started work at both ends of a nine-mile, $600 million tunnel through Mount Macdonald in the Rogers Pass area of the Selkirk Mountains in British Columbia. The crews were slated to join up four years later, eliminating a major bottleneck on the treacherous Rocky Mountains haul to the West Coast. Greater access to tidewater from the landlocked plains of Western Canada was being opened up by the largest rail building program since the completion of the transcontinental railway.

If reform of the Crow was the catalyst that spurred that activity, after years of neglect and heavy cost in lost export opportunities, it was a hard-won victory. The Crow died hard in a long, emotionally charged, bitterly fought struggle. The final chapter on its demise remained to be written after this history was completed.

One commentator reviewing that reform commented: "Prairie farmers gave the government in Ottawa the initial push, then stood back in horror at the results, realizing too late that it could not be switched off." [16]

The battle of the Crow was joined in earnest on February 8, 1982, when Transport Minister Jean-Luc Pepin announced the appointment of Dr. J.C. Gilson, an Agricultural Economist at the University of Manitoba, as the federal representative to lead consultation among major agricultural organizations and the national railways in an effort to reach consensus on Crow reform. Pepin set a deadline of June 1, 1982, for Western farm organizations to negotiate a new cost-sharing formula between producers, the railways and government to cover the cost of shipping grain.

The process was marked by dissension from the start, with the National Farmers Union refusing to take part in the discussions. They, and the national wing of the New Democratic Party, vowed to fight for retention of the 85-year-old Crow Rate declaring it to be "a crucial part of the bargain of Confederation for the Prairie Provinces."

While the final outcome of the grain freight rate debate bears implications for the future operations of the Canadian Wheat Board, there is no doubt the continuing campaigns in the saga of the Crow Rate will be chronicled elsewhere in the future. Consequently, only a cursory summary of events will be undertaken here. It should be noted however that the main thrust of the battle hinged on the method of payment by the federal government of what became known as the "Crow gap." As a quid-pro-quo for abolition of the Crow Rate, the federal government pledged to recompense Western farmers annually by an amount, based on 1981-82 calculations, equivalent to the shortfall between the railway cost of moving grain and the Crow Rate.

Central to the dispute was the contention that the Crow Rate had created a distortion in agricultural production on the Prairies by giving a financial incentive to the growing of export oriented grains. This, it was contended, was to the disadvantage of secondary, value-added production such as livestock, specialty crops and establishment of processing industries in the West. The powerful Prairie Pools remained adamant that the federal government payment toward the Crow shortfall be made directly to the railways into the future. Other factions, represented by the Palliser Wheat Growers Association, the Prairie Farm Commodity Coalition, Western Barley Growers Association, United Grain Growers and others, contended that the federal payment should be made directly to all farmers in Western Canada in order to promote "resource equity."

In June 1982, Gilson presented his report on the consultations. He recommended that the Crow shortfall, estimated at $644.1 million, be paid directly to the railways in 1982-83. Thereafter, an increasing proportion of the payment would go directly to the producers until 1989-90, at which time 81 per cent would be going directly to the producers and 19 per cent to the railways.

Rather than producing the hoped for western consensus, the 53-page Gilson Report generated renewed feuding between the commodity groups in the West. When Pepin indicated the federal Cabinet preferred the Gilson formula, producers in Quebec, backed by their provincial government, entered the fray. Fearing that acreage-based federal payments to farmers would give Western livestock producers a cost of production advantage, Quebec added its powerful political voice to the advocates of the "pay-the-railway" formula.

Prairie provincial governments, although denied participation in the consultative process, took conflicting stands. The Conservative Alberta government backed the Gilson solution while the NDP government in Manitoba called for retention of the Crow. In Saskatchewan the legislature voted unanimously to reject Pepin's proposal to adopt the Gilson recommendations, but did not rule out some other means of amending the Crow Rate.

As the controversy swirled, with a variety of proposals and counter-proposals on acreage-based "pay-the-farmer" formulas emerging, the structure of provincial umbrella farm organizations affiliated to the Canadian Federation of Agriculture began to crumble. At their annual meeting in November 1982, Manitoba Pool Elevator's delegates voted to withdraw from the Manitoba Farm Bureau over the stand taken by the MFB during the Gilson consultations. In January, 1983, the opposing forces collided head on at the annual meeting of the Western Agricultural Conference in Regina. Rent by dissension over the method of Crow reform, that meeting marked the last time representatives from the three Prairie Provinces gathered to hammer out a united Western stand to carry to the CFA, a process carried out since 1940.

The Canadian Wheat Board had, of necessity, steered clear of the acrimonious debate, but in the same week that the WAC disintegrated in Regina, the Producer Advisory Committee to the Board entered the politically sensitive Crow debate. The Committee passed a resolution informing Ottawa that they rejected the Gilson recommendations. Two of the nine members present, Henry Dechant and Lorne Parker, dissented, maintaining that government policy was out of the Committee's domain.

When the CFA annual meeting convened in Ottawa on February 7, 1983, the Prairie voice was fractured. Delegates from the other regions sat back and watched the Western combatants battle each other, then overwhelmingly voted for payment of the Crow benefit directly to the railways. Only United Grain Growers and the Manitoba Farm Bureau delegates dissented. Within the year, U.G.G. had withdrawn from the Canadian Federation of Agriculture and the Manitoba Farm Bureau foundered without the financial support of Manitoba Pool.

In the interim, on January 31, 1983, Pepin had announced in Winnipeg that the federal government was opting for the Gilson solution. Outlining the proposed legislation, Pepin said a Crow benefit of $651.6 million would be paid directly to the railways for 1982-83. Thereafter, an increasing percentage would go directly to the farmers, by way of an acreage-based payment, until 1985-86. By that time, the federal government payment would be split equally between the farmers and the railways. A major review would then take place to decide whether to proceed to the eventual Gilson solution, with 81 per cent going to farmers by 1990-91.

Still adamant in their pay-the-railway stance, the Prairie Pools mounted a sustained lobbying effort in Ottawa. They were joined by Quebec farm organizations, which met with the powerful Liberal Caucus from that province. Following that meeting, Consumer Affairs Minister André Oullet announced that he, and 73 other Quebec caucus members, would oppose the Gilson solution. The beleaguered Transport Minister now faced a possible revolt within Cabinet and the Liberal Caucus.

On May 4, 1983, Pepin called an Ottawa press conference and conceded defeat. The federal Crow payment would be paid to the railways. While agreeing that opposition from Prairie farmers to the Gilson solution was strong, he conceded that internal dissent among Liberal MPs from Quebec was the deciding factor in amending the proposed legislation: "I couldn't have had a majority in the House of Commons, it's as simple as that. There's no shame in that. I'm not feeling embarrassed or ashamed." [17]

The next week Bill C-155, the Western Grain Transportation Act, began its stormy passage through the House of Commons. It would not fall to Pepin to pilot it through to its final stage. After almost two months of debate and procedural wrangling, the government threatened to recall Parliament for the entire summer if the Bill was not given second reading. The opposition conceded and the legislation passed to the Standing Committee on transportation. There was to be no respite. Throughout the summer the arguments were reheard and rehashed as the Committee travelled across the country hearing representations, primarily on the payment formula.

The Canadian Wheat Board now had a number of concerns with certain sections of Bill C-155, chief among them being the possibility that the Board's power to co-ordinate grain transportation might be shifted to the Grain Transportation Agency by Order-in-Council. Appearing before the Committee on August 18, Esmond Jarvis made two principal points:

> In closing, I will review the two points which have been the focus of this presentation. First, transportation and sales are inextricably linked. But transportation must effectively serve sales needs. It cannot be otherwise or Canada will lose an important edge it now has in world markets. The current system with GTA making the initial splits in car allocations (between board and non-board and off-board grains) has not been too cumbersome. But a danger exists. Policy makers should be very careful in not separating further the vital link needed between transportation and sales.
>
> Secondly, I have tried to place the limited financial support given to Canadian grain farmers into an international context. Western grain producers receive much less government support than producers in competing countries. But, in the long term such support is very important in maintaining a viable Canadian farm sector. This sector has been a much needed stimulus to the entire Canadian economy during the current recession, and at all times it is a major earner of foreign exchange. [18]

While Jarvis had avoided making a direct contribution to the Crow benefit payment dispute, his latter point may have tactfully conveyed the message of where the Board's preference lay.

The blunt-spoken Charlie Gibbings, who had retired as a Commissioner of the Board on January 31, 1982, to be replaced by the appointment of the Sales Manager of the the Alberta Wheat Pool, W.H. "Bill" Smith, the following April, was not as diplomatic. In a written submission to the Transport Committee, Gibbings argued against the pay-the-producer concept:

> The government is mistakenly trying to solve a specific problem — the need to expand grain export capacity — with a non-specific solution which will theoretically lead to economic development in other areas. A group of individuals want to see the transportation system in a certain configuration, and they expect farmers, the grain companies, the wheat board, and our customers to adjust to accommodate it.
>
> I suggest the reverse approach be taken. Let the transportation system develop to meet the needs of the people who are using it. That is the approach that makes real economic sense, and the government should allow it to proceed by keeping bureaucracy out of the grain business. [19]

When Parliament re-convened on September 12, Lloyd Axworthy had replaced Pepin as Transport Minister, and it fell to the Winnipeg MP to pilot the legislation through its final stormy stages. The end came on November 14, 1983, when the government invoked closure on debate, and Bill C-155 cleared the House. After three days of debate in the Senate, Supreme Court Justice Brian Dickson formally gave Royal Assent to the *Western Grain Transportation Act*. Following almost six months of Committee hearings and emotional debate, the Crow was dead at age 86. But, the debate lingered on. Section 62 of the new Act called for a review of the payment format on or before April 1, 1984.

In its final form, Bill C-155 had gone through some 80 amendments. In summary, the *Western Grain Transportation Act* provided for an annual Crow benefit payment to the railways of $658.6 million from the federal Treasury, representing the difference between the estimated full cost of grain transportation by rail and what producers paid under the statutory Crow's Nest Pass Rate in 1982. A base volume, or "cap," of 31.5 million tonnes was placed on distribution of the federal funds. Producers were to pay full costs on all grain shipments above the base volume. Future increases in rail rate costs were to be shared between the producer and the government, with the producer paying three per cent of inflationary costs on the base volume in the crop years up to 1985-86, and six per cent thereafter. The government was to pay all annual cost increases in excess of those percentages. A "safety net" was incorporated to protect the producer in the event of distressed grain prices. It provided that, by 1988, the freight rate paid by producers could not exceed 10 per cent of the calculated price of a basket of six major grains.

The concerns of the Wheat Board, over co-ordination of the grain transportation system, were relieved by the government's pledge that those powers would be retained by the Board. However, an enlarged Senior Grain Transportation Committee, representing a broad spectrum from the grain industry, government agencies, producers, shippers and the railways, was given powers to advise and make recommendations to the Minister of Transport, or Grain Transportation Authority Administrator, on any matter respecting the transportation, shipping or handling of grain.

When Axworthy, in early February 1984, announced the appointments to the 21-member committee, he also announced the appointment of CNR Chairman Jack Horner to a four-year term as head of the Grain Transportation Authority. The appointment of Horner was greeted with some consternation in the grains industry. First elected as a Progressive Conservative MP, representing the Alberta riding of Crowfoot, in 1958, Horner crossed the floor in 1977 and was given the portfolio of Industry, Trade and Commerce in the Trudeau Liberal Cabinet. He went down to defeat as a Liberal candidate in the 1979 general election.

The GTA had been headed by acting administrators for over three years when Horner's brother, Dr. Hugh Horner, tendered his resignation in September 1980, after only one year as Administrator. In its first year of operation, the GTA came under heavy fire after open market stocks of unpriced rapeseed piled up in Vancouver and it was forced to reduce the number of cars available for such shipment. An indication of the "no win" situation previously faced by the Canadian Wheat Board, before the GTA began to make the initial split between Board and non-board car allocations, was given at a public meeting in Winnipeg to discuss the bottleneck. Despite the obvious evidence that too many cars had been allocated to the movement of unpriced rapeseed, John Channon, Chairman of the Alberta Grain Commission, charged the GTA was aggravating the situation by its "pig-headed refusal" to allocate sufficient cars to the non-board shipments. The GTA was now serving as a "lightning rod" deflecting charges of self-interest previously levelled against the Wheat Board.

When the new grain freight rate regime went into effect on January 1, 1984, the immediate effect was minimal with the average weighted rail costs paid by farmers for wheat shipment rising from $4.66 to $5.16 a tonne for the 1983-84 crop year.[20] However, estimates were that the farmers' costs of moving grain under the new formula would double by 1985-86 and increase fivefold by 1990-91. By that latter date it was estimated the producer would be bearing 60 per cent of the actual costs of moving grain.

It was by no means certain, however, that the pay-the-railroad format would remain in effect. A five-man Committee of Inquiry on the Crow benefit payment, chaired by Mr. Justice Gordon C. Hall of the Manitoba Court of Appeal, was appointed by Order-in-Council on April 24, 1984. Announcement of the new enquiry was made by Axworthy. However, when the report of the inquiry was forwarded to Ottawa on March 29, 1985, it was addressed to Transport Minister Don Mazankowski. In the interim the Liberals had been swept from power in Ottawa.

When Canadians went to the polls on September 4, 1984, both the Liberals and Conservatives had chosen new leaders. Brian Mulroney had ousted Joe Clark as Leader of the Progressive Conservative Party at a convention. John Turner had succeeded Trudeau, who retired from politics. In a pre-election Cabinet shuffle, Turner chose Axworthy to succeed Senator Argue as Minister Responsible to Parliament for the Canadian Wheat Board on June 30, 1984.

Under Mulroney, the Conservatives were given a massive majority, winning 211 of the 282 seats in the House of Commission. The Liberals won 40 seats, the NDP 30 and one independent was elected. Charlie Mayer, a Manitoba farmer, was appointed Minister of State Responsible for Reporting to Parliament on the Canadian Wheat Board.

Finding advantages and disadvantages with both the pay-the-railways and the pay-the-producer formats, the Hall Committee report introduced yet another formula for payment of the Crow benefit. It found that, among other things, the pay-the-railway formula masked the real transportation costs from the producer and reduced incentives for farmers to seek greater efficiency in the grain handling and transportation system. On the other hand, the commission said spreading the benefit among all producers with land capable of producing statutory grains would dilute the benefit, so that those who actually grew and shipped grains for export would receive inadequate compensation for freight rate increases.

The Hall commission opted for a "Grain Transportation Refund," to be administered through the Western Grain Stabilization Administration. It recommended that the Crow benefit be paid out quarterly to producers in the Wheat Board designated area, on the basis of net sales of eligible grains in each crop year. Thus, the benefit would be paid on grain sold farm-to-farm and to such outlets as feed mills, rather than solely on grain moved by rail out of the Prairies.

The new formula failed to find universal favour, with the Prairie Pools remaining firmly wedded to the pay-the-railway formula. As 1985 closed, yet another review of the *Western Grain Transportation Act* was under way with hearings taking place across Western Canada. This time, the Grain Transportation Authority was delegated, under terms of the Act, to conduct the review and report on possible amendments — including the method of payment of the Crow benefit.

As the disruptive legacy of the Crow was unfolding, attention was also riveted on the equally divisive domestic feed grains policy. As early as July 1980, the Producer Advisory Committee had urged the Wheat Board to cease offering feed grains into the domestic market under the corn-competitive formula, which based prices on U.S. corn landed in Montreal. On December 21, 1981, the Board announced that it was withdrawing from the domestic market when feed barley fell to a discount to what could be obtained by the Board on the export market. Under pressure, the Board agreed to continue to supply the domestic market at the formula price for 60 days, pending a review of the policy.

In March, 1982, the federal government announced that, from the opening to the close of navigation on the Great Lakes in 1982, it would provide for reimbursement of losses up to eight million dollars against the difference between the Board's domestic and export sales prices. At the same time, No. 3 CWRS and No. 1 Canada Utility wheats were removed from the corn-competitive pricing system. Despite payment of the eight million dollars, Wheat Board sales into the domestic market below the current world prices cost Western farmers $2.4 million in 1982, when the Board's losses on domestic sales mounted to $10.4 million vis-a-vis prices obtainable on the export market.

In December, 1982, Ottawa announced it would extend its policy of compensating the Board for losses on domestic sales from the opening of navigation in 1983 at Thunder Bay to July 31, 1983. However, during most of that period, export feed grain prices fell to a discount to those on the domestic market, and the federal government paid out only $8,000 of the eight million dollars committed.

A promised, review of the domestic feed grain policy dragged on with continuing meetings between the government, the Advisory Committee of the Wheat Board, and the Canadian Livestock Feed Board of Canada in an attempt to resolve the issue. In 1984, losses again began to mount on barley sales made at formula prices, and the Board became concerned that sales to the domestic market would reduce supplies available for export commitments. Another contentious point was that formula prices caused distortions in the open market, driving prices down to meet the formula discounts.

Finally, after meeting with provincial Agriculture Ministers, farmers and feed grains users, Mayer announced on August 1, 1985, the corn-competitive pricing formula would no longer be used, and the Wheat Board would be able to sell Prairie feed grains into the domestic market at competitive prices. Outlining the new policy, Mayer noted that production and consumption patterns had changed dramatically over the previous 10 years, with Ontario becoming a surplus producer of feed grains and Quebec becoming almost 70 per cent self-sufficient. Only about 1.5 million tonnes of Prairie feed grains moved east in 1983-84, compared to 2.3 million tonnes 10 years previously.

Relieved of one of the last political restraints to its autonomy to act as an independent marketing agency for Western Canadian grain producers, the Board was free to pursue its primary function of negotiating sales in the world marketplace. In his first major address to Western Canadian farmers, after becoming Minister Responsible for the Board, Mayer affirmed the role of the Canadian Wheat Board in pursuing that objective. Speaking to the 1984 annual meeting of Manitoba Pool Elevators in Winnipeg, the new minister promised a hands-off approach:

> Unlike some of my predecessors, I do not intend to try to bask in the reflected glory of the Board's sales successes. Seldom has a cabinet minister ever made a grain export sale; although many have jumped at the chance to appear to have been involved. [21]

Late in the anniversary year, the Board's long relationship with Exportkhleb, built up over many years of hard work and mutual understanding, paid off again. On December 5, 1985, another long-term agreement was announced. Under it the Soviet Union was to purchase a minimum of 25 million tonnes of Canadian wheat and feed grains between August 1, 1986, and July 31, 1991. Previous to that agreement the Soviet Union had purchased 75,105,620 tonnes of grain dating back to the 1957-58 crop year. Included in that total were 56,827,709 tonnes of wheat, 7,481,368 tonnes of durum, 10,529,305 tonnes of barley, and 267,238 tonnes of oats. [22]

Two weeks later the Wheat Board announced the final results for the 1984-85 crop year. Despite the widespread apprehension that there would be little or no final payment due to the tight and competitive market, there were surpluses in all the pools. A final payment of 58 cents brought the total realized price of No. 1 CWRS wheat to $5.08 a bushel, basis Thunder Bay or Vancouver. With a final payment of 67.6 cents, total returns for top grade durum amounted to $5.58 a bushel. No. 1 Feed barley earned a 13.7 cent final payment, bringing total returns to $2.86 a bushel in highly competitive feed grains market. [23] Thus, in spite of a drought reduced 1984 crop and lower than normal grades, Wheat Board sales returned over $4.1 billion to the Western economy.

Reaction from Prairie spokesmen to the Board's performance in a tough world market was highly favourable. Western Canadian farmers could look to the south at the fractious political manoeuvring and growing grain mountains, and then contemplate their own near empty bins. Prices were far from satisfactory on world markets, but their marketing agency had proven that, given improvements in the transportation and handling system, it could meet the competition and sell whatever might be produced. Criticism of the Canadian Wheat Board, even among some of the previously vociferous minority commodity groups, had all but abated as the Board celebrated its 50th anniversary year.

While facing severe near-term problems in a world market beset by intensifying subsidy wars, the Canadian Wheat Board in 1985 was still able to look to the future with optimism. The Board's annual Report to Producers on the 1984-85 crop year noted that the "modest celebration" of its first half-century had not coincided with a good year for Western Canadian producers:

> The year was one which showed that no sales, handling, or transportation system, no matter how efficient, can counter the effects of Mother Nature and a fiercely competitive international market.
>
> The Prairie harvest of 1984 was a bitter disappointment. Drought, especially across the south, reduced the crop by 18 per cent below the average of the previous three years. Export availability dropped accordingly, and Prairie exports dropped by almost 25 per cent from the 1983-84 record. Carryovers were brought to the lowest level in over 30 years. Revenue loss from the reduced volume was compounded by a continuing slide in grain prices. Wheat Board sales revenue dropped by over a billion dollars from the previous year.
>
> This report covers the marketing of your 1984 grain crop. As you receive it, the Board is in the midst of facing even greater challenges in marketing your 1985 crop. With the recent passage of a new U.S. farm bill, which lowers world prices but maintains U.S. farm income, we cannot offer hope for an immediate improvement in prospects for our producers.
>
> While this is the unfortunate reality for the near term, we are not as pessimistic as some about the longer term. There is a "herd instinct" in the world grain market and, at the moment, the instinct is to be pessimistic, even though the facts sometimes indicate otherwise. With a continuing growth in world population, and continued improvements in living standards in developing countries, world grain consumption has nowhere to go but up. The increase may be more moderate than in the past, and it will continue to be marked by year-to-year fluctuations, but the trend will still be there.[24]

Footnotes: Chapter Ten

1. Accumulated from Reports of the Canadian Wheat Board, Crop Years 1935-36 up to 1984-85 inclusive.

2. John I. McFarland, *Address to the Winnipeg Canadian Club*, April 11, 1935, p. 6.

3. USDA Foreign Agriculture Grain Circular, November 1985.

4. *Canadian Wheat Board Report to the Producers on the 1983-84 Crop Year*, p. 3.

5. Esmond Jarvis, Address to Saskatchewan Agricultural Conference, October 28, 1985, p. 2.

6. *The Manitoba Co-operator*, December 19, 1985, p. 34.

7. Esmond Jarvis, Address to Saskatchewan Agricultural Conference, October 28, 1985.

8. *The Manitoba Co-operator*, October 11, 1984, p. 6.

9. *Ibid*, March 28, 1985, p. 5.

10. *Ibid*.

11. *Report of the Canadian Wheat Board, Crop Year 1983-84*, p. 25.

12. Grain Elevators in Canada, Canadian Grain Commission, 1985-86, pp. 90, 91.

13. Report of the Hall Commission, Grain and Rail in Western Canada, Vol. 1, 1977, p. 134.

14. Reports of the Canadian Wheat Board, Crop Years 1962-63 and 1983-84.

15. Statistics Canada. Figures between years are not necessarily comparable since the definition of a "census farm" was revised for census counts.

16. *The Manitoba Co-operator*, November 24, 1983, p. 5.

17. *Ibid*, May 12, 1983, p. 5.

18. Canadian Wheat Board Files, Brief to the House of Commons Standing Committee on Transportation, August 18, 1983.

19. *The Manitoba Co-operator*, October 6, 1983, p. 4.

20. *Report of the Canadian Wheat Board, Crop Year 1983-84*, p. 23.

21. *The Manitoba Co-operator*, November 15, 1984, p. 1.

22. Minister's Canadian Wheat Board Press Release, December 5, 1985.

23. Canadian Wheat Board Press Release, December 20, 1985.

24. The Canadian Wheat Board, Report to Producers on the 1984-85 Crop Year, pp. 2,3.

A PERSONAL ASSESSMENT

It is a general popular error to imagine the loudest complainers
for the public to be the most anxious for its welfare.

— Edmund Burke

At the time of the final editing of this second volume of the history of the Canadian Wheat Board, the largest and most fundamental change in the evolution and form of the Board was underway. As the Board approached the new millenium, a new Board of Directors had taken over from the slate of up to five federally appointed Commissioners who oversaw and conducted the affairs of the Canadian Wheat Board.

In late 1998, farmers across Western Canada, in a mail-in vote, elected ten new Directors to chart the future actions of the Wheat Board. They were joined by five additional Board members appointed by the federal government from the business community. That Board of Directors, now headed by a Chief Executive Officer, replaced both the former Commisioners and the farmer-elected Advisory Committee to the Board.

Some 65,000 ballots were cast by Western Canadian farmers in the election of the majority of the members of the first ever Board of Directors to head the Wheat Board. That new administrative body was the principal change in a series of amendments to the *Canadian Wheat Board Act* authorized by Parliament.

Without going into detail on all of the amendments to the Act, it might be pertinent to briefly examine the general tide of events leading to that milestone.

Since the completion of the main body of this work some 12 years ago, the role of the Canadian Wheat Board had come under increasing scrutiny, due perhaps in part to the volatile and changing world market situation described in this volume, which has persisted to the present. Adding to that continuing uncertainty has been the final demise of the Crow Rate resulting in Western grain farmers facing heavily increased transportation charges. That, in turn, pre-

cipitated a search for cropping alternatives and secondary production alternatives to offset decreasing returns from export grains. Principal among those
alternatives was an increasing interest in livestock, particularly in intensified hog
production. Inevitably that, at least temporarily, affected production of what has
traditionally been the mainstay of Western Canadian agriculture — high-quality, high-protein wheat.

*Marketing issues became the main topic of debate among farmers in the
nineties. This photo was taken in August 1996 during a Winnipeg rally by
farmers to support CWB marketing.*

Concurrent with those changes was an aggressive move by a number of organizations for a "dual marketing" option. Those groups were vociferous in their demand to be permitted to market all of their grain outside of the monopoly provisions of the Canadian Wheat Board. While the most militant have normally been minority factions, the thrust for a dual marketing system has also been backed by the provincial government in Alberta and the Western Canadian Wheat Growers Association.

The most militant organization to emerge titled themselves Farmers For Justice, a group of producers primarily living close to the Canada - U.S. border. With the advent of the North American Free Trade Agreement, members of this militant group in effect counselled civil disobedience on the part of its adherents by advocating the transporting of grain across the border for sale without first obtaining an export permit from the Canadian Wheat Board.

Drawn by domestic American grain prices, which were consistently above world market prices due to the multiplicity of government support programs south of the border, increasing numbers of the dissidents began "running the border." Ignoring the anomaly of openly exporting grain into the largest of the world's grain exporters, which was in turn more often than not using export subsidies to relieve its own troublesome surpluses, the Farmers for Justice and their supporters contended it was a large and lucrative market ready for unlimited individual entrepreneurship.

As the inevitable tide of protest arose from American farmers who saw Canadian trucks lined up at U.S. border grain elevators, there was also concern and misgivings expressed by most Western Canadian farmers. As has been outlined in this volume, the Canadian Wheat Board had in the past, and has continued, to export grain into niche markets in the United States through accredited agents. Any such premiums earned in that market were therefore pooled in the Wheat Board accounts and distributed to all Board permit holders delivering similar grains by inclusion in any final payments.

While the dissident farmers mounted a strident campaign claiming intrusion into their fundamental right to market their own grain in whatever manner they saw fit, the majority defenders of the Canadian Wheat Board saw their actions as not only jeopardizing the premium American market, but also as diluting the returns of the majority of the producers. The Farmers For Justice became derisively labelled as "Farmers For Just Us."

One Wheat Board defender likened the actions of the border runners as being similar to a few diners at a communal dinner snatching all the choice meat from a pot of stew by virtue of their inalienable right of being closest to the kitchen.

Charges were laid against a number of the farmers trucking grain into the United States without first obtaining of an export permit from the Board and with breaches of the *Customs Act*. When one persistent offender charged with failing to produce an export permit at the border, and who subsequently disobeyed a court order, chose to go to jail rather than pay the fines levied against him, the rhetoric heightened. In the simplistic interpretation of the dissidents,"farmers were being thrown in jail for selling their own wheat," a phrase that found favour in much of the urban oriented media.

As the dissident voices mounted, marketing choice referendums were held both provincially in Alberta and across the Prairie Provinces by the federal government. There was a wide variance in the results. In Alberta, where opposition to the Wheat Board's monopoly powers was most evident, the questions posed the alternative of a dual marketing system. That of the federal government more realistically rejected such an option. Given the choice of a totally open market or maintaining the Board's monopoly on exports of wheat and barley, a wide majority of producers voted on the side of retaining the Canadian Wheat Board.

Of particular interest in the context of this history is the tenor of many of the presentations made both during and leading up to the referendums and at the hearings into proposed amendments to the *Canadian Wheat Board Act*. Proponents of the marketing choice concept produced papers purporting to prove, through historic references, that dual marketing systems had operated with marked success during the early years of the Canadian Wheat Board. Such an inference was contrary to historic fact, as readers of this work and its predecessor may well have concluded. In most cases allegedly academic studies widely distributed in Western Canada were based on extremely selective, distorted, or incomplete quotations. It is hoped that what has appeared here, and in the previous volume on the history of the Canadian Wheat Board, may serve to set the record straight.

Despite all of the rhetoric, and sometimes adverse publicity for the Canadian Wheat Board, the dissident voices appeared to have been muted by the outcome of the late 1998 mail-in ballot by farmers. While anti-monopoly forces fielded candidates in all of the ten districts, the final count saw eight pro-monopoly farmers elected to the Board of Directors.

The essence of the majority of Western Canadian farmers appreciation of the Canadian Wheat Board, and its monopoly powers, may have been best defined by an American Professor of History and Director of Canadian Studies at Duke University, North Carolina. In a rebuttal to an anti-Wheat Board study of the monopoly buying powers of the Board by two Alberta-based academics, John Herd Thompson, as a Distinguished Visiting Professor of History at the University of Alberta, set the record straight.

Apparently referring to the plethora of selective and often out-of-context pamphlets dealing with the past history of the Wheat Board, he wrote:

> "At some future date, a majority of Western Canadian producers, speaking directly and/or through their elected repre-

sentatives, may decide that a monopoly Canadian Wheat Board is no longer the best answer to the complex question of how to market their wheat crop. But contemporary Canadian grain growers who want to change should not delude themselves about the past to justify new directions they may wish to take in the future. A rationale for ending the CWB monopoly in the 1990s cannot be found in the history of the creation of the monopoly between 1919 and 1967."

It is hoped that this volume and its predecessor will serve to illuminate the past history of the Canadian Wheat Board without resorting to selectivity or omission as may future volumes to follow.

The CWB's head office at 423 Main Street in Winnipeg.

COMMISSIONERS OF THE CANADIAN WHEAT BOARD
1935 – 1998

Chief Commissioners

John I. McFarland	August 14, 1935 – December 3, 1935	
James R. Murray	December 3, 1935 – July 1937	
George H. McIvor	July 1937 – April 30, 1958	
	December 3, 1935 – July 1937	Assistant Chief Commissioner
W.C. McNamara	June 1, 1958 – October 5, 1970	
	September 1945	Appointed Commissioner
	February 1947	Assistant Chief Commissioner
G.N. Vogel	March 4, 1971 – September 30, 1977	
	September 1, 1964	Appointed Commissioner
	July 1, 1969	Assistant Chief Commissioner
W. Esmond Jarvis	October 3, 1977 – November 1, 1990	
L. F. Hehn	December 1, 1990 – December 31, 1998	

Commissioners

D.L. Smith	August 14, 1935 – December 3, 1935	Assistant Chief Commissioner
H.C. Grant	August 14, 1935 – December 3, 1935	
A.M. Shaw	December 3, 1935 – August 31, 1938	
R.C. Findlay	July 1938 – October 26, 1939	Assistant Chief Commissioner
W. Charles Folliott	August 1938 – March 13, 1943	
C. Gordon Smith	October 26, 1939 – December 1944	Assistant Chief Commissioner
D.A. Kane	June 1, 1943 – September 1945	
	December 1944 – September 1945	Assistant Chief Commissioner

C.E. Huntting	December 1944 – February 1947	
	September 1945 – February 1947	Assistant Chief Commissioner
F.L.M. Arnold	February 1947 – May 1948	
T.W. Grindley	July 1948 – July 1950	
William Riddel	August 1, 1950 – September 30, 1965	
	June 1958 – September 1965	Assistant Chief Commissioner
W. Earle Robertson	November 1952 – December 31, 1964	
John T. Dallas	September 1, 1958 – January 1, 1961	
J.B. Lawrie	December 22, 1961 – June 30, 1969	
	October 1, 1965 – June 30, 1969	Assistant Chief Commissioner
D.H. Treleaven	October 1, 1965 – December 31, 1975	
	March 4, 1971 – December 31, 1975	Assistant Chief Commissioner
R.L. Kristjanson	October 1, 1965 -	
	January 1, 1976 – August 1, 1990	Assistant Chief Commissioner
C.W. Gibbings	July 1, 1969 – December 31, 1982	
R.M. Esdale	April 1, 1971 – December 31, 1975	
J.L. Leibfried	January 1, 1976 – December 31, 1985	
F.M. Hetland	January 1, 1976	
	October 10, 1990 – January 16, 1995	Assistant Chief Commissioner
W.H. Smith	April 7, 1983 – June 10, 1992	
R.H. Klassen	September 15, 1988 – December 31, 1998	
G.P. Machej	October 10, 1990 – December 31, 1998	
K. Beswick	February 22, 1993 – April 30, 1996	

CANADIAN WHEAT BOARD
ADVISORY COMMITTEE
1935 – 1998

First Advisory Board appointed August 14, 1935, but disbanded on December 3, 1935: Paul F. Bredt, L.C. Brouillette, Brooks Catton, Lew Hutchinson, Robert McKee, C.H.G. Short, Sidney Smith.

Advisory Board reconstituted August 27, 1940, appointed by the Governor-In-Council.

Elected Advisory Committee

During the 1974-75 crop year the appointments of members of the previous Advisory Committee were terminated and a new committee was elected by producers in eleven electoral districts. Successful candidates were appointed for a four-year term by the Governor-in-Council in accordance with Section 10 of the *Canadian Wheat Board Act*.

District 1:

L.E. Parker, Ste. Agathe, MB	May 1975-January 1987
W. A. Harder, Lowe Farm, MB	January 1987-December 1998

District 2:

D. Mitchell, Douglas, MB	May 1975-January 1983
B. McDonald, Strathclair, MB	January 1983-January 1987
L. N. Maguire, Elgin, MB	January 1987-January 1995
W. Nicholson, Shoal Lake, MB	January 1995-December 1998

District 3:

E. Murphy, Estevan, SK	May 1975-January 1979
C. A. Hookenson, Kisbey, SK	January 1979-January 1987
T. L. Hanson, Fillmore, SK	January 1987-December 1998

District 4:

V. Althouse, Kelvington, SK	May 1975-January 1979
M. G. W. Halyk, Melville, SK	January 1979-December 1998

District 5:

E. K. Turner, Regina, SK	May 1975-January 1983
H. Yelland, Porcupine Plain, SK	January 1983-January 1987
J. H. Gjesdal, Birch Hills, SK	January 1987-January 1990
J. Clair, Radisson, SK	January 1990-December 1998

District 6:

R. R. Atkinson, Landis, SK	May 1975-January 1995
W. Rosher, Smiley, SK	January 1995-December 1998

District 7:

A.Sahl, Mossbank, SK	May 1975-January 1990
D. Dewar, Hazlet, SK	January 1990-December 1998

District 8:

T. Strain, North Battleford, SK	May 1975-January 1987
G. Pike, Lloydminster, SK	January 1987-January 1990
L. Pattison, Marshall, SK	January 1990-December 1998

District 9:

O. Reber, Burdett, AB	May 1975-January 1983
C. F. Thurston, Bow Island, AB	January 1983-January 1987
D. Cutforth, Baron, AB	January 1987-December 1998

District 10:

G. L. Harrold, Lamont, AB	May 1975-December 1977
A. Smith, Red Deer, AB	March 1978-January 1979
K. D. Galloway, Fort Saskatchewan, AB	January 1979-January 1990
L. Erickson, Donalda, AB	January 1990-January 1995
R. Ponto, Galahad, AB	January 1995-December 1998

District 11:

W. D. Lea, Jarvie, AB	May 1975-January 1979
H. A. Dechant, Fairview, AB	January 1979-January 1987
A. W. Macklin, Grande Prairie, AB	January 1987-December 1998

MINISTERS RESPONSIBLE TO PARLIAMENT FOR THE CANADIAN WHEAT BOARD
1935 – 1998

W.D. Euler	Minister of Trade and Commerce, (Lib.)	October 31, 1935 – May 10, 1940
James A. MacKinnon	Minister of Trade and Commerce, (Lib.)	May 10, 1940 – January 18, 1948
C.D. Howe	Minister of Trade and Commerce, (Lib.)	January 18, 1948 – June 21, 1957
Gordon Churchill	Minister of Trade and Commerce, (PC)	June 21, 1957 – October 11, 1960
Alvin Hamilton	Minister of Agriculture, (PC)	October 11, 1960 – April 22, 1963
Mitchell Sharp	Minister of Trade and Commerce, (Lib.)	April 22, 1963 – November 3, 1966
Robert H. Winters	Minister of Trade and Commerce, (Lib.)	November 3, 1966 – April 22, 1968
Charles M. Drury	Minister of Industry, Trade and Commerce, (Lib.)	April 22, 1968 – July 5, 1968
Jean-Luc Pepin	Minister of Industry, Trade and Commerce, (Lib.)	July 5, 1968 – October 15, 1969
Otto E. Lang	Minister responsible for the Canadian Wheat Board (PC)	October 15, 1969 – June 4, 1979
	Minister Without Portfolio, (Lib.)	July 1968 – September 1970
	Minister of Manpower and Immigration	September 1970 – January 1972
	Minister of Justice	January 1972 – June 1975
	Minister of Transport	September 1975 – June 1979
		October 15, 1969 – June 4, 1979
Donald Mazankowski	Minister of Transport, (PC)	June 4, 1979 – March 3, 1980
Senator Hazen Argue	Minister of State, (Lib.)	March 3, 1980 – June 30, 1984
Lloyd Axworthy	Minister of Transport, (Lib.)	June 30, 1984 – September 17, 1984

Charles Mayer	Minister of State for the Canadian Wheat Board, (PC)	September 17, 1984 – November 4, 1993
	Minister of State for Grains and Oilseeds	August 1987 – January 1993
	Minister of Western Economic Diversification	January 1989 – January 1993
	Minister of Agriculture, Small Communities and Rural Areas	January 1993 – June 1993
	Minister of Agriculture and Agri-Food	June 1993 – November 1993
	Minister of Small Communities and Rural Areas	June 1993 – November 1993
Ralph Goodale	Minister Responsible for the Canadian Wheat Board (Lib.)	November 4, 1993 –
	Minister of Agriculture and Agri-Food	November 4, 1993 – June 11, 1997
	Minister of Natural Resources	June 11, 1997 –

WEIGHTS & MEASURES

Throughout this volume various, and sometimes apparently arbitrary, references appear in relation to tonnages and volume of grain in the area of sales, production and inventories; i.e., tons, long tons, metric tons (tonnes). This is occasioned in large part by the use of imperial weights and measures on the domestic scene in the past, and before the introduction and use of metric calculations in Canada. Since there is some uncertainty as to the preciseness of the terminology in the documents examined, we have used the exact words encountered in the archival material. It has been quoted precisely as written at the period in question. For the guidance of readers, the more commonly used weights and measures for agricultural commodities in domestic and world markets are set out here along with conversion factors.

1 short ton = 2,000 pounds

1 long ton = 2,240 pounds

1 tonne (metric ton) = 2,204.622 pounds

Bushel weights: wheat, soybeans = 60 pounds;

corn, sorghum, rye, flaxseed = 56 pounds;

barley, buckwheat = 48 pounds;

oats = 38 pounds.

Factors for converting domestic and metric weights

wheat, soybeans; 1 tonne = 36.7437 bushels

corn, rye, sorghum, flaxseed; 1 tonne = 39.368 bushels

barley, buckwheat; 1 tonne = 45.9296 bushels

oats, 1 tonne = 58.016 bushels

Example: wheat at $160 a tonne - $160 divided by 36.7437 = $4.3544 per bushel.

SELECTED BIBLIOGRAPHY

General Works

Britnell, George E. and Fowke, Vernon C. *Canadian Agriculture in War and Peace*. Stanford, CA: Stanford University Press, 1962.

Colquette, R. D. *The First Fifty Years: A History of United Grain Growers Ltd.* Winnipeg: Public Press, 1957.

Davidson, Clive B. *Wheat, Politicians and the Great Depression: Two Memoirs*. Winnipeg: Natural Resources Institute, University of Manitoba, 1976.

Ellis J. H. *The Ministry of Agriculture in Manitoba, 1870-1890*. Winnipeg: Manitoba Department of Agriculture, Economics and Publication Branch, 1970.

Fairbairn, Garry Lawrence. *From Prairie Roots: The Remarkable Story of Saskatchewan Wheat Pool*. Saskatoon: Western Producer Prairie Books, 1984.

Finlayson, R. K. *That Man R. B. Bennett*. [n.p., n.d.]

Fowke, Vernon C. *Canadian Agricultural Policy, The Historical Pattern*. Toronto: University of Toronto Press, 1946.

_____ *The National Policy and the Wheat Economy*. Toronto: University of Toronto Press, 1957.

Grains & Oilseeds: Handling, Marketing, Processing. 3rd edition, revised. Winnipeg: Canadian International Grains Institute, 1982.

Hadwiger, Don F. *Federal Wheat Commodity Programs*. Ames, Iowa: Iowa State University Press, 1970.

Hamilton, Fred W. Service at Cost: A History of Manitoba Pool Elevators, 1925-1975. Saskatoon: Modern Press, 1978.

Josling, Tim. *Intervention and Regulation in Canadian Agriculture: A Comparison of Costs and Benefits Among Sectors*. Ottawa: Economic Council of Canada, 1981. (Technical Report No. E/14).

MacGibbon, Duncan Alexander. *The Canadian Grain Trade*. Toronto: The MacMillan Company of Canada Ltd., 1932.

_____ *The Canadian Grain Trade 1931-1951.* Toronto: University of Toronto Press, 1952.

Moorhouse, Hopkins. *Deep Furrows.* Toronto and Winnipeg: George J. McLeod Ltd., 1918.

Morgan, Dan. *Merchants of Grain.* New York: Penguin Books, 1980.

Nesbitt, Leonard D. *The Story of Wheat.* Calgary: Alberta Wheat Pool, 1953.

_____ *Tides in the West.* Saskatoon: Modern Press, [1962?]

Patton, Harald S. "The Canadian Wheat Board in Prosperity and Depression". Article reprinted from: *Economics, Sociology and the Modern World: Essays in Honor of T. N. Carver* / N. E. Himes, editor. Cambridge: Harvard University Press, 1935. (Central Selling Agency booklet).

_____ *Grain Growers' Co-operation in Western Canada.* Cambridge: Harvard University Press, 1928.

Swanson, W. W. and Armstrong, P. C. *Wheat.* Toronto: MacMillan, 1930.

Wilson, Barry. *Beyond the Harvest.* Saskatoon: Western Producer Prairie Books, 1981.

Wilson, Charles F. *A Century of Canadian Grain: Government Policy to 1951.* Saskatoon: Western Producer Prairie Books, 1978.

_____ *C.D. Howe: An Optimist's Response to a Surfeit of Grain.* Ottawa: Grains Group, 1980.

_____ *Grain Marketing in Canada.* Winnipeg: Canadian International Grains Institute, 1979.

Wood, Louis Aubrey. *A History of Farmers' Movements in Canada.* Toronto: Ryerson Press, 1924.

Government Documents, Publications and Reports

Canada. House of Commons. *An Act to Provide for the Constitution and Powers of the Canadian Wheat Board.* George V, July 5, 1935.

Canada. House of Commons. *Hansard.* Selected years 1930 to 1984.

Canada. House of Commons. Special Committee on Bill 98, Canadian Grain Board Act. *Proceedings and Evidence.* Ottawa: King's Printer, June 28, 1935.

Canada. House of Commons. Wheat Committee of Cabinet Minutes, 1946.

Canada. Privy Council. Office files.

Canada. Report of the Inquiry Into the Distribution of Railway Boxcars. Ottawa, 1958.

Canada. Report of the Royal Commission to Enquire Into Charges Against Manitoba Pool Elevators. Ottawa, 1931.

Canada. Report of the Royal Grain Inquiry Commission. Ottawa, 1938.

Canada. Senate. *Hansard.* Selected years 1930 to 1984.

Canada. Transport Canada. *Western Grain Transportation: Report on Consultations and Recommendations,* (J. C. Gilson).

Canada. Transport Canada. Report of the Committee of Inquiry on Crow Benefit Payment. March 1985 (Mr. Justice Gordon C. Hall).

Canada. Transport Canada. Grain Handling and Transportation Committee. *Grain and Rail in Western Canada, 1977* (Mr. Justice Emmett Hall).

Canadian Wheat Board. *Minutes of the Advisory Committee to the Canadian Wheat Board.* Crop years 1940-41 to 1983-84.

Canadian Wheat Board. *Minutes of the Canadian Wheat Board.* Crop years 1935-36 to 1984-85.

Canadian Wheat Board. *Reports of the Canadian Wheat Board.* Crop years 1935-36 to 1984-85.

Canadian Wheat Board. Trade and Commerce files.

Drummond, W. M. and Mackenzie, W. *Progress and Prospects of Canadian Agriculture.* Ottawa: Queen's Printer and Controller of Stationery, 1957.

Forbes, J. D.; Hughes, R. D.; Warley, T. K. *Economic Intervention and Regulation of Canadian Agriculture. A Study Prepared for the Economic Council of Canada and its Institutes for Research and Public Policy.* Ottawa: Canadian Government Publishing Centre, 1982.

R. B. Bennett papers. Public Archives of Canada.

United States. Congress. House. Subcommittee on Livestock and Grains of the Committee on Agriculture. *Sale of Wheat to Russia.* 92nd Cong. 2nd sess., 1972.

United States. Congress. Senate. Committee on Government Operations. Permanent Subcommittee on Investigations. *Russian Grain Transactions.* 93rd Cong. 2nd sess., 1974.

W. L. Mackenzie King papers. Public Archives of Canada.

Winnipeg Grain Exchange. *Minutes of the Council,* 1934.

Winnipeg Grain Exchange. *Wheat Marketing Fallacies.* [n.p., 1922?]

Newspapers

Free Press Evening Bulletin, 1933.

The Manitoba Co-operator, 1935 to 1985.

The Western Producer

Western Weekly Reports

The Winnipeg Free Press, 1930 to 1984 (Manitoba Archives).

Interviews

Taped Interviews: George McIvor; Honourable Otto Lang; R. L. Kristjanson; Frank T. Rowan; C. Gordon Earl.

Verbal Interviews: Douglas L. Campbell, Henry Monk.